OXFORD
UNIVERSITY PRESS

ASPIRE
SUCCEED
PROGRESS

Complete
20th Century History
for Cambridge IGCSE®
Revision Guide

D1421699

Ray Ennion

Oxford excellence for Cambridge IGCSE®

OXFORD

OXFORD
UNIVERSITY PRESS

Great Clarendon Street, Oxford, OX2 6DP, United Kingdom

Oxford University Press is a department of the University of Oxford. It furthers the University's objective of excellence in research, scholarship, and education by publishing worldwide. Oxford is a registered trade mark of Oxford University Press in the UK and in certain other countries

British Library Cataloguing in Publication Data
Data available

978-0-19-833260-2

10 9 8 7

Paper used in the production of this book is a natural, recyclable product made from wood grown in sustainable forests. The manufacturing process conforms to the environmental regulations of the country of origin.

Printed in India by Manipal Technologies Limited

Acknowledgements

IGCSE is the registered trademark of Cambridge International Examinations. Past paper questions are reproduced by permission of Cambridge International Examinations. Cambridge International Examinations bears no responsibility for the example answers to questions taken from its past papers which are contained in this publication. The example answers, marks awarded and/or comments that appear in this book were written by the author. In examination, the way marks are awarded to questions like this may be different.

The publishers would like to thank the following for permissions to use their photographs:

Cover image: Michael Nicholson/Corbis; p9: ©George Strube/Express Newspapers/N&S Syndication; p9: Paul Dwight-Moore/fotoLibra; p14: Epic/CCI/Mary Evans; p14: Punch Limited; p21: David Low/Evening Standard, 19 January 1933/Associated Newspapers Ltd./Solo Syndication/British Cartoon Archive, University of Kent, www.cartoons.ac.uk; p27: 360b/Shutterstock; p38: Media Wales Ltd.; p41: Photo12/UIG/Getty Images; p46: Hulton Archive/Getty Images; p48: Illustrated London News Ltd/Mary Evans; p53: David Low/Daily Herald, 28 June 1950/Associated Newspapers Ltd./Solo Syndication/British Cartoon Archive, University of Kent, www.cartoons.ac.uk; p54: David Low/Daily Herald, 18 October 1950/Associated Newspapers Ltd./Solo Syndication/British Cartoon Archive, University of Kent, www.cartoons.ac.uk; p55: David Low/Daily Herald, 27 Jun 1952/Associated Newspapers Ltd./Solo Syndication/British Cartoon Archive, University of Kent, www.cartoons.ac.uk; p62: Punch Limited; p68: Topham/Picturepoint; p70: Bettman/Corbis; p75: Punch Limited; p78: Herbblock/Library of Congress, Prints & Photographs Division, [reproduction number, e.g., [LC-USZ62-123456];

p80: World History Archive/Alamy; p83: Nicholas Garland/Telegraph Media Group Limited 1981/British Cartoon Archive, University of Kent, www.cartoons.ac.uk; p85: Punch Limited; p96: Nicholas Garland/Independent, 8th August 1990/British Cartoon Archive, University of Kent, www.cartoons.ac.uk; p98: Dennis Brack/Danita Delimont, Agent/Alamy; p100: Popperfoto/Getty Images; p103: special acknowledgement for permitting the reproduction of a substantial amount of material ©Philip A. Sauvain from his book Key Themes of the Twentieth Century, Nelson Thornes, 1996; p107: Eduard Thony/Mary Evans Picture Library; p113: Grenville Collins Postcard Collection/Mary Evans; p121: Punch Limited; p122: Punch Limited; p127: Punch Limited; p135: ©George Strube/Express Newspapers/N&S Syndication; p138: War posters/Alamy; p141: SZ Photo/Süddeutsche Zeitung Photo; p141: Hugo Jaeger/Timepix/The LIFE Picture Collection/Getty Images; p142: War posters/Alamy; p146: Overcrowded shack in Caroline County, Virginia, 1941 (b/w photo), American Photographer, (20th century) / Private Collection / Peter Newark Pictures / Bridgeman Images; p150: Courtesy of the WGBH Media Library & Archives; p155: Universal History Archive/Rex Features; p156: The Buffalo News; p157: Granger, NYC — All rights reserved.; p161: The Buffalo News; p167: Popperfoto/Getty Image; p177: Punch Limited; p182: Popperfoto/Getty Images.

Illustrations by Adrian Barclay, OUP and QBS Learning

The authors and the publisher are grateful for permission to reprint extracts from the following copyright material:

Contains Parliamentary information licensed under the Open Parliament Licence v1.0, http://parliament.uk/site-information/copyright/open-parliament-licence/.

Brian Reid for MIA, 2008 (transcription/markup): adapted from https://www.marxists.org/reference/archive/stalin/works/1946/03/x01.htm, J. V. Stalin on Post-War International Relations, Soviet News 1947, Marxists Internet Archive.

Pravda: *Pravda*, 2 November 1956, http://english.pravda.ru/news/russia.

Evening Standard: Headline 'Arab terrorists gun down Israelis in Munich village – hold 13 as hostages. Murder at the Olympics', *The Evening Standard*, 5 September 1972, reprinted by permission of The Evening Standard.

Although we have made every effort to trace and contact all copyright holders before publication this has not been possible in all cases. If notified, the publisher will rectify any errors or omissions at the earliest opportunity.

Contents

Introduction iv

Core

1 Were the peace treaties of 1919-23 fair? 1

2 To what extent was the League of Nations a success? 13

3 Why had international peace collapsed by 1939? 24

4 Who was to blame for the Cold War? 40

5 How effectively did the USA contain the spread of communism? 51

6 How secure was the USSR's control over Eastern Europe, 1948-c. 1989? 73

7 Why did events in the Gulf matter, c. 1970-2000? 87

Depth Study

8 The First World War, 1914-18 100

9 Germany, 1919-45 124

10 The USA, 1918-41 144

11 Israelis and Palestinians since 1945 165

Index 190

Introduction

How to use this book

This revision guide provides the information you need to revise and refresh your knowledge of Cambridge IGCSE History, in order to work to your best abilities throughout the course and in assessment.

It provides comprehensive coverage of the latest syllabus together with examples of tasks similar in style to those which you will face in the examination.

The revision guide

The book is divided into eleven sections. The first seven sections cover the 20th Century Core section of the syllabus. The final four sections cover the more popular Depth Study syllabus sections. Each section covers the historical detail related to the topic and, where appropriate, gives an explanation to aid understanding. This approach allows you to develop your responses to tasks and questions to go beyond simple description into explanation and evaluation.

When covering a topic, the book summarises the main detail. It does not go into the depth of detail covered by your textbook and lesson notes.

In each section you will find the following useful features:

Key Ideas

A summary of what the section is about. This gives the principles and issues of the period covered allowing you to see the 'big message' rather than the narrow detail.

Background

A short introduction to the section to enable you to put your studies fully into the context of the period being studied.

Exam-style questions

At the end of each section there are related questions to help you test yourself to see how much you have learnt and understood. This will help assess how thorough your revision has been.

Tasks

Throughout each chapter, you will find tasks ✓ to do in groups or on your own to ensure that you are applying what you're learning. Some of these relate to a source provided, to help prepare you for source-based questions in the examination.

The examination

The work you have to do in the examination is wide-ranging and demanding. This revision guide will help you to develop the necessary knowledge, understanding and skills. The Cambridge IGCSE History course requires all students to be able to demonstrate evidence of the following three objectives:

1   *An ability to recall, select, organise and deploy knowledge of the syllabus content.*

    Selection means:

    - Considering the question being asked and what is needed to produce an answer. This material should be useful and relevant.
    - Selecting material that will allow the construction of, and support for, an argument.

    Organising your knowledge means:

    - Your answer needs to be coherent, tackling the question in a logical manner. You should avoid jumping around from point to point.
    - Your argument should be clear and consistent.
    - You should reach an overall conclusion.

    Deployment of knowledge means that:

    - Once relevant material has been selected, it should be used in a relevant way to answer the question. This requires more than just producing description or narrative.
    - Each paragraph should add more to an answer in terms of supporting the argument.

    You should remember that the key is to answer the question as set. For source-based questions, the answer should relate to significance – the significance of one aspect as compared to the significance of other aspects in relation to the demands of the question.

2   *An ability to construct historical explanations using an understanding of:*

    - *cause and consequence, change and continuity, similarity and difference.*
    - *the motives, emotions, intentions and beliefs of people in the past.*
    - *significance.*

    This means:

    - Showing an understanding of how and why things happened in the past.
    - The ability to go beyond description to explain and evaluate as part of a developed argument.
    - Being aware of reasons why people acted as they did.
    - Understanding why events and actions had the consequences they did.
    - Understanding why situations and policies sometimes remain constant and also change.
    - Being able to explain differences and similarities between actions, events, developments, ideas and policies.

- The ability to assess the importance and significance of events, developments and individuals. Here it is important that you are aware that there are no right answers. Views need to be supported by sound, accurate knowledge and relevant, carefully chosen examples.
- Significance goes beyond explanation of both sides to look at the width and nature of impact across time as well as the impact over time.

3 *An ability to understand, interpret, evaluate and use a range of sources as evidence in their historical context.*

This means:

- Being able to use different pieces of source material with confidence.
- An ability to interpret what the source is saying.
- The ability to compare sources for agreements and disagreements.
- Deciding the usefulness or reliability of sources for specific investigations.
- The ability to reach conclusions by using a range of source material critically.

Examination preparation techniques

- Make a revision plan.
- Revise regularly using the content sections from this book and by preparing answers to the examination-style questions provided. Try techniques such as:
  - o highlighting key words;
  - o summarising causes and consequences in spider diagrams;
  - o using acronyms.
- Know what a good answer looks like and how it will be marked. Remember the best answers are those which show your knowledge and understanding relevant to that specific question. This requires being flexible in your thinking – there is no set answer to a history question.
- When you have finished revising a section you should be able to write at length about the statements in the KEY IDEAS box.
- During your revision sessions write responses to the examination-style questions. Keep asking yourself 'Is my answer focused on the question?' Every point should relate directly to the question set, including any dates. Do not use pre-prepared responses to questions on a similar topic; make sure you are focused on the question being asked.
- Develop an understanding of the requirements of key words used in questions, including 'Describe', 'Explain', 'How far', 'Useful'. They all demand different types of answer.
- Wherever possible support the point you are making with an example so as to improve the overall quality of your answer.
- Practise writing answers against the clock to ensure appropriate use of time. Papers 1 and 2 allow two hours, and if you are doing Paper 4, the time limit is one hour.

Style of questions

You will encounter a number of different styles of question throughout your studies and in assessment. Try to familiarise yourself with what questions look like, and what they are asking you to do.

Some questions ask you to recall historical facts. They might look like this:

(a) *In what ways was the Treaty of Versailles designed to restrict Germany's ability to attack France? (5 marks)*

> *Cambridge IGCSE History 0470 Paper 11 Q5a June 2011*

Your answer should relate directly to the question as set. It is not necessary to give lengthy explanations and context. A strong answer, which gets straight to the point, might start like this:

The Treaty stated that Germany could only have 100,000 men in its army and they had to be volunteers, as conscription was banned by the Treaty...

This response shows sound recall of knowledge in relation to the terms of the Treaty. It is important that the answer does not stray from the focus of the question. An example of failure to focus would be:

The Treaty took the Saar from Germany for fifteen years.

Whilst this is a correct historical fact, it is not an answer to the question set.

A question paper might then go on to questions which ask you to produce explanation as opposed to description or narrative. Answers to these kinds of question often benefit from making a plan before you start writing your answer. This helps to focus your thinking on the specific demands of the question. For example:

(b) *Why was the Berlin Wall built in 1961? (7 marks)*

> *Cambridge IGCSE History 0470 Paper 11 Q8b June 2012*

<u>Plan</u>
- To hide the prosperous west from East Germans.
- To stop the brain drain.
- To pick a fight with Kennedy.
- To stop negative propaganda.

The plan gives you the outline detail. Each point identified should be developed into an explanation.

Berlin was important in the Cold War. Overnight on the 13 August 1961 Berlin was split in two by the erection of a barbed-wire barrier. This separated East from West. This barrier was later made more permanent by the erection of a wall made from concrete.

This part of an answer shows good historical detail about the erection of the Wall and could be used as an introduction, but it fails to focus on *why* the Wall was built.

One reason for the Berlin Wall being erected was to prevent the mass movement of people from East to West. Around 15% of the population had moved between 1949 and 1961. Many of those moving were skilled workers such as engineers, teachers and lawyers. This movement became a drain economically on the communists. The large number moving gave a bad impression making communism look unpopular as people wanted to escape. Khrushchev was determined to stop this loss of talent.

This answer shows more understanding than the first example as it explains one reason *why* the Wall was built.

A third type of question invites you to explore different views about an historical issue, event or person etc. The issues and arguments presented should be explained, not just listed. To fully answer this type of question, you should include some form of evaluation in your response. This evaluation may take place throughout an answer or at the end as a conclusion.

An example of this question style is:

(c) *'The League of Nations was destroyed by the Depression of the 1930s.' How far do you agree with this statement? Explain your answer. (8 marks)*

Cambridge IGCSE History 0470 Paper 12 Q6c November 2012

A student might start to tackle this question with a brief plan, such as:

Plan

One side:

    The economic depression
- rise of dictators (Hitler)
- self-interest in difficult economic times
- weakness of imposing sanctions (role of US)

Other side:

    Manchuria
- attitude of Japan
- weaknesses of League – Lytton
- attitude of Britain and France re military

    Abbyssinia
- use of sanctions
- failure to act – Suez Canal
- Hoare–Laval
- retaining Mussolini's support against Hitler

    Inherent defects
- absence of USA
- lack of army
- idea of 'toothless'

    Evaluation
- idea of most important
- attitudes towards League

Imagine the first part of this student's response has demonstrated good understanding of both sides of the argument. The student concludes their response with the following paragraph:

The Depression alone cannot be blamed for the failure of the League. It is a number of reasons acting on the League. The League was weakened by its own inbuilt weaknesses which meant it lacked the power to exercise control over other strong countries at a time of great economic difficulty. The events in Manchuria did not help as the League was shown to lack power in dealing with a strong nation, Japan, which was not prepared to do what the League wanted. This was copied by Mussolini in Abyssinia. Seeing what went on in Manchuria also encouraged Hitler to leave the League. Weaknesses shown by Britain and France in relation to their own self-interests did not help the way in which the League was viewed and they acted outside the League in relation to Hoare-Laval. They also found it difficult to operate within the League at a time when their own countries were economically threatened. As I have explained earlier a strong argument can be put for each of the reasons I have identified.

This evaluation is not just a summary of what has gone previously but an attempt to put the issues into the bigger picture of the time, whilst showing there is some relationship between reasons. This would be a strong conclusion.

Source-based questions also feature in the examination, and cover a range of skills using source material. Answers should focus on the demands of the question, but you should use your knowledge to support an answer. The questions vary for each examination session. In the past, questions have tested:

Interpretation of sources – Here answers should go beyond surface information looking for attitudes, points of view, bias, etc. You should think carefully about the 'big message' of a source. Styles of questions to test interpretation will vary. In the past use has been made of approaches such as:

> What does this source tell you about...?
>
> What impression does this source give of…?
>
> What is the cartoonist's message?
>
> What point is the cartoonist making about...?
>
> Would Y have been happy with this source?
>
> Who published this source, X or Y?
>
> Would X have been happy with the report in this source?

Purpose – Answers to purpose questions should explain the message of a source, why the author/artist wanted to communicate that message at that particular time and the intended impact on the audience. It is useful to consider the tone of language used. Purpose questions have taken the form of the following question:

> Why was this source published in…?

Reliability / usefulness – There is no one way of evaluating sources for reliability and usefulness. It will depend on the question and the source(s). In producing an answer it is necessary to go beyond surface information and consider views, beliefs and attitudes. To do this it is possible to use the tone and language of a source on some occasions. Other approaches depend on the use of contextual knowledge to consider purpose and motives of the author. Approaches used in the past have included:

> Do you believe what this source says about…?
>
> How far do these sources prove…?
>
> Is X telling the truth about…?
>
> Which of these sources is more useful in understanding…?
>
> How reliable is source X...?
>
> How far does this source help you understand why...?

Using sources together – This type of question requires the overall message or purpose to be established. This is more than just comparison of surface detail. Sometimes sources will agree on some points of detail yet disagree on overall message or purpose. Answers should point these differences, and similarities, and you may wish to use quotes from the sources. Some questions require more than evaluation but also comparability for reliability or usefulness. Questions may look similar to the following:

> How far do these sources agree about…?
>
> How different/similar are these sources?
>
> Is one of these sources more useful as evidence about…?
>
> Which source do you trust more as evidence about...?
>
> Is one source more useful/reliable than the other for...?

Are you surprised? – Here it is necessary to use contextual knowledge about the person or organisation to work out whether or not you are surprised by the message, purpose or action within the source that relates to that person or organisation.

The final question – Source-based question papers will include sources which support the hypothesis in the question and others which disagree. You should look at each supporting source in turn and explain clearly - with evidence - how that that particular source supports the hypothesis. The same process should then be followed for those sources which do not support the hypothesis. In both instances your reasons should be supported by evidence. Remember that these questions are about the sources and how far they support the hypothesis and not whether the hypothesis is correct. Your answer must be based on the sources; your contextual knowledge should be used only to improve and inform your analysis of the sources.

Importance / Significance – Here, answers must demonstrate an ability to assess the importance and significance of events, developments and individuals. An example of this approach might be:

> How significant was the opposition of big business in limiting the impact of Roosevelt's New Deal? Explain your answer.

This question asks about the significance of big business. A good answer to this question might assess the impact in terms of what was achieved by big business opposition and also consider where big business opposition was less successful. This might involve the nature of impact such as 'how powerful was the impact?'. This would then allow consideration that the New Deal continued in spite of opposition, since this was not sufficiently drastic.

Throughout this revision guide, you will find examples of the different types of questions listed here, to allow you to practise and get familiar with the different styles of questions. Your teacher should also be able to provide past papers to help you prepare for examination.

1 Were the peace treaties of 1919–23 fair?

KEY IDEAS

This section will:

→ Describe the roles of the "Big Three" in the peacemaking process.

→ Examine the reasons for their individual motives and aims.

→ Analyse to what extent each of them achieved their aims.

→ Consider the impact of the treaties on Germany and its allies.

→ Evaluate the view that the treaties were "justified at the time".

Background

The First World War came to an end in November 1918. By the end of the war over 15 million people had been killed, the economy of Europe was in ruins and both the Russian and Austro-Hungarian empires had collapsed. In Russia the Bolsheviks had come to power.

In January 1919 delegates from 32 countries were invited to meet in Paris at the palace of Versailles. Each nation present wanted a settlement that would last. The defeated nations and Soviet Russia were not invited to attend.

At this conference five treaties were drawn up and referred to collectively as the Versailles Settlement. The main one was the Treaty of Versailles which dealt with Germany. The other treaties dealt with Germany's allies.

The leaders of Britain, France and the United States played a significant part in the decision-making and became known as the "Big Three".

Each of these leaders had his own motives and they all had different outcomes in mind. Woodrow Wilson from the United States believed his objectives could be achieved through his "Fourteen Points". Georges Clemenceau representing France wanted future security for his country while David Lloyd George from Britain wanted to avoid intense German grievance.

However, differences in opinion on how this should be achieved led to disagreements and compromises being made that resulted in fierce criticism of the Versailles Settlement, and especially the Treaty of Versailles.

Germany felt that they had been treated too harshly and that they should seek revenge. Others thought the punishment should have been harsher.

The background to the Versailles Settlement

At the end of the First World War, Germany and its allies—Austria-Hungary, Turkey and Bulgaria—had failed in their attempt to dominate Europe. There were several key factors at play as the Versailles Settlement was discussed.

Every country involved wanted to prevent another war: Four years of war had devastated many parts of Europe. Millions of soldiers on both sides were killed or injured.

Towards the end of the war the defeated powers sought an armistice. This meant hostilities were suspended. The armistice terms had an important effect on the terms of the peace treaties themselves, as the principle of reparations was established.

There had been a revolution in Russia: The Bolsheviks had come to power following a revolution. A left-wing group often known as communists, they pledged to destroy capitalism throughout the world.

Germany had dealt with the Russians in the Treaty of Brest-Litovsk: the treaty took large amounts of land and 25% of the population. The Allies believed that if Germany had won they would have done the same to Britain and France.

The mood within countries in 1919: There was strong feeling in Britain and France that Germany should be held responsible for the war and should pay for all the damage and destruction.

1.1 What were the motives and aims of the Big Three at Versailles?

The roles of the "Big Three" in the peacemaking process

Clemenceau's motives and aims were:

- to ensure the future security of France as Germany had attacked France twice in the previous 50 years
- to punish Germany severely, leaving it weak
- the permanent disarmament of Germany
- a very high level of reparations to pay for the destruction caused by Germany
- the return of Alsace-Lorraine to France
- the Rhineland to become an independent state so that France no longer shared a common border with Germany
- the Saar Basin to be transferred to France.

▲ Fig. 1.1 Clemenceau

Wilson's motives and aims were:

- a fair and lasting peace to prevent Germany seeking revenge
- aimed to allow nations to decide their own political future (self-determination)
- international cooperation with countries working together to settle disputes peacefully in the future
- his 'Fourteen Points'.

Lloyd George's motives and aims were:

- a "just and firm" peace which avoided Germany seeking revenge but satisfied the British people
- a share of Germany's colonies
- the economic revival of Europe and the German economy so trade would be re-established
- to reduce the threat of the spread of communism from Russia
- to maintain the strength and power of the British navy to protect Britain's colonies
- to persuade Clemenceau to make key concessions to ensure France did not become the dominant power in Europe.

▲ Fig. 1.2 Wilson

▲ Fig. 1.3 Lloyd George

1.2 What were the main terms of the Treaty of Versailles?

Key terms of the Treaty of Versailles

War Guilt (Article 231): Germany was forced to accept total responsibility for starting the war.

Reparations: Germany had to accept liability for the damage caused by the war and pay reparations. The figure for reparations was not decided at Versailles. It was finally agreed in 1921 and was set at £6,600 million.

The Rhineland: The Rhineland was to be a **demilitarised** zone. German troops were not allowed in the area as it formed the border between Germany and France. In addition there was to be an Allied army of occupation on the west bank of the Rhine for 15 years.

Anschluss: Germany and its former ally Austria were not allowed to unite.

Disarmament: The Germany army was limited to 100,000. The soldiers had to be volunteers as **conscription** was banned. No tanks or heavy artillery, military or naval air force, or submarines were permitted. The navy was restricted to 36 warships including 6 battleships and 15,000 sailors.

League of Nations: An international police force was to be set up to prevent future wars.

> **Reparations**
> The payment for damage caused during the war.

> **Demilitarised**
> No troops, armaments or fortifications present.

> **Conscription**
> Compulsory military service.

Decisions about territory under the terms of the Treaty of Versailles

Territory	Decision
Alsace-Lorraine	Returned to France.
The Saar Basin	To be administered by the League of Nations for 15 years. After that time a **plebiscite** would be held to decide if it should belong to France, to Germany or remain under League control.
Danzig	Was to become a Free City administered by the League of Nations. Poland could use the port and the strip of land known as the "Polish Corridor".
Eupen, Malmedy and Moresnet	Transferred to Belgium.
North Schleswig	Transferred to Denmark.
West Prussia, Posen and parts of Upper Silesia	Transferred to Poland.
Memel	Transferred to Lithuania.
Estonia, Latvia and Lithuania	Set up as independent states.
German colonies	Became **mandates** of the League of Nations, which effectively meant that Britain and France controlled them.

▲ Table 1.1 The treaty of Versailles and territories

> **Plebiscite**
> A vote by the people of a country or region on an important issue.

> **Mandate**
> The authority, given by the League of Nations, to Britain and France to govern the former German colonies.

> ✔ Produce your own chart to show how the main German and Turkish colonies were distributed under the Versailles Settlement.

1.3 Why did all the victors not get everything they wanted?

As each of the Big Three wanted such different outcomes regarding the treatment of Germany, it was virtually impossible to devise a settlement to satisfy all parties.

France

The Versailles Treaty satisfied a number of demands:

- the demilitarisation of the Rhineland secured its eastern frontier
- Germany's economic power and military capacity was reduced
- Alsace-Lorraine was returned to France
- France was to be a major recipient of reparations
- France was to gain some of Germany's colonies.

To avoid France becoming a dominant power in Europe, Lloyd George persuaded Clemenceau to:

- abandon the idea of an independent Rhineland state
- avoid giving the scale of reparations in the treaty
- abandon the idea that Danzig be given to Poland
- abandon the French claim to the Saar Basin
- abandon the French President's idea of splitting Germany into a collection of smaller states.

France wanted an Anglo-American Treaty of Guarantee to assist them if Germany became aggressive again. This did not materialise as America withdrew into isolation and Britain would not act independently.

United States

Wilson was pleased with some points of the settlement:

- reference to a League of Nations was included in each of the peace treaties
- there was partial satisfaction with the requirement that the defeated nations should disarm
- the Rhineland was to remain part of Germany, allowing a return of economic strength and trading possibilities.

Wilson was less happy with others:

- he thought that the Versailles Treaty was too harsh on Germany
- the principle of free navigation of the seas was abandoned at Britain's insistence
- Britain, France and Japan had rewarded themselves with Germany's former colonies
- self-determination failed to apply in some areas such as the Sudetenland
- the US Congress failed to approve the treaties and the League of Nations.

Britain

Lloyd George was satisfied with some decisions:

- he had successfully persuaded Clemenceau to moderate his approach towards Germany
- he was able to extend the British Empire
- Germany would be able to contribute to the future economic prosperity of Europe which was reassuring for those who feared the spread of communism.

Lloyd George did not approve, however, of the decision to place German-speaking peoples under the rule of other countries.

1.4 What was the impact of the Treaty of Versailles on Germany up to 1923?

The impact of the Treaty of Versailles on Germany

A fragile new government, the Weimar Republic, had been set up at the end of the war. It was forced to sign the hated Treaty of Versailles, making it even more unpopular.

An attempted revolt against this democratically elected government by the Freikorps, led by Kapp, failed but left Germany in chaos.

The Republic was under threat from the Spartacists who wanted a system of government based on communism, as recently established by the Bolsheviks in Russia.

When the reparations figure was announced, Germany claimed it could not afford to pay. It made a payment in 1921 but not in 1922, resulting in French and Belgian troops occupying the Ruhr. Armed resistance to the invasion was not possible, so the response was peaceful strike action.

As revenue declined, the German government began to print more money. This stoked up the existing inflation into hyperinflation. The German Mark became worthless.

German reaction to the Treaty of Versailles

The German people and government were horrified at the harshness and injustice of the Treaty of Versailles. They were forced to sign the War Guilt Clause even though they believed they had not caused the war.

They were treated as a defeated nation. Many were not aware that Germany had surrendered; they thought they had stopped fighting to make peace. They objected to the "diktat" or imposed peace, as they thought they should be allowed to participate in the discussions.

They were being punished twice. Firstly through reparations and secondly by being deprived of important industrial areas, such as the Saar, to provide the resources needed to pay the reparations.

The reduction in armaments brought a loss of pride and resentment. This also contributed to a feeling of insecurity as the size of the army was thought to be too small to defend against a possible French attack.

Some German people were now living under foreign rule resulting in a loss of pride.

It was seen as insulting that they were not invited to join the League of Nations.

Was German reaction to the treaty justified?

Germany was accused of operating a double standard. The call for fair treatment was difficult to accept in view of the treatment of Russia at Brest-Litovsk.

Germany's economic problems were self-inflicted as they had intended to pay for the war by imposing reparations themselves if they had won.

While the reparations sum was large, it was only 2% of Germany's annual production.

The harshness of the treaty should not have been a surprise given the terms of the armistice.

Germany complained that their treatment did not recognise the Fourteen Points. Self-determination was applied to some countries but not to Germans in new countries such as Czechoslovakia.

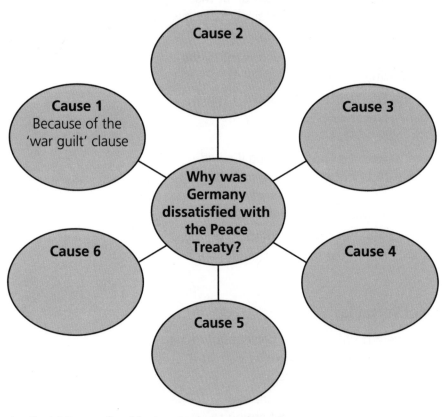

▲ Fig. 1.4 German dissatisfaction with the Treaty of Versailles

✔ Copy the chart in figure 1.4
1. Complete each of the circles with one explained reason.
2. In groups of two or three, discuss each of the reasons and decide which reason would upset Germany the most. Continue your discussions until you have a full rank order.
3. Present to other members of the class your arguments (reasons) for your choices.

1.5 How were Germany's allies affected by the other peace treaties?

The other peace treaties affected Germany's allies. These treaties had a number of features in common with the Treaty of Versailles, including:

- a war guilt clause;
- an obligation to pay reparations;
- reduction in armaments;
- acceptance of the Covenant of the League of Nations.

The Treaty of St Germain with Austria, 10 September 1919	The Treaty of Trianon with Hungary, 4 June 1920
<ul><li>Austria had to accept the break-up of the Austro-Hungarian Empire and was separated from Hungary.</li><li>Austria had to recognise the new independent states of Hungary, Czechoslovakia, Yugoslavia and Poland.</li><li>Territory from the former Empire was transferred to Czechoslovakia, Poland, Yugoslavia and Italy and Romania.</li><li>Union between Austria and Germany was forbidden (Anschluss).</li></ul>Austria was no longer a leading European power, it was now a land-locked nation surrounded by hostile states. Austria suffered economic problems after the war. It resented Anschluss. An attempt had been made to give eastern Europeans self-determination and freedom to rule themselves, although three million Sudeten Germans were placed under Czech rule. Italy was disappointed as it thought it should have received more land.	<ul><li>Hungary had to accept the break-up of the Austro-Hungarian Empire.</li><li>Hungary had to recognise the independence of Yugoslavia and Czechoslovakia.</li><li>Territory from the former Empire was transferred to Czechoslovakia, Yugoslavia and Romania .</li></ul>Like Austria, Hungary was now a landlocked nation. Under the terms of the treaty, it had lost, 70% of its territory and one-third of its population.

The Treaty of Neuilly with Bulgaria, 27 November 1919	The Treaty of Sèvres with Turkey, 10 August 1920
• Bulgaria had to recognise the independence of Yugoslavia. • Bulgaria lost territory to Greece, Yugoslavia and Romania. Bulgaria regarded the treaty as a national catastrophe, despite being treated less harshly than its allies for having played only a relatively small part in the war.	• Turkey had to recognise the independence of the Kingdom of Herjaz and Armenia. • Turkey lost its provinces in the Middle East to Britain (Palestine, Iraq and Transjordan) and France (Syria) under League mandates. • Turkey lost territory to Greece and Italy. • The Dardanelles Strait was to become an international waterway. The loss of Smyrna to Greece outraged Turkish national feeling as the principle of self-determination was being ignored. This sparked a national movement led by Mustapha Kemal. He challenged the peace treaty by using force to drive the Greeks out of Smyrna, forcing the treaty to be re-negotiated. **The Treaty of Lausanne with Turkey, 24 July 1923** • Turkey confirmed the loss of its provinces in the Middle East. • Most of Turkey's lost European territory was returned. • The Dardanelles Strait was to return to Turkish sovereignty. • Restrictions on armed forces were removed and the payment of reparations no longer applied.

1.6 Could the treaties be justified at the time?

Source 1

Although the Treaty seemed severe to many Germans it could have been much worse. If Clemenceau had had his way, the Rhineland would have become an independent state, the Saarland would have been given to France and Danzig to Poland. However, the Germans were not inclined to count their blessings in 1919. Most of all they resented being forced to sign the war guilt clause and a non-negotiated, but dictated, peace in humiliating circumstances.

▲ Written by an historian in 2014

Source 2

The atmosphere at Versailles was emotionally charged. Calls by allied statesmen such as 'Hang the Kaiser' and 'squeezing the German lemon until the pips squeak' were typical of the desire of many to go beyond a guarantee of future security to bring about the humiliation of Germany.

▲ Written by an historian in 2014

Source 3

> It must be a peace without victory. Victory would mean peace forced upon the loser, a victor's terms imposed upon the defeated. It would be accepted in humiliation, and would leave resentment and a bitter memory upon which terms of peace would rest. Not permanently, but only as if built on sand. Peace without victory was the only sort of peace that the peoples of America could join in guaranteeing.

▲ President Wilson speaking to the American Senate prior to the peace conference

Source 4

THEIR TURN NEXT.

▲ A cartoon published in the Daily Express, a British newspaper, in May 1919.

Source 5

◄ A cartoon published in Germany in July 1919. It was entitled 'Clemenceau the Vampire'.

Source 6

> There will be strong attempts to persuade the government to depart from the strict principles of justice, in order to satisfy some shameful principles of either revenge or greed. We must resist that.

▲ Lloyd George speaking during the 1918 election campaign.

Source 7

> We propose to demand the whole cost of the war from Germany.

▲ Lloyd George speaking immediately prior to the Peace Conference of 1919.

Source 8

> He (Lloyd George) was especially interested in the question of reparations, saying that if I helped him out in this direction he would be extremely grateful. By 'helping him out' he meant to give a believable reason to the British people for having misled them about the question of war costs, reparations etc. He admitted he thought Germany could not pay anything like the amount of reparations which the British and French demanded.

▲ From an American delegate's note of a conversation with Lloyd George during the peace negotiations in 1919.

Other reactions

The Germans did not think the treaties could be justified. They tried hard to convince the world that the terms were harsh and unfair.

Many people agreed with Germany. One was the British economist Keynes, who criticised the idea of reparations. Many historians argued that the Treaty of Versailles made future war more likely.

Some argued that the terms did not punish Germany harshly enough for starting a war which caused so much damage and which brought over 9 million British and French casualties. Many thought that given the complexities and demand for revenge, the terms could have been harsher, particularly following Germany's treatment of Russia.

In the armistice Germany had agreed to reductions in armed forces, losses of territory and the principle of reparations.

> ✔ Given that Germany had agreed to certain terms as part of the armistice, why were they surprised by the treaty?

Source 9

> In the view of the allied powers this war was the greatest crime against humanity that any nation ever committed. Germany's responsibility is not limited to having planned and started the war. She is also responsible for the savage and inhuman manner in which it was fought. No less than seven million dead lie buried in Europe. There must be justice for the dead. There must be justice for those who suffer war debts. There must be justice for those millions whose homes and lands German savagery has destroyed.

▲ From the Allied statement to the German delegation at Versailles, June 1919.

Source 10

> The historian, with every justification, will come to the conclusion that we were very stupid men. We arrived determined that a Peace of justice and wisdom should be negotiated: we left conscious that the treaties imposed on our enemies were neither just nor wise.

▲ A leading British official at the conference writing in his diary in 1919.

Source 11

> This is not a peace treaty; it is an armistice for twenty years.

◄ A comment by Marshall Foch at the signing of the Treaty of Versailles, 1919. Foch was the French commander-in-chief of the Allied armies in the final year of the war.

Source 12

Vengeance!

German Nation!

Today in the Hall of Mirrors in the Palace of Versailles the disgraced Treaty is being signed. Do not forget it. On the spot where, in the glorious year of 1871, the German Empire in all its glory began, today German honour is dragged to the grave. The German people will unceasingly press forward to regain its status among nations to which it is entitled. Then will come revenge for the shame of 1919.

▲ A translation of part of the front page of a German newspaper. It was published on the day of the signing of the Treaty of Versailles, 28 June 1919.

Exam-style questions

1. What terms of the Treaty of Versailles affected Germany's ability to pay reparations?

2. What problems did the Treaty of Sèvres bring?

3. Why were Clemenceau and Lloyd George in disagreement over how to treat Germany?

4. Why was Austria unhappy with their treatment under the terms of the peace settlement?

5. German reaction to the Treaty of Versailles was justified. How far do you agree with this statement?

6. Study sources 1 and 2. How far do these sources agree? Explain your answer using the sources.

7. Study sources 3 and 4. Does source 3 make you surprised by what is shown in the cartoon (source 4)? Explain your answer using the sources and your knowledge.

8. Study source 5. Why was this cartoon published in Germany in 1919? Use the source and your knowledge to explain your answer.

9. Study sources 6, 7 and 8. Do these sources prove Lloyd George could not be trusted? Use the sources and your knowledge to explain your answer.

10. Study all the sources. How far do they show that the peacemakers at Versailles wanted to treat Germany harshly? Use the sources to explain your answer.

2. To what extent was the League of Nations a success?

KEY IDEAS

This section will:

→ Consider the strengths and weaknesses of the structure and organisation of the League of Nations.

→ Analyse the degree to which it was successful in peacekeeping during the 1920s.

→ Consider the impact of the League's humanitarian work.

→ Evaluate the impact of the World Depression on the League.

→ Examine the reasons for failure in Manchuria and Abyssinia.

Background

At the Peace Conference of 1919 Wilson demanded as one of his "Fourteen Points" the establishment of a general association of nations. Each peace treaty contained an acceptance of the Covenant of the League of Nations. The Covenant was the constitution or charter of the League. This stated that the primary aim was to preserve world peace. The Covenant laid out the structure, rules and procedures of the League.

The League was organised around a structure of Assembly, Council and Secretariat.

At its inception there were 42 members. The League was originally made weaker by the absence of America, Germany and Soviet Russia and by the withdrawal of certain countries, including Germany, Japan and Italy, in the 1930s. Britain and France were the only major countries to remain members throughout the time of the League's existence.

Collective security was the intended means to maintain peace. There were three stages to this—moral disapproval, economic sanctions and military sanctions. The League did not have an army of its own.

The 1920s proved to be a relatively successful period for the League, although even during this period it adopted the role of passive bystander. However, the League used agencies and commissions to address issues of disease, poverty and exploitation and achieved a lot in the 1920s.

The 1930s saw the work of the League made more difficult by the World Depression. This decade also saw the League fail in its peacekeeping role in Manchuria and Abyssinia.

The aims of the League

The aims of the League were set out in the Covenant. They were:

- to achieve international peace and security
- to promote international cooperation, especially in business and trade
- to encourage nations to disarm
- to improve living and working conditions for the people of all nations
- to uphold and enforce the Treaty of Versailles.

Source 1

◀ The League of Nations and his deterrent power. Published in French magazine Le Rire, France, in 1919.

Source 2

OVERWEIGHTED.

President Wilson. "HERE'S YOUR OLIVE BRANCH. NOW GET BUSY."
Dove of Peace. "OF COURSE I WANT TO PLEASE EVERYBODY; BUT ISN'T THIS A BIT THICK?"

▲ Published in the British magazine *Punch*, March 1919.

> ✔ How similar are the messages of these cartoons (source 1 and 2) about the League of Nations?

The organisation and structure of the League

The League of Nations was created through the peace treaties at the end of the First World War. It was based in Geneva, Switzerland. It started work in 1920.

The Assembly	• Met annually at the League's headquarters. • All members of the League were represented. • Considered matters of general policy and recommended action to the Council. • Fixed the budget. • Every member of the League had one vote. • Decisions had to be unanimous.
The Council	• Met four times a year and for emergencies. • Had both permanent and non-permanent members. • In 1920 the permanent members were Britain, France, Italy and Japan. • The non-permanent members were elected by the Assembly for three-year periods. • In 1926 Germany became a permanent member. • The number of non-permanent members increased from four in 1920 to nine in 1926 and eleven in 1936. • Each member country had one vote. Decisions had to be unanimous.
The Secretariat	• Performed all the administrative and financial work of the League. • Organised conferences and meetings. • Kept records and prepared reports.
Agencies, committees and commissions	• The Mandates Commission ensured that Britain and France acted in the interests of the people of the former colonies of Germany and her allies. • The Refugees Committee assisted in the return of refugees to their original homes following the end of war. • The Slavery Commission worked to abolish slavery around the world. • The Health Committee began to educate people about health and sanitation and started to deal with dangerous diseases.

▲ Table 2.1: The organisation and structure of the League

Outside the League, but affecting its operation, was the Conference of Ambassadors. This was a group of senior diplomats representing the Allied powers. It was established in 1920 to deal with matters arising from the peace settlements. It duplicated some of the functions of the League and played a major role in the Corfu incident.

The powers of the League

The League could take action in three ways to try to solve a dispute.

1. **Moral condemnation**—putting pressure on a guilty country by bringing world opinion against it.	2. **Economic and financial sanctions**—members of the League could refuse to trade with the guilty country.	3. **Military force**—armed forces from member countries could be used against an aggressor.

▲ Fig. 2.1 Powers of the League

2.1 How successful was the League in the 1920s?

Why was the League able to achieve some successes in the 1920s?

Most of the major countries had joined believing that conflicts could be avoided. People and governments did not want a repeat of a horrific conflict like the First World War and so there was a high level of goodwill towards the League.

Disputes were often between smaller countries. They were willing to give the League a chance and readily accepted the League's decision, an example of this being the dispute over the Aaland Islands.

Countries were rebuilding after the First World War and were in no position, economically or militarily, to enter into further conflict.

The League of Nations was new and countries were willing to give it a chance to be successful. It was led by the victors of the First World War (except America). This gave the League some credibility.

Success in settling political disputes	Success in dealing with humanitarian issues
• Sweden and Finland fought over the Aaland Islands (1921); resolved by giving them to Finland. • Dispute between Germany and Poland over Upper Silesia (1921); the area was divided between the two following a plebiscite. • Dispute between Turkey and Iraq over the province of Mosul (1924). • Greece and Bulgaria fought over their borders (1925); Greece was ordered to withdraw and pay Bulgaria £45,000 compensation. • In South America differences were settled between Peru and Columbia and between Bolivia and Paraguay.	• Refugees—After the war around 400,000 prisoners and refugees were successfully returned to their homelands from Russia and Greece. • Health organisation—Helped Soviet Russia to prevent a typhus epidemic in Siberia; worked hard to defeat leprosy; started an international campaign to exterminate mosquitoes, reducing the spread of malaria and yellow fever. • Transport—Made recommendations for the marking of shipping lanes; produced an international highway code for road users. • Economic and financial—Devised a plan to deal with Austria's economic problems by stabilising the currency; devised similar plans for Hungary, Greece and Bulgaria. • Social issues—Freed 200,000 slaves in British-owned Sierra Leone; it challenged the use of forced labour on the Tanganyika railway in Africa, reducing the death rate from 50% to 4%; blacklisted large international companies involved in illegal drug selling. • Working conditions—Banned poisonous white lead from paint; limited the working hours for young children.

▲ Table 2.2 Successes of the League in the 1920s

What were League's failures in the 1920s?

Failure to deal with aggressors	Failure to implement disarmament	Agreements made outside the League
• Poland and Lithuania fought over Vilna (1920). Poland was clearly the aggressor but did not withdraw. The French would not act against Poland as they saw them as a possible future ally. • Italy and Greece dispute over Corfu (1923). Here Mussolini went behind the back of the League to the Conference of Ambassadors, persuading it to change the League ruling.	• All attempts at international disarmament failed, despite the efforts of the Disarmament Commission. The French regarded disarmament as a threat to their security. This encouraged Germany to argue that they had a right to rearm to protect themselves.	• There was limited faith in the League's ability to deal with any major challenge in the 1920s as the resolution of disputes was in relation to minor countries. • France was the country most concerned about its security, making mutual assistance pacts with other countries including Poland and Czechoslovakia. • The Locarno Treaties of 1925 provided guarantees for the frontiers of north-eastern Europe. • The Kellogg-Briand Pact had 65 signatories of countries renouncing war by 1928.

▲ Table 2.3 Failures of the League in the 1920s

2.2 How far did weaknesses in the League's organisation make failure inevitable?

Membership

Wilson had intended the League to be a general assembly of nations but this was never achieved. The United States refused to join and this meant that the League was missing the world's wealthiest and most powerful country. This reduced the ability of the League to take action against aggressive countries either militarily or by considering economic and trade sanctions.

Germany was only allowed to join the League in 1926 after it had demonstrated its peaceful intentions. This had the effect of creating a view that the League was a club created for victorious powers closely associated with the Treaty of Versailles.

Soviet Russia was not invited to join the League because it was communist. Russia was the third of three significant world powers not in the League.

Britain and France were the only major powers that were members of the League throughout its existence but they were both greatly weakened by the First World War. Britain was trying to maintain its empire while France was primarily concerned with increasing security against Germany. The League took second place.

Japan and Italy were both original members but left after disputes with the League. Japan left in 1933 following criticism for invading Manchuria and Italy left in 1937 following the imposition of sanctions over Abyssinia.

Collective security

The League did not have an army of its own and so relied heavily on **collective security**. If military sanctions were to be imposed, member countries would be asked to contribute towards a fighting force. This created uncertainty as an appropriate army would be difficult to assemble since member states would be reluctant to send their army to participate in a dispute in which they were not directly involved.

In theory this appeared to be a good idea for the preservation of peace but often nations looked to the League to take action when they were not willing to take action themselves.

The absence of the United States reduced its effectiveness as the League was deprived of a powerful army and strong financial backing in support of sanctions.

The League's Covenant demanded **unanimous decisions** in both the Assembly and the Council. This made it difficult to take decisive action against any country acting in a war-like manner.

Collective security represented an idealistic approach. It was unrealistic to expect nations to obey it while at the same time failing to give it the power to enforce its will.

> ✅ Discuss the following statement in groups: The League of Nations was more successful in the 1920s than many expected.

> **Collective security**
> This was the intended means by which the League aimed to maintain peace. It depended on the willingness of the members of the League to work together to deal with aggression. There were three stages: moral disapproval, economic sanctions and military sanctions.

> **Unanimous decisions**
> These were in place to prevent the League from being dominated by stronger, more powerful, countries. This gave all members an equal say in the running of the League.

✔ Was the League of Nations successful?
By 1925 many people were able to see both good and bad points in relation to the League of Nations. Complete a table to show the successes and failures of the League. One has been started for you below.

Key issue	Success	Failure
Decision-making	Gained credibility in relation to the handling of Upper Silesia where a plebiscite was held and the interests of the population met.	
Role of Britain and France		Showing self-interest. An example of this was in relation to Vilna. Here...
Membership		

2.3 How far did the Depression make the work of the League more difficult?

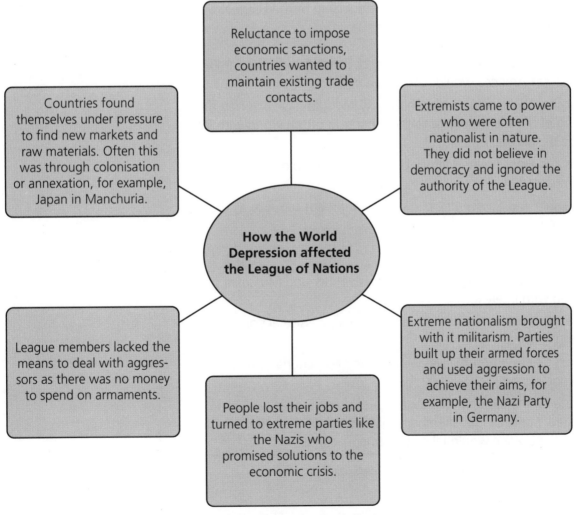

▲ Fig. 2.2 The effects of the World Depression on the League of Nations' effectiveness

2.4 How successful was the League in the 1930s?

Japan's invasion of Manchuria

Japan had a powerful army and navy and strong leaders who often dictated government policy. Japan faced a declining export market for its silk as demand decreased resulting in a growing economic crisis. Invading Manchuria provided an answer to Japan's need for food and raw materials.

Response of the League

Action

- The League instructed Japan to withdraw, but was ignored and the invasion continued.

- China was in a state of anarchy so the League was to some degree willing to allow Japan to "sort it out".

- A commission of enquiry was set up, led by Lord Lytton. This concluded that the invasion was not justified. The commission did not present its report until 1932, a full year after the invasion. The findings were considered by the League in February 1933 and were accepted by a vote of 42 to 1.

- Japan responded by terminating its membership of the League.

Failure to introduce sanctions

- No European country wanted to cut back its trade with the Far East, especially as America would have taken over.

- Military sanctions were less appealing as it would have involved the sending of a naval task force to the other side of the world with little chance of success.

- Britain and France feared attack on their Far East colonies if sanctions were imposed.

- The League was Eurocentric in nature and did not see Asia as vital for Europe.

Result

- Japan got away with blatant aggression as Hitler and Mussolini watched with interest.

- The League looked weak when faced with aggressive action taken by a strong country.

- To avoid taking action the League regarded Manchuria as a Japanese sphere of interest.

- As these events took place in East Asia the League was less damaged. Some League members believed that if the action was in Europe the League would take appropriate action.

▲ Table 2.4 The League's response to Japan's invasion of Manchuria

Source 3

> Manchuria showed that the League was toothless. The failure of the League to stop aggression in Manchuria had grave consequences in Europe too. The lesson was obvious; there was no power in the world to stop a determined aggressor.

▲ Extract from *Essential Modern World History* by Steven Waugh published in 2001.

Source 4

▲ A cartoon published in Britain's *Evening Standard*, 19 January 1933.

Italy's invasion of Abyssinia

In October 1935 Italy invaded Abyssinia. Mussolini was looking for ways to boost his popularity in Italy following a period of economic recession and unemployment. The primitive nature of Abyssinia's defences were no match for the modern Italian army and air force.

✔ Read source 3 and look at source 4. How far would the cartoonist have agreed with source 3?

The League and Abyssinia

Action

- The League immediately condemned the unprovoked aggression of Italy and imposed economic sanctions which immediately banned arms sales to Italy (but not Abyssinia), monetary loans to Italy, imports from Italy and exports to Italy of rubber, tin and metals.

Failures of the League

- The League failed to ban oil and coal exports to Italy as it was thought America would not support this and that the economic interests of League members would be affected.
- It did not close the Suez canal to Mussolini's supply ships for fear of reprisals against the British colonial possessions of Gibraltar and Malta.

Result

- Britain and France showed self-interest—if coal had been included in the sanctions it was reported that 30,000 British coal miners would lose their jobs. Also the behind-the-scenes Hoare-Laval Pact was leaked to the French press. This was disastrous for the League as its members were seen as committing an act of treachery, with the League losing all credibility. Furthermore, France had made secret agreements with Italy giving them economic concessions in North Africa and Mussolini may well have thought France would not object to him taking over Abyssinia.
- The League was powerless when its most important members failed to take effective action against Italy as they were desperate to keep Italy's friendship. They feared Mussolini would ally with Hitler.
- On 7 March 1936 Hitler remilitarised the Rhineland. The French would now not support sanctions as they were desperate to gain the support of Italy.
- On 9 May 1936 Mussolini formally annexed the whole of Abyssinia. The League watched helplessly.
- Collective security was now dead as was the existence of the League as a peacekeeping organisation.
- In November 1936 Mussolini and Hitler signed the Rome–Berlin Axis.

▲ Table 2.5 The League's response to Italy's invasion of Abyssinia

Source 5

Economic sanctions against Italy were serious, but not a great problem. Banning the sale of weapons and rubber simply made Italy look for suppliers who were not members of the League. The biggest worry was a ban on selling oil. If that happened in 1935 the invasion of Abyssinia would have halted in a week.

▲ Extract from *Mussolini* by Denis Mack Smith published in 1983.

Source 6

> Could the League survive the failure of sanctions to rescue Abyssinia? Could it ever impose sanctions again? Probably there had never been a clear-cut case for sanctions. If the League had failed in this case there could probably be no confidence that it could succeed again in the future.

▲ Anthony Eden, British Foreign Minister, speaking to members of the government about the crisis in Abyssinia, May 1936.

✔ Discuss the following statement in groups and present your findings to the whole class.

'Events in Abyssinia were more important factors in the failure of the League failing than those in Manchuria.'

Exam-style questions

1. Describe the methods available to the League to uphold their aims.

2. In what ways did the League of Nations lose credibility?

3. Why was it difficult for the League to achieve its aims?

4. Why did the League fail in Corfu?

5. 'The League of Nations was doomed to failure from the start.' How far do you agree with this statement?

6. 'The League of Nations failed because of Britain and France.' How far do you agree with this statement?

7. Read sources 5 and 6. Having read source 6 are you surprised by source 5?

8. Look at sources 1 to 6 in this chapter. How far do these sources support the view that the League of Nations failed because of the aggression of Japan and Italy? Use the sources to explain your answer.

3 Why had international peace collapsed by 1939?

KEY IDEAS

This section will:

→ Examine the long-term consequences of the Treaty of Versailles.

→ Examine the consequences of the failure of the League of Nations.

→ Consider how far Hitler's foreign policy was to blame for the outbreak of war.

→ Evaluate the policy of appeasement.

→ Raise understanding of the importance of the Nazi-Soviet Pact.

Background

In the 1920s the existence of the League of Nations, as well as a series of international agreements such as Locarno, brought a period of relative calm and stability. Some people were even suggesting an age of peace and tranquility.

Despite this, few were surprised that war broke out again in 1939. The 1930s was an age of increasing tension and conflict in Europe, starting with the invasion of Manchuria by Japan in 1931.

What had gone wrong?

The peace treaties had left many countries resentful and determined to reverse the terms. The most significant country affected was Germany. The people, encouraged by the **"stab in the back" myth**, turned to the Nazi Party. The Nazi Party led by Hitler followed a foreign policy which was designed to destroy the hated Treaty of Versailles. Additionally he made aggressive demands such as "**lebensraum**" and the destruction of communism.

The Great Depression brought militarist extremists to power. In Germany many people turned to the Nazis as they promised work and food.

It was clear by the summer of 1936 that the League had failed and with it the idea of collective security. An alternative had to be found to preserve world peace. Britain and France turned to **appeasement** while at the same time rearming as a matter of urgency.

It was clear that appeasement had failed when Hitler occupied Czechoslovakia in March 1939. The next country to be invaded by Germany would be Poland. Britain and France promised assistance should Germany decide to attack.

In late August 1939 the most unlikely agreement was made between two ideologically opposite countries—Nazi Germany and Soviet Russia. This non-aggression pact suited both countries in the short-term. In effect it sealed the fate of Poland.

On 1 September 1939 Hitler invaded Poland knowing that he would not face opposition from Soviet Russia. It was clear that he was aiming for European domination. Germany ignored the British ultimatum demanding withdrawal.

On 3 September 1939 Britain declared war on Germany.

"Stab in the back" myth

After the First World War the myth developed that Germany had been betrayed by a group of weak, unpatriotic politicians. The myth gained popularity, giving rise to the thinking that if the war had not really been lost then the peace settlement was unnecessary and should be overturned.

Lebensraum

Living space for German people, especially in eastern Europe.

Appeasement

The policy of Britain and France that saw them making pacts and deals with the dictators in order to satisfy their demands without going to war.

Main causes of the outbreak of war in 1939

▲ Fig. 3.1 The main causes of war in 1939

> ✔ Copy the causes of the Second World War from figure 3.1 on to six separate pieces of card. In groups, place the cards in order to show which was the most important reason for war, which was the second most important and so on. Explain why you have made these decisions.

3.1 What were the long-term consequences of the peace treaties of 1919–23?

The Paris Peace Settlement left many nations dissatisfied and wanting revisions to the treaties. Both Japan and Italy had expected to receive greater shares of the spoils.

The most dissatisfied nation was Germany. Most Germans wanted to reject the Treaty of Versailles as they did not agree with the territorial provisions, disarmament, war guilt and reparations. This dissatisfaction stemmed from the "stab in the back" myth.

Although the Treaty of Versailles was harsh on Germany, it failed to completely disable the country militarily and economically. This gave Germany the opportunity to rebuild when the time was right.

Hitler promised to destroy the treaty and this promise assisted his rise to power. To carry out this promise would require the rise of Germany as a strong military nation. This was forbidden by the treaty.

Britain and France disagreed about how to treat Germany. The British thought the treaty had been too harsh and were prepared to make concessions; the French were afraid of Germany becoming strong again.

3.2 What were the consequences of the failure of the League of Nations in the 1930s?

Japan

The Japanese invasion of Manchuria brought the first major failure of the League of Nations. It showed that the League was weak in the face of aggression by a great power, encouraging further acts of aggression. It also demonstrated the Eurocentric nature of the League.

Japan withdrew from the League and moved closer firstly to Hitler and then to Mussolini through the Anti-Comintern Pact. The results of the invasion of Manchuria encouraged Italy and Germany to think that their territorial ambitions were achievable.

Italy

The League would have to take action against Italy's invasion of Abyssinia, but this depended on Britain and France. Both countries needed Mussolini's friendship as they saw him as an ally against Hitler.

When Italy invaded Abyssinia in October 1935, the League took action by imposing economic sanctions. However, these sanctions failed to include essential commodities such as oil and coal. They also failed to close the Suez Canal. These actions, together with the Hoare-Laval Pact, showed the limitations of the League. League members (Britain and France) were incapable of putting internationalism before national interests. Hitler was delighted. He continued to take steps to destroy the Treaty of Versailles, knowing he would not face opposition.

Disarmament

One of the aims of the League of Nations was to persuade countries to disarm and so reduce the chance of conflict. At the Disarmament Conference of 1932–33 the Germans stated they would disarm if every nation disarmed. The French would not accept this. This gave Hitler the excuse he needed. He left the conference while at the same time pretending that Germany wanted peace. Hitler had in fact been rearming almost from the time he came to power. Germany left the League.

Appeasement

The failure of the League led to intensive rearmament programmes for Britain and France. Following the recession neither of these countries had spent enough on their defences.

By summer 1936 it was clear that rearmament was a priority. As it would take several years for full rearmament to be achieved, a short-term approach was required. Both countries adopted a policy of appeasement towards the dictators.

3.3 How far was Hitler's foreign policy to blame for the outbreak of war in 1939?

What were Hitler's foreign policy aims?

Hitler's foreign policy aims were originally set out in *Mein Kampf* which he began writing while in prison in 1924 following the unsuccessful Munich Putsch.

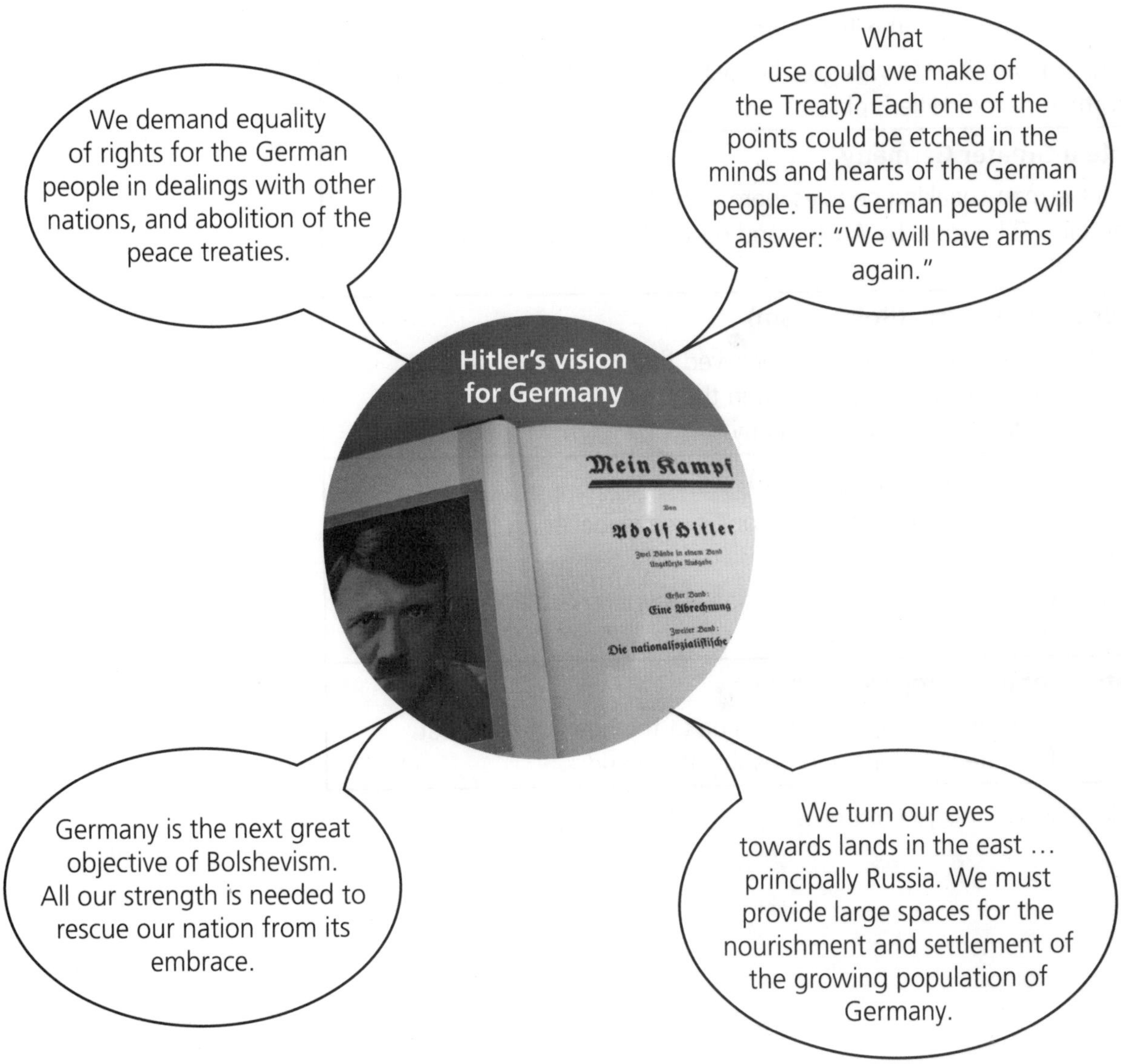
We demand equality of rights for the German people in dealings with other nations, and abolition of the peace treaties.
What use could we make of the Treaty? Each one of the points could be etched in the minds and hearts of the German people. The German people will answer: "We will have arms again."
Hitler's vision for Germany
Mein Kampf
Adolf Hitler
Eine Abrechnung
Germany is the next great objective of Bolshevism. All our strength is needed to rescue our nation from its embrace.
We turn our eyes towards lands in the east … principally Russia. We must provide large spaces for the nourishment and settlement of the growing population of Germany.

▲ Fig. 3.2 Hitler's foreign policy

When Hitler became Chancellor of Germany in January 1933 his foreign policy objective was to make Germany great again. How was he to achieve this?

Destroy the Treaty of Versailles
• The disarmament clause would be broken by introducing conscription and building up Germany's armed forces.
• The demilitarised Rhineland would be remilitarised, strengthening Germany's western frontier.
• Territory lost under the Treaty would be regained.
• Uniting with Austria was specifically banned by the Treaty but now formed part of Hitler's plans.
Create a Greater Germany
• All German-speaking peoples were to be brought into a German empire. This would be Austria and parts of Czechoslovakia and Poland.
Destroy communism (Bolshevism)
• Hitler was anti-communist. He believed that Bolsheviks were responsible for Germany's defeat in the First World War and that they wanted to take over Germany.
Acquire lebensraum (living space)
• Hitler wanted extra living space for Germans, believing this was their entitlement.
• This would be achieved by expansion eastwards into Poland and Soviet Russia.
Create a central European empire
• Having achieved his aims he would be at the head of the most powerful state in Europe and possibly the world.

▲ Table 3.1 Hitler's foreign policy objectives

What foreign policy actions were taken by Hitler from 1933 and 1936?

Hitler's actions during this period reflected more an attempt to achieve equality with Britain and France than they were steps on the road to war.

Date	Event/Action
1933	• Germany refused to pay any more reparations. • Hitler walked out of the Disarmament Conference (October). • Hitler withdrew Germany from the League of Nations (October). • The rearmament of Germany began in secret.
1934	• A non-aggression pact was agreed with Poland (January). This ensured that if Germany decided to attack Austria or Czechoslovakia, Poland would not intervene. • Hitler attempted union (Anschluss) with Austria (July) but backed down after Mussolini showed his disapproval by moving Italian troops to the Brenner Pass.
1935	• Hitler announced that conscription would be reintroduced (March). • A massive rearmament rally was held in Germany, boosting Nazi support. Britain and France believed that the constraints of the treaty were too great and also a strong Germany was a buffer against communism. • Germany signed a naval agreement with Britain (June) allowing Germany to have a navy up to 35% of the size of the British navy. The French were unhappy with this. • A plebiscite was held in the Saar (January) in accordance with the terms of the treaty of Versailles. Over 90% were in favour of a return to Germany. Germany had regained its first piece of lost territory by legal and peaceful means. It was a tremendous propaganda success for Hitler.
1936	• Germany remilitarised the Rhineland (March). Britain and France made no effort to stop them. It was suggested Germany was marching into "its own backyard". • Hitler developed closer relations with Italy by agreeing an informal alliance, the Rome–Berlin Axis. • The Anti-Comintern Pact committed Germany and Japan to hostility towards Soviet Russia. Neither Germany nor Japan would assist Soviet Russia if it attacked either country.

▲ Table 3.2 Hitler's foreign policy actions before 1937

> ✔ Hitler hated the Treaty of Versailles. Which parts of the Treaty had he destroyed by 1935?

Hitler's true intentions—the steps to war, 1936–1939

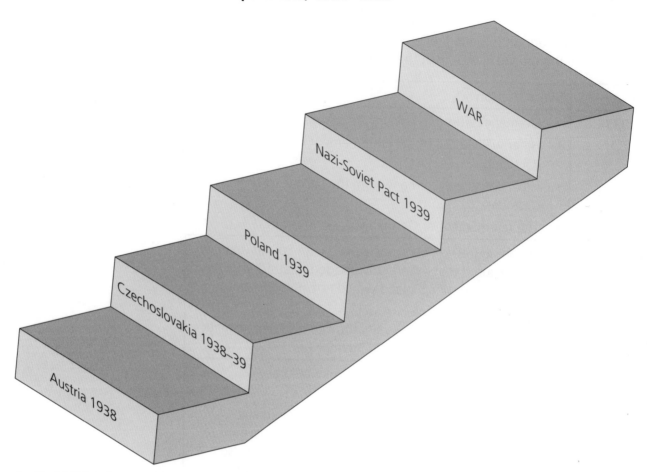

▲ Fig. 3.3 Hitler's foreign policy actions leading to war in 1939

The Spanish Civil War

- Italy and Germany supported Franco's nationalists in the Spanish Civil War, hoping that if they were successful Spain would become a German ally.

- This gave Hitler an opportunity to test his new military equipment. His Luftwaffe was tested and committed a ruthless assault on Guernica.

- Hitler saw it as an opportunity to fight against communism.

- Hitler succeeded in establishing Mussolini as an ally. They formed the Rome-Berlin Axis.

- Britain and France decided not to become involved. Soviet Russia supported the Republicans.

Anschluss with Austria, 1938

Reasons for union with Austria

- Hitler had stated in *Mein Kampf* that he felt the two countries belonged together as one German nation.

- Hitler was born in Austria.

- One of Hitler's aims was to form a Greater Germany which would include all German-speaking peoples. Austria had the largest number of German speakers outside Germany.

- Many in Austria supported the idea of union as their country was economically weak after it had been reduced in size by the Treaty of St Germain.

- This was an opportunity to further break the Treaty of Versailles as it had forbidden Anschluss.

- From 1934, Hitler's relationship with Mussolini had improved enough that he now had Mussolini's support.

Events

- In early 1938 Hitler encouraged the strong Nazi Party in Austria to stir up trouble. They staged demonstrations and started riots encouraging union with Germany.

- Hitler forcefully told the Austrian Chancellor Schuschnigg that political union was the only way to sort out the problems. Hitler persuaded Schuschnigg to agree but then Schuschnigg changed his mind, ordering a plebiscite to be held among the Austrian people.

- Hitler was furious, ordering Schuschnigg to withdraw the plebiscite and resign. At the same time Hitler ordered invasion plans to be drawn up.

- The new Austrian leader Seyss-Inquart asked Germany to send troops into Austria to restore law and order. On the 12 March 1938 German troops invaded and two days later Austria was made a province of Germany.

- On 10 April, under the watchful eye of the Nazis, 99% of the Austrian people voted for Anschluss.

- Britain and France took no action. Chamberlain, the British Prime Minister, felt that Austrians and Germans had a right to be united.

Results

- Germany broke another term of the Treaty of Versailles. Britain and France were not prepared to defend what they saw as a flawed treaty. Also they did not wish to go against the views of the Austrian people.

- Hitler had increased German territory, population and resources.

- Hitler's confidence in his plans was increasing, particularly as he had the support of Mussolini.

- Austria's soldiers and weapons increased the strength of the German military.

- Hitler had declared his intentions and would not stop at Austria. Czechoslovakia would be next.

▲ Table 3.3 Hitler takes Austria

Anschluss

Refers to the political and/or economic union of one government or territory with another. The union of Germany and Austria was prohibited by the Treaty of Versailles.

Was appeasement a good idea or the wrong policy?

Many people agreed that the Treaty of Versailles was unfair and that Hitler should be allowed to get back what was rightfully Germany's.

Soviet Russia under Stalin was seen as a much greater threat than Germany. The British people hoped that a strong Germany would stop the spread of communism.

Britain and France were not ready to fight as they were militarily weak and were still coping with the impact of the Great Depression. Appeasement would give time for rearmament.

It was hardly surprising that Britain and France wanted to avoid war. Memories of the horror of the First World War were still vivid. People were naturally horrified at the thought of more bloodshed. Britain was also concerned that its Commonwealth countries might not give support.

It was thought that support would not be forthcoming from America. Would Britain and France be able to survive without this support?

Arguments for appeasement

▲ Fig. 3.5 Arguments for appeasement

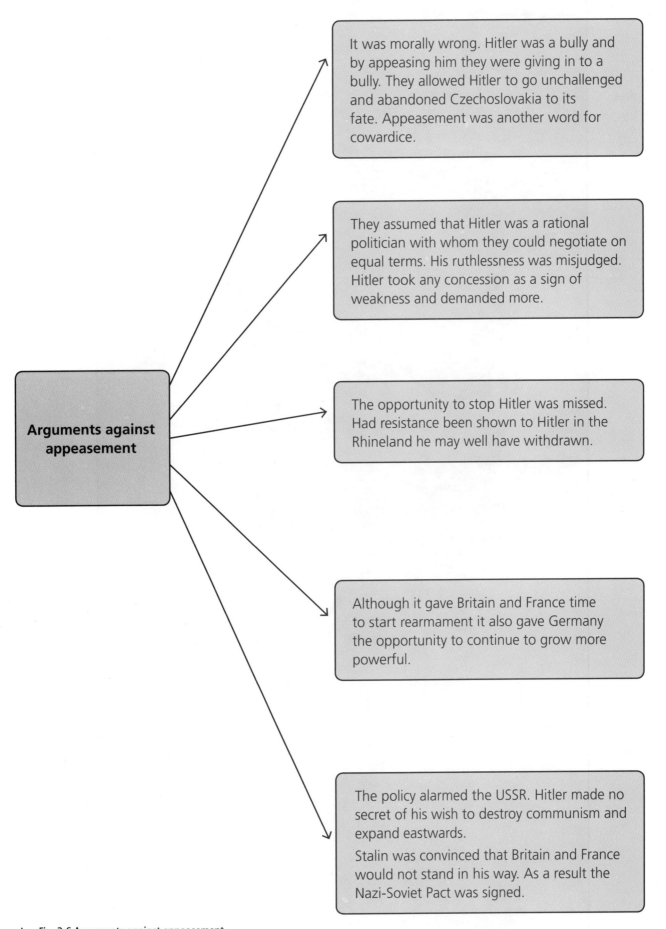

It was morally wrong. Hitler was a bully and by appeasing him they were giving in to a bully. They allowed Hitler to go unchallenged and abandoned Czechoslovakia to its fate. Appeasement was another word for cowardice.

They assumed that Hitler was a rational politician with whom they could negotiate on equal terms. His ruthlessness was misjudged. Hitler took any concession as a sign of weakness and demanded more.

Arguments against appeasement

The opportunity to stop Hitler was missed. Had resistance been shown to Hitler in the Rhineland he may well have withdrawn.

Although it gave Britain and France time to start rearmament it also gave Germany the opportunity to continue to grow more powerful.

The policy alarmed the USSR. Hitler made no secret of his wish to destroy communism and expand eastwards.
Stalin was convinced that Britain and France would not stand in his way. As a result the Nazi-Soviet Pact was signed.

▲ Fig. 3.6 Arguments against appeasement

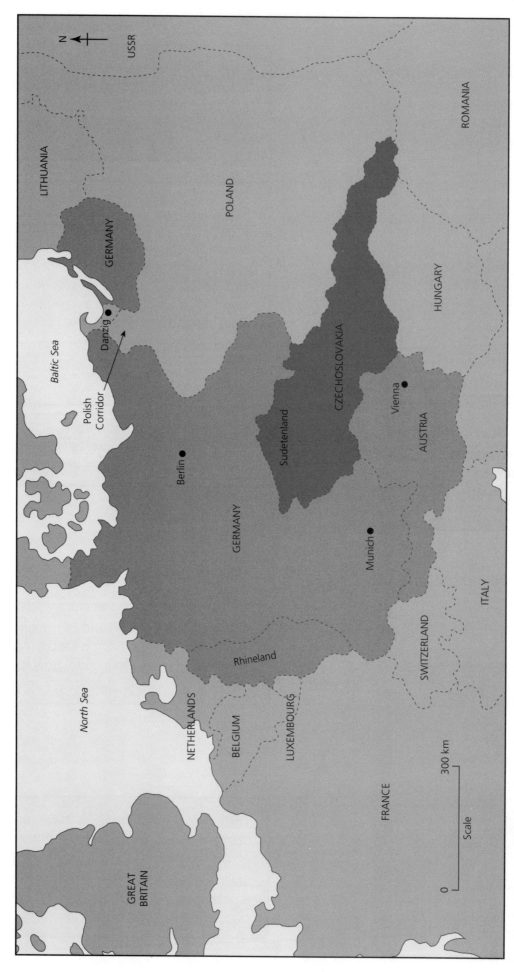

▲ Fig. 3.4 Map of central Europe after Austrian Anschluss (1938)

The Sudetenland

Czechoslovakia had been created by the Treaty of St Germain. Three and a half million Germans lived in the Sudetenland area of Czechoslovakia. The Sudetenland formed the border area between Germany and Czechoslovakia. The Sudeten Germans complained of discrimination by the Czech government. In 1938, Hitler demanded that Germany be given the Sudetenland. If this happened Czechoslovakia would be defenceless against a German attack.

The British Prime Minister, Chamberlain, wanted to find a peaceful solution to the problem rather than allowing Hitler to use force. Two summit meetings took place between Hitler and Chamberlain.

Where?	Berchtesgaden, Bavaria 15 September 1938	Bad Godesberg, Rhineland 22 September 1938
What happened?	Areas of the Sudetenland where the majority of the population was German should be handed over to Germany. This was to be subject to the approval of the British, French and Czech governments.	Chamberlain reported that approval had been given. Hitler had changed his mind and wanted the whole of the Sudetenland by the 1 October 1938 or there would be war.

▲   Table 3.4 Summit meetings between Hitler and Chamberlain to discuss the Sudetenland

Chamberlain was appalled by Hitler's change of heart. Europe was on the brink of war.

The Munich Conference, 29 September 1938

This conference was attended by Chamberlain (Britain), Hitler (Germany), Mussolini (Italy) and Deladier (France). Czechoslovakia and the USSR were not invited.

Hitler got what he had demanded at Bad Godesberg. The Czechs were forced to accept the agreement or face the full force of the German army on their own.

The following day, Chamberlain and Hitler signed a declaration promising that their countries would never go to war. Chamberlain returned to Britain saying "I believe it is peace in our time". He received a hero's welcome.

Outcomes of the conference

Britain and France had abandoned Czechoslovakia. On 1 October 1938 German troops marched into the Sudetenland. During October and November, Hungary and Poland took parts of Czechoslovakia.

In March 1939 Hitler took over the rest of Czechoslovakia. There was no resistance from the Czechs. Britain and France did not help.

Appeasement had failed. Poland would be Hitler's next target. Britain promised Poland it would guarantee its independence.

Source 1

> We have suffered a total defeat. I think that in a period of time Czechoslovakia will be overrun by Nazis. The whole balance of power in Europe has been upset. And I do not think this is the end. This is only the beginning.

▲   From a speech made by Winston Churchill to the House of Commons in 1938. The speech was made soon after the Munich Agreement.

Source 2

> It was thanks to Mr Chamberlain's courage that a senseless war was
> avoided. As I wrote to him then: 'Millions of mothers will be blessing
> your name tonight for having saved their sons from the horrors of war.'
> I also wrote at the time: 'The day may come when we may be forced to
> fight Germany. If we have to do so, I trust that the cause may be one in
> which the honour and vital interests of Britain are clearly at stake.' This
> was not the case in September 1938.

▲ From Sir Neville Henderson's account, published in 1940, of his time as British Ambassador to Germany from 1937 to 1939.

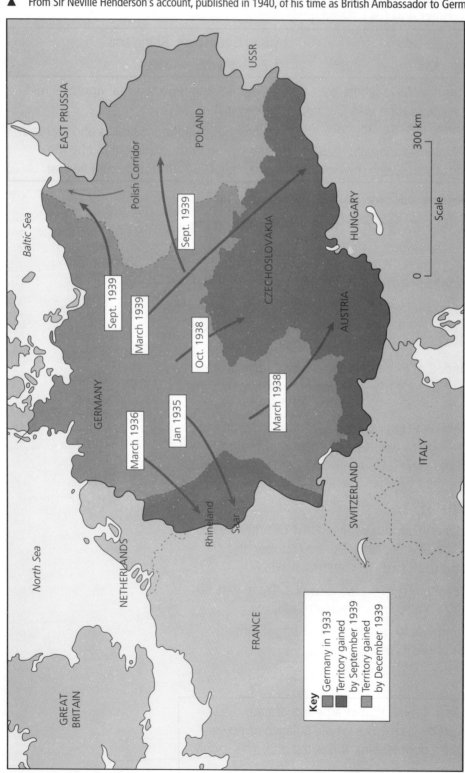

▲ Fig. 3.7 Map of Europe showing Hitler's territorial gains, 1935–39

3.5 How important was the Nazi-Soviet Pact?

The background to the Nazi-Soviet Pact

Ever since 1933, when Hitler came to power, Stalin had been concerned about the threat Germany posed. Hitler had openly stated his wish to crush communism and to gain land as lebensraum.

Stalin had failed to reach a lasting agreement with Britain and France in the 1930s. He had joined the League of Nations in 1934 but the League had shown it was toothless over Abyssinia. Some people in Britain thought a strong Germany would be an asset in the fight against the spread of communism.

Stalin signed a treaty with France in 1935. The treaty stated that France would help the USSR if Germany invaded the Soviet Union. But Stalin was not sure, particularly when France failed to stop Germany when they remilitarised the Rhineland, an area on their own border.

Stalin's concerns were increased by the Munich Agreement in 1938. He had not been invited to the conference nor had he been consulted. He concluded that Britain and France were happy to allow Hitler to take land in the east.

Discussion with Britain and France over the spring and summer of 1939 came to nothing.

The importance of the Nazi-Soviet Pact

On 23 August 1939, astounding news was announced which was to make war inevitable. The two most ideologically opposed countries had signed a 10-year non-aggression pact.

Poland was doomed. Secretly Germany and Russia decided to split Poland between them. Stalin was interested in sections of eastern Poland and wanted the Baltic States which had once been part of Russia.

The pact gave Stalin time to build up his armed forces, which were weak following the purges, as he realised that eventually Hitler would break his promise and attack the Soviet Union. Stalin also feared the threat of Japan which would mean war on two fronts.

The pact gave Hitler the confidence to invade Poland, knowing he would not have to fight a war on two fronts.

Hitler did not believe Britain and France would go to war over Poland. This belief was shaken momentarily by Britain signing a formal alliance with Poland on 25 August 1939. Hitler assumed that Anglo-French opposition would not be any more serious than it had been over Czechoslovakia. Also Hitler's position had been strengthened by Italy signing the Pact of Steel in May 1939, thus becoming a formal ally.

On 1 September, ignoring Britain's warnings, Hitler invaded Poland. On 17 September Soviet forces invaded from the east, occupying the Baltic states of Lithuania, Estonia and Latvia. Within three weeks Poland had been defeated.

Hitler had taken one gamble too many. On 3 September Britain declared war on Germany.

Source 3

In 1939, the USSR stood alone in the face of growing Fascist threat. The USSR had to make a treaty of non-aggression with Germany. Some British historians tried to prove that this treaty helped to start the Second World War. The truth is it gave the USSR time to strengthen its defences.

▲ A Soviet historian writing in 1981

Source 4

▲ A cartoon published in Britain in 1939. Britain is represented by a growling bulldog.

Why was Poland important to Hitler?

Under the terms of the Treaty of Versailles, the "Polish Corridor" (German land) was given to Poland in order to provide an outlet to the sea and Danzig was put under the control of the League of Nations. Hitler wanted this land back. The demand to return Danzig was not unreasonable as it was mainly German speaking.

The destruction of Poland was an essential preliminary to the invasion of Russia, the destruction of communism and the acquisition of 'lebensraum'.

3.6 Why did Britain and France declare war on Germany in September 1939?

Germany ignored ultimatums from both Britain and France demanding that the German army be withdrawn from Poland. The Poles failed to take the opportunity to negotiate with Germany over the disputed areas of the Polish Corridor and Danzig.

It was clear that Germany was making a bid for European dominance and not just establishing the principle of self-determination for German-speaking peoples. Events in Czechoslovakia had shown Hitler's real aim of European dominance by force.

On the 31 March 1939 a British-French guarantee was given promising that Poland would receive support and assistance if attacked. They were forced to do just that, as Hitler had pushed them to the point where they had to resist. Otherwise, they faced humiliation and acceptance that Germany would dominate Europe.

As Germany had not responded to the ultimatum, on 3 September 1939 Britain and France declared war on Germany.

Exam-style questions

1. What happened in the Saar in 1935?
2. What actions had Hitler taken by 1936 to prepare for war?
3. Describe events in 1938 relating to Czechoslovakia.
4. Why did Britain and France not want to go to war with Germany?
5. Why did some people argue that appeasement was the wrong policy?
6. Why did Stalin agree to the Nazi-Soviet Pact?
7. 'Hitler achieved his foreign policy aims.' How far do you agree?
8. 'The Spanish Civil War was more important to Hitler than the remilitarisation of the Rhineland.' How far do you agree?
9. 'Hitler was an opportunist rather than a planner.' How far do you agree?
10. Study sources 1 and 2. Does source 2 show that Churchill was lying to Parliament? Explain your answer using the sources and your knowledge.
11. Study source 4. Why did the cartoonist draw this cartoon? Explain your answer using the cartoon and your knowledge.
12. Study all the sources. How far do these sources provide convincing evidence that war in Europe was inevitable? Use the sources to explain your answer.

Who was to blame for the Cold War?

Background

By the end of 1944 it was becoming obvious that Germany was going to lose the war and that the Soviet Union was going to play a greater part in world affairs. By this time the ideological differences between the United States and the USSR were re-emerging, as were the tensions between the former allies. The United States was a democracy with a capitalist economy. The USSR followed a system based on communism, with one-party rule and no political opposition allowed. The economy was controlled by the state.

The United States, the USSR and Britain set up two conferences in 1945, one at Yalta (February) and one at Potsdam (July). At the conferences it was evident that there were major differences over the future of eastern Europe.

The USSR believed that the West wanted the recovery of Germany which would make it a threat to the USSR. The United States suspected the USSR of trying to spread communism to as many countries as possible. The USSR was now regarded by the West as the main threat to peace.

The United States followed a policy of containment, introducing the Truman Doctrine and Marshall Plan in an attempt to prevent the expansion of the "Iron Curtain".

Matters came to a head when Stalin blockaded routes into West Berlin. This action completed the breakdown of relations between East and West.

NATO, a defensive alliance, was set up by the West in 1949.

4.1 Why did the USA–USSR alliance begin to break down in 1945?

Removal of the common enemy: There was no longer a common enemy, Germany, and so no need for the Allied cooperation which had been extensive during the war.

Ideological differences: The ideological differences between the USA and the USSR began to re-emerge. The United States followed a democratic, capitalist approach opposed to the communist ideology of the USSR. This made it more difficult to build up trust between the two.

History of hostility: There was a long history of mistrust going back to 1918 and the intervention of the West in the Russian Civil War against the Bolsheviks. In the 1930s Stalin thought that the West saw Hitler and the

Nazis as the buffer against the spread of communism. In addition, Stalin was not invited to the Munich Conference.

The USSR in world affairs: By early 1945 it was obvious that the Soviet Union's "sphere of influence" was growing. Stalin was included with other European leaders in important conferences at Yalta (February 1945) and Potsdam (July 1945).

What were the issues to be addressed at Yalta and Potsdam?

It was clear by early 1945 that Germany would be defeated. The Allies needed to focus on the problems that the defeat of Germany would bring. The challenges faced by the USA, the USSR and Britain were:

- what to do with a defeated Germany and its leaders
- what to do with countries formerly occupied by Germany, many of which were in eastern Europe
- to decide the future of Poland
- how war with Japan could be ended as soon as possible
- to discuss how a lasting peace was to be maintained.

The Yalta Conference, February 1945

Roosevelt, Churchill and Stalin met at Yalta in the Ukraine to discuss these issues.

Source 1

▲ A British cartoon published in February 1945. It shows Roosevelt, Stalin and Churchill.

ISSUE	WHAT WAS DECIDED?
What to do with a defeated Germany	• Surrender was to be unconditional. • Germany and its capital Berlin were to be temporarily divided into four occupation zones. • Germany's eastern border was to be moved westwards. • War criminals were to be hunted down and punished. • Germany had to pay reparations.
What to do with countries formerly occupied by Germany	• Following liberation they were to be allowed to hold free elections to decide how they were to be governed.
The future of Poland	• A provisional government was to be established comprising of pro-Soviet Lublin Poles and exiled London Poles who had fled in 1939. • Poland's border was to be moved westwards into German territory. • Free elections were to be held.
How war against Japan could be ended	• Stalin agreed to intervene in the war against Japan after Germany was defeated. • In return Russia was to receive land in Manchuria and territory lost to Japan during the 1904–05 Russo–Japanese War.
How a lasting peace was to be maintained	• An organisation to be known as the United Nations was to be set up.

▲ Table 4.1 The Yalta Conference

What changed between the Yalta Conference and the Potsdam Conference?

In the United States: President Roosevelt died in April and was replaced by Harry S. Truman. Truman was strongly anti-communist but inexperienced in international affairs.

In Britain: Churchill's Conservative Party was defeated in a general election. He was replaced by Labour leader Clement Attlee.

The Soviet Union had liberated eastern Europe and was installing sympathetic governments. They failed to hold "free" elections.

On the eve of Potsdam, Truman informed Stalin that the United States had successfully tested an atomic weapon.

The Potsdam Conference, July–August 1945

Truman, Attlee and Stalin met at Potsdam near Berlin in July 1945. There was much disagreement and little agreement.

AGREEMENTS	DISAGREEMENTS
• The Polish–German border was to be the Oder–Neisse Line formed by two rivers. • The Nazi Party was to be banned. • Germany was to be denazified and war crime trials held. • The decision to split Germany and Berlin into four zones was confirmed. • Each country was to take reparations from its own zone.	• No agreement was reached over the future government of Poland. • There was disagreement over Germany. Stalin wanted Germany crippled to prevent future threat. • The USSR wished to intervene in the war against Japan but was refused by Truman.

▲ Table 4.2 The Potsdam Conference

The results of the Potsdam Conference—from wartime alliance to Cold War

The USA and the USSR emerged from the Second World War as superpowers and were prepared to face each other head on. The failures at Potsdam highlighted the increasing differences between these two superpowers, causing tension to increase.

Winston Churchill, the former British Prime Minister, referred to an "iron curtain" descending across Europe, dividing eastern Europe from western Europe, democracy from communism.

Source 2

A shadow has fallen upon the scenes so lately lighted by the Allied victory. From Stettin on the Baltic to Trieste on the Adriatic, an iron curtain has descended. Behind that line lie all the states of central and eastern Europe. The Communist parties have been raised to power far beyond their numbers and are seeking everywhere to obtain totalitarian control. This is certainly not the liberated Europe we fought to build. Nor is it one which allows permanent peace.

▲ Adapted from a speech by Winston Churchill, March 1946.

Stalin accused Churchill of trying to provoke war against the Soviet Union. The Soviet Union had been invaded from the West twice in 30 years. Stalin was determined to set up a "buffer zone" of protective states to ensure invasion never happened again. His reply to Churchill's speech was robust.

Source 3

Mr Churchill now takes the stance of warmonger. The following circumstances should not be forgotten. The Germans made their invasion of the USSR through Finland, Poland and Romania. They were able to make their invasion through these countries because, at the time, governments hostile to the Soviet Union existed in these countries. What can there be surprising about the fact that the Soviet Union, anxious for its future safety, is trying to see that governments loyal in their attitude to the Soviet Union should exist in these countries?

▲ Stalin replying to Churchill's speech, 1946.

> ✔ Read carefully what Churchill and Stalin are saying in sources 2 and 3. Explain why their views differ so much?
>
> Who benefited most from the conferences held at Yalta and Potsdam, the United States or the USSR? Explain your answer.

4.2 How had the USSR gained control of Eastern Europe by 1948

Soviet expansion in eastern Europe

Towards the end of the war the Soviet Red Army advanced through large areas of Eastern Europe as it drove back the Germans. After the end of the war Soviet troops remained in much of Eastern Europe.

As agreed at the Yalta Conference, elections were held in the eastern European countries. By 1948 all these countries had communist governments. This had been achieved through rigged elections and intimidation. The countries now under Soviet control became "satellite" states.

An alliance of communist countries called COMINFORM was set up in 1947. This tightened Stalin's hold on the satellite states, further restricting their contact with the West. Only one eastern bloc country, Yugoslavia, rejected Stalin's leadership, although it remained communist.

> ✔ Produce a spider diagram which shows the outcomes of the Yalta and Potsdam Conferences. In groups discuss these outcomes. Select the three most significant and explain your findings to the class.

Soviet troops remained after liberation.
New government formed in June 1945 dominated by "Lublin" Poles.
Opposition leaders arrested and murdered.
Rigged elections in 1947 gave communists 80% of the vote.

Soviet troops remained after liberation.
Communists won 17% of the vote in November 1945 elections.
Used secret police to discredit and persecute rival politicians and parties.
Rigged elections in 1947 gave communists control of a coalition government.
Social Democratic Party and Communist Party merged in 1948.

Soviet troops remained after liberation.
Soviets accepted a coalition government in 1945, accepting key positions for communists.
Rigged elections in 1946 gave the communists and their allies 90% of the vote.

Soviet troops left after the war.
Post-war elections gave communists leadership of a balanced, coalition government.
Foreign Minister Jans Masaryk, a popular and non-communist politician, murdered in May 1947.
All non-communist members of the government resigned in February 1948, with communists filling vacant positions.

Not liberated by Red Army.
Marshal Tito elected President in 1945.
Not prepared to take orders from Stalin.
Expelled from Cominform in 1948.
Accepted aid from the West.

Soviet troops remained after liberation.
Initially joined a coalition with other parties.
Monarchy abolished in 1946.
New constitution in 1947 effectively destroyed parliamentary democracy.

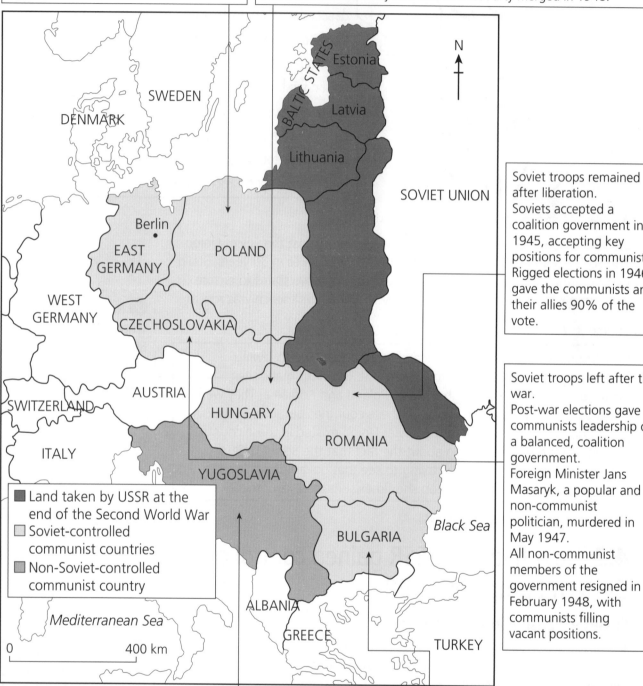

Land taken by USSR at the end of the Second World War
Soviet-controlled communist countries
Non-Soviet-controlled communist country

▲ Fig. 4.1 Map of Soviet expansion 1945–48

4.3 How did the United States react to Soviet expansion?

The Truman Doctrine

The immediate view held by the United States of the Soviets was that they were attempting to spread communism around the world. They feared that Greece and Turkey might be the next countries to fall to Stalin. The Truman Doctrine was explained by the President in March 1947, when he stated:

> I believe that it must be the policy of the United States to support all free people who are resisting attempted subjugation by armed minorities or by outside pressures. I believe that we must help free peoples to work out their own destiny in their own way.

Truman persuaded the American Congress to provide aid in the form of arms and money for Greece and Turkey. In Greece, the communists were eventually defeated in 1949 following a civil war.

The United States became committed to a policy of stopping the spread of communism. This was the policy of "containment".

Marshall Aid

Truman believed that countries which suffered from poverty were vulnerable. Many countries in Europe were struggling to cope with the after-effects of the war and were facing economic collapse.

In addition, if Europe became prosperous again it could become a trading partner for America.

In June 1947 following a visit to Europe, the American Secretary of State George Marshall announced an economic recovery plan which provided aid to build up Europe's economy. This became known as the Marshall Plan.

gave to communist countries who were struggling

Source 4

> The United States should do whatever it is able to do to assist in the return of normal economic health to the world. Without this there can be no political stability and peace. Our policy is directed not against any country or idea but against poverty, hunger, desperation and chaos. Its purpose should be the rival of a working economy to permit the emergence of conditions in which free institutions can exist.

▲ George Marshall speaking in June 1947

To help war-torn Europe recover, the United States offered money, machinery, food and technological equipment. In return, European countries would buy American goods and allow American investment in their industries.

Sixteen western European states accepted the offer. Between 1948 and 1952 the United States gave $13 billion of aid.

Stalin refused Marshall Aid for the USSR and banned eastern European countries from receiving it. To counter the effects of the Marshall Plan, Stalin set up COMINFORM in 1947. This aimed to develop economic cooperation between communist countries.

Source 5

▲ An American cartoon published in 1949

4.4 What were the consequences of the Berlin Blockade?

Tensions over Germany

Following the Yalta and Potsdam conferences in 1945 the Allies had agreed to divide Berlin into four zones of occupation. Berlin, which was deep inside the Soviet zone, was also divided into four zones.

The war had left Germany devastated. The United States and Britain wanted to help Germany recover quickly. The USSR, however, wanted a weak Germany.

Stalin was using German resources to rebuild the USSR.

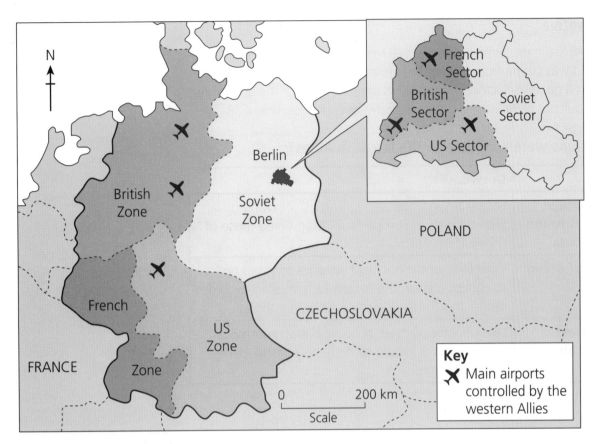

▲   Fig. 4.2 Germany in 1948

Causes of the blockade

Long-term causes of the blockade	Short-term causes of the blockade
• Within the Soviet zone, Soviet troops were able to control all access. • The USSR believed the western Allies had no right to be in Berlin. The western Allies were seen as a threat as they had a base inside the Soviet zone. • The western Allies needed to be there to prevent the USSR fully controlling Berlin. • The West could spy on Soviet activity behind the Iron Curtain.	• In January 1947 Britain and the United States combined their zones to form "Bizonia". France joined a year later. Stalin felt threatened by this, fearing he was being forced out. • Western Germany began to recover with the help of Marshall Aid. In East Germany there was poverty and hunger. • In 1948 the western Allies introduced a new currency into western Germany. Stalin refused to introduce it in the Soviet zone.

▲   Table 4.3 Causes of the Berlin blockade

Stalin's motive

In June 1948 Stalin retaliated by blocking all road and rail links into West Berlin. Berlin was cut off from all supplies. He increased the pressure by turning off all gas and electricity supplies. His aim was to force the other three powers to pull out of Berlin, making Berlin fully dependent on the USSR.

What options were available to the western Allies?

Option	Drawbacks
Driving armed convoys through the blockade	Highly provocative with strong risk of war. Russian armed forces in Europe far outnumbered those of the western Allies.
Pull out of Berlin	Countries would not trust America to stand up to communism in the future. Failure to act would render the Truman Doctrine an empty threat.
Supply West Berlin by air	Less risky than armed convoys but an enormous undertaking. It would be extremely costly. Planes could be shot down.

▲ Table 4.4 The options of the Allies

The airlift

The airlift lasted for 11 months and involved nearly 300,000 flights. Cargo carried included coal, food, medicines and petrol. Planes were landing in West Berlin at the rate of one every two minutes.

Although they did not fire on incoming aircrafts, the Soviets used obstruction tactics, including jamming radios and shining search lights to temporarily blind pilots.

Stalin lifted the blockade in May 1949 having failed to achieve his goal.

Source 6

◄ The Millionth Ton of Supplies reaches Berlin, 1949.

The consequences of the blockade

The West had successfully stood up to the Soviet Union. In May 1949 it was announced that the Federal German Republic, West Germany, had been formed by the merging of the zones of the Western allies. It did not include West Berlin which was protected by British, American and French forces. In October 1949 Stalin retaliated by turning the Soviet zone into the German Democratic Republic. This meant Germany was divided, with hostility between the two parts. East Berlin was part of East Germany. The division would last for 40 years.

In April 1949, the North Atlantic Treaty Organisation (NATO) was set up. Membership included the United States.

In January 1949, COMECON was created with the object of directing the national economies of the Soviet bloc. This proved to be more favourable to the USSR than to its other members.

In May 1955, the Warsaw Pact was formed with eight communist countries unifying their armed forces under a central command. This was a direct response to the rearmament of West Germany and its incorporation into NATO.

4.5 Who was the most to blame for starting the Cold War: the USA or the USSR?

In what ways was the USSR to blame?

- The communist ideology was expansionist and universal and therefore the Soviet Union could not co-exist with capitalism. It intended to impose its own system of government throughout the world.
- Stalin did not abide by the agreements made at Yalta. He installed a communist government in Poland and went on to impose Soviet systems throughout Eastern Europe.
- The creation of COMECON ensured that each Eastern European country followed the Soviet model of economic policy.
- Stalin frequently used ideological language when condemning the West and justifying his own actions.
- The establishment of COMINFORM was a clear sign that he intended to undermine capitalist society.
- He was the only leader to remain in power from the pre-war era through to the division of Europe in 1949. He often adopted a confrontational approach to relations with other countries.
- Stalin's concerns for Soviet security at the end of the war stemmed from historical fears about invasion from the west. These fears came from:
  - the events of the Russian Civil War
  - the belief that Britain and France encouraged Nazi Germany to expand eastwards during the late 1930s
  - the belief that the Western allies deliberately delayed opening a second front in order to weaken the Soviet Union
  - Britain refusing to share the German secret Enigma codes.

- In an attempt at one-upmanship the United States tried to keep secret the testing of an atomic bomb.
- There was deep concern over the future of Germany. The Allied plans to unify their three zones, together with the significant losses experienced by the USSR in the war, fuelled the desire to impose a communist system for protection. This provoked Stalin into drastic action over Berlin in 1948.

In what ways was the USA to blame?

- It can be argued that the true purpose of Marshall Aid was to provide a market for US goods and to ensure the preservation of a capitalist, free market system.
- The Marshall Plan promised aid to countries willing to stand up to the communist threat.
- The creation of Bizonia and the introduction of a new currency into the western zones of Germany was a clear breach of the Potsdam Conference agreement and an attempt to impose a capitalist system.
- Truman was very aggressive in his dealings with officials from the Soviet Union and felt that as a powerful, atomic power he should be allowed to dictate terms at the Potsdam Conference.
- NATO was set up as a military alliance to defend its members against possible communist attack.

Exam-style questions

1. Describe how Germany was dealt with at the Yalta and Potsdam Conferences.
2. Would Stalin have been pleased with the outcomes of the two conferences?
3. Study source 1. What was the cartoonist's message? Explain your answer using details of the source and your knowledge.
4. Study sources 2 and 3. Is either of these two sources useful for studying events at that time? Explain your answers using details of the sources and your knowledge.
5. Study sources 4 and 5. Are you surprised these two sources give such different views of the Marshall Plan? Explain your answers using the sources and your knowledge.
6. Study source 5. Is this cartoon supporting or criticising the Marshall Plan? Use details of the cartoon and your knowledge to explain your answer.
7. Look at source 6. To what extent does this picture suggest that the Berlin Blockade was a mistake for Stalin?
8. Study all the sources. Do these sources provide convincing evidence that the Soviet Union was responsible for the beginning of the Cold War? Use the sources to explain your answer.

5 How effectively did the USA contain the spread of communism?

KEY IDEAS

This section will:

→ Examine American reaction to North Korea's invasion of South Korea.

→ Consider American reaction to the Cuban revolution and the aftermath.

→ Study American involvement in Vietnam.

→ Consider the effectiveness of American involvement in these areas in containing the spread of communism.

Background

When the Second World War came to an end, the USA became increasingly concerned about the threat of communism, seeing it as a Russian attempt to dominate first Europe and then the world. This posed a challenge to American economic, political and ideological interests.

The fall of Korea to communism in 1948 and China in 1949 led to a real concern that Asia would be engulfed. The USA wanted to stop this growth and was willing to go to war to prevent it.

The spread of communism also threatened American interests in Cuba, while Vietnam presented a challenge to American influence.

5.1 America and events in Korea, 1950–53

The background to events in Korea

From 1910 Korea had been controlled by the Japanese. At the end of the Second World War in 1945, the Japanese troops based in the north of Korea surrendered to the Soviet Union while those based in the south surrendered to the Americans. A temporary dividing line was drawn up between the north and south along the 38th parallel of latitude (38° north). Free elections were to be held for a united, democratic Korea.

In 1948 separate elections were held. The south became the Republic of Korea, a capitalist dictatorship. In the north, now called the Democratic People's Republic of Korea, there was a communist dictatorship, supported by China and the Soviet Union.

On the 25 June 1950 North Korean soldiers, armed with Russian weapons, invaded South Korea.

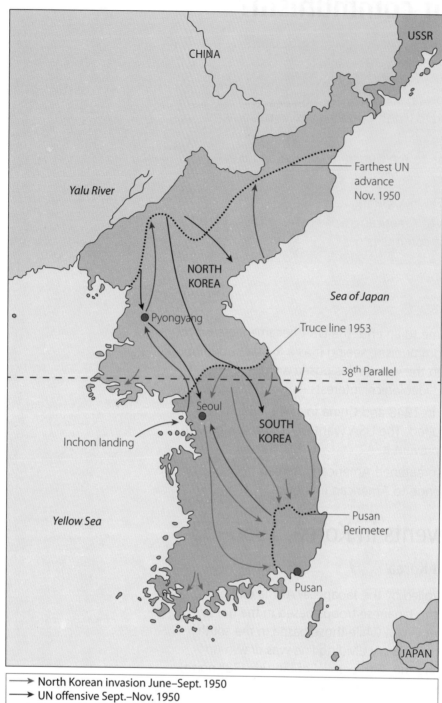

North Korean invasion June–Sept. 1950
UN offensive Sept.–Nov. 1950
Communist Chinese offensive

▲ Fig. 5.1 The Korean War, 1950–3

Why did North Korea invade South Korea in June 1950?

Kim Il-Sung wanted a united Korea under communist rule. He had good reason to assume that in 1950 he would be successful with the support of Stalin (Soviet Union) and Mao Zedong (China). North Korea's armed forces, using weapons supplied by the Soviet Union, were stronger than the armed forces of South Korea.

Now China and the Soviet Union had the atom bomb, Kim thought an American response unlikely. Korea was not a major American priority. Public statements by leading American politicians contributed to this belief.

Source 1

HONEST, MISTER, THERE'S NOBODY HERE BUT US KOREANS

▲ A cartoon published in Britain in June 1950. Stalin is shown talking to some of his friends.

> ✅ Explain why the cartoon in source 1 was published.

How did the United Nations become involved?

President Truman, seeing the North Korean invasion as a communist plot, acted quickly. He sent the US Seventh Fleet to try to prevent a Chinese attack on Formosa (Taiwan). He ordered General MacArthur to go to Korea with military supplies.

The United Nations Security Council met on the day that North Korean troops crossed the border into South Korea. An American resolution was passed at the United Nations demanding the withdrawal of the North Koreans. Its passing was made possible by the absence of the Soviet representative on the Security Council. At that time the Soviets were not present as a protest against America's treatment of communist China. There were no Russians present to use the veto.

As North Korea had no intention of withdrawing, a second American resolution was put forward on the 27 June. A third resolution 10 days later made clear how military forces were to be deployed.

Troops from America and 15 other countries were sent to assist South Korea.

What was the attitude of the USA to the invasion of South Korea?

As they had been closely involved in the establishment of the Republic of Korea they gave support. Under their policy of containment, the USA was determined to halt further communist expansion. The actions of North Korea were seen by America as part of Moscow's attempt to gain world domination.

The US feared that success in South Korea would encourage communist China to attack Formosa. If South Korea and Formosa fell to the communists, Japan would come under threat. From America's point of view, the fall of South Korea, Formosa (the base of the non-communist Chinese), and Japan to the communists would represent a major shift in world power balance. The most effective way to prevent this was to oppose the North Korean invasion of South Korea.

If the UN had not acted, it is likely America would have acted on its own. America gave full support to the UN. The UN forces were commanded by the American General, MacArthur, who took his orders directly from Truman rather than from UN officials. Half the ground forces were American, together with over 90% of the air forces and over 85% of the naval forces.

Source 2

> In South Korea the government forces were attacked by invading forces from North Korea. The UN Security Council called on the invading troops to cease hostilities and withdraw to the 38th parallel. This they have not done, on the contrary they have continued to attack. I have ordered US air and sea forces to give Korean government troops cover and support.
>
> The attack upon Korea makes it plain that communism will now use armed invasion and war.

▲ President Truman speaking to the American people on 27 June 1950

Source 3

JUST A CHANGE OF VEHICLE   WEDNESDAY October 18 1950

▲ A cartoon published in Britain, October 1950. On the left is President Truman.

> ✓ What is the cartoonist's message in source 3? Explain your answer.

The course of the war

By September 1950 only a small corner of Korea was not controlled by the communists but following UN troops landing at Inchon the communists were pushed back into North Korea. Truman decided to pursue the communists and so the UN troops invaded North Korea.

The Chinese leader Mao Zedong was angered by this action, sending a large Chinese army to attack MacArthur's army. In 1951 the UN army was forced to retreat back into the South, followed by the communists.

A UN counter-attack forced the Chinese and North Koreans back to the 38th parallel. President Truman did not want a lengthy or costly war in Asia but MacArthur wanted to carry on into China. He even suggested the use of the atomic bomb. Truman dismissed MacArthur in April 1951.

In 1953 a ceasefire was agreed which left Korea as two separate countries. Truman settled for communism being contained in North Korea.

Source 4

▲ A British cartoon published in 1962.

✔ Why was the cartoon in source 4 published?

What were the results of the Korean War for the United Nations?

The UN had used military sanctions against an aggressor, showing that it was more purposeful than the League of Nations had ever been.

The UN had failed in its objective of a "unified, independent and democratic government" for Korea.

The massive involvement and influence of the USA made it look more like an American action than one by the UN.

UN support for the American motion had only been achieved by chance: when the Korean War began, Russia was boycotting the UN Security Council and so there were no Russian delegates to veto the UN decision.

What were the results of the Korean War for the USA?

- Forty thousand troops died but many more would have perished if MacArthur had got his way.
- The US policy of containment had been successful as the spread of communism into South Korea had been prevented.
- After MacArthur's invasion of the North, the Soviet Union could say with some justification that the USA was an expansionist country.
- Many American Republicans felt the USA had missed an opportunity to destroy communism in China. This feeling contributed towards the excesses of McCarthyism in America.
- American relations with China, as well as with the Soviet Union, were now strained, bringing a new dimension to the Cold War.

Source 5

> The American military intervention in Korea in the Summer of 1950 made the already tense situation even worse. The United States was seeking to gain control of the whole country.
>
> By unleashing a civil war in June 1950 the South Koreans, backed by the United States, turned Korea into a place of fierce international conflict but in the end failed to achieve the aims of their Washington masters. Soviet and Chinese assistance to the People's Democratic Republic of Korea frustrated the plan to take over North Korea.

▲ From a Soviet history book published in 1984.

Exam-style questions

1. What part did the United Nations play in the events in Korea?
2. What did America fear might happen if it did not get involved in Korea?
3. Why was the United Nations involved in Korea?
4. How successful was America in Korea?

5.2 America and events in Cuba, 1959–62

Background to events in Cuba

Cuba was important to the USA for a number of reasons:

- Cuba served an economic purpose for America. The Cubans were forced to sell their raw materials to America for low prices. Also Cuba bought American manufactured goods.
- The USA invested heavily in the Cuban economy. The railway industry was run by the USA who also controlled the telephone system and tobacco plantations.
- Guantanamo Bay was an important US naval base.
- The US influenced Cuban politics, ensuring policy was favourable to America. Unhappiness with this was increasing.
- Cuba was a holiday island for rich Americans.
- The American mafia controlled much of the gambling, horse racing and hotels in Cuba.

It was the height of the Cold War. In 1961 tension rose again. The Soviets built the Berlin Wall to prevent East Germans escaping to the West.

President Kennedy was inexperienced and viewed by Khrushchev as being weak.

Why did tensions develop between Cuba and America?

In 1959 there was a revolution in Cuba. The unpopular President Batista was overthrown by revolutionary Fidel Castro. Castro promised to end American influence and control.

The US was worried by this, as it had supported Batista. They feared Castro would turn out to be a communist.

Castro negotiated trade agreements with the Soviet Union to export sugar and Khrushchev sent Castro advisers, military equipment and economic aid.

How did the USA react to the Cuban revolution?

The relationship between the countries was tense and frosty.

In response to Cuban trade links with the Soviet Union the USA banned all trade with Cuba and in January 1961 cut off diplomatic relations.

In April 1961 President Kennedy made available weapons and transport for an attempt to overthrow Castro. In this invasion 1,500 Cuban exiles landed at the Bay of Pigs to find themselves faced with 20,000 Cuban troops armed with weapons supplied by the USSR. The anticipated support from the Cuban people did not materialise and the exiles were killed or taken prisoner. The invasion was a dismal failure.

In June 1961 Khrushchev met Kennedy in Vienna. The US was concerned as Kennedy was thought to be weak and would not back the containment policy with force.

In July 1961 Castro nationalised all American industries. In September 1961 Khrushchev publicly announced that he would provide arms to Cuba.

In September 1962 Khrushchev told Kennedy that he had no intention of placing nuclear missiles on Cuba. It was a lie. The Americans became increasingly alarmed about the Soviet military build-up in Cuba. The tension was heightened when, on 14 October 1962, a US spy plane photographed the construction of nuclear missile sites on Cuba.

Why did Khrushchev put nuclear missiles into Cuba?

Placing missiles in Cuba would reduce the advantage held by the USA: The USA had missiles in Western Europe and had recently placed missiles in Turkey, which bordered the Soviet Union.

To act as a deterrent: Cuba was an ally of the Soviet Union. Missiles on Cuba would act as a deterrent against another attack. Cuba was the only communist country in the western hemisphere.

To send out a message of strength to the USA: Khrushchev was seen by some within the Soviet Union as not being strong enough in his dealings with the USA. Missiles close to America would give Khrushchev increased bargaining power.

The Soviet Union wanted a base close to America for its medium-range missiles: Cuba was only 90 miles away and would be able to reach the USA.

To "close the gap": Khrushchev wanted to increase the number of Soviet warheads. Medium-range weapons were cheaper to produce and could threaten America from Cuba.

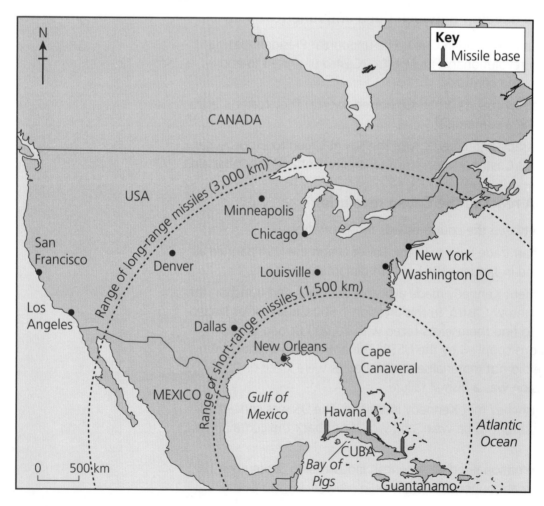

▲ Fig. 5.2 The threat to US cities posed by missiles on Cuba.

What options did Kennedy have?

In the days following Kennedy receiving the spy plane photographs he met with his advisers to discuss a response. There were several options.

Diplomatic measures

To use negotiation rather than aggression to help find a solution. This could be through the United Nations.

The USA would be seen as weak as it was backing down.

Do nothing

He did not want another disaster like the Bay of Pigs.

Overreaction to the situation might cause a nuclear war.

Not doing anything might be seen by the Soviets as weakness and result in other challenges, such as Berlin.

Threaten Castro

To warn Castro as to what will happen if the missiles are not removed.

Likely to be ignored with the US looking weak and ineffectual.

Full ground invasion

Would remove the missiles and Castro as well.

Almost certainly this would lead to a Soviet response to protect Cuba or even a takeover of Berlin.

Air strikes

These would destroy the missiles before they could be used.

To be effective all the bases had to be destroyed. This could not be guaranteed.

Inevitably there would be loss of life and almost certainly the Soviet Union would retaliate.

Naval blockade

To prevent missiles reaching Cuba by introducing a blockade enforced by the American navy forcing negotiation.

It gave the opportunity for both sides to consider their next move.

▲ Fig. 5.3 Kennedy's options

Thirteen days

On 14 October 1962 a U2 spy plane took photographs over Cuba. The following day American intelligence staff analysed the photographs. This confirmed that nuclear missiles had been placed in Cuba. From the 16 October Kennedy and his advisers met for thirteen days and nights.

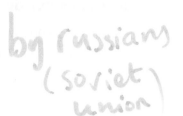
by russians (soviet) union

Tue 16 October 1962
President Kennedy is informed of the missiles on Cuba. A group of advisers called EX-COMM meet in secret to discuss the US response.

Wed 17 October 1962
EX-COMM continues to work on a response to the crisis.

Thur 18 October 1962
Kennedy meets with the Soviet Foreign Minister. The minister denies the presence of missiles on Cuba. Kennedy keeps quiet about what he has discovered.

Sun 21 October 1962
Kennedy decides to impose a blockade of Cuba. This decision is taken despite some members of EX-COMM favouring a show of force.

Mon 22 October 1962
In a live broadcast on American television, Kennedy informs the American public of the missiles and that he is going to impose a blockade. He asks Khrushchev to withdraw the missiles from Cuba.

Tue 23 October 1962
Khrushchev replies stating that there are no nuclear missiles on Cuba. He calls the blockade an act of piracy. Soviet ships sail towards the American blockade. If the blockade is ignored America will fire on the ships. War is certain to follow. The world holds its breath!

Wed 24 October 1962
The Soviet ships reach the blockade. Kennedy stands his ground. One is allowed through, the others turn back. One crisis has been averted! The missiles still remain on Cuba.

Fri 26 October 1962
Good news – Khrushchev admits to the existence of missiles on Cuba! Kennedy receives a letter from Khrushchev saying the Soviet Union will remove the missiles from Cuba if Kennedy agrees to lift the blockade and promises never to invade Cuba.

Sat 27 October 1962
Bad news! A second letter from Khrushchev to Kennedy in which he revises his proposals of the first letter. His new condition for the removal of missiles from Cuba is the withdrawal of US missiles from Turkey.

Another challenge for Kennedy! An American spy plane is shot down over Cuba, killing the pilot. The advice to launch an immediate reprisal attack is ignored by Kennedy.

Delaying tactics! Kennedy ignores the second letter but agrees to the demands made by Khrushchev in his first letter.

Secret talks! Robert Kennedy informs Soviet ambassador that US will not invade Cuba and that the missiles in Turkey will be removed within six months.

Sun 28 October 1962
Good news! Khrushchev agrees to remove the missiles from Cuba.

Phew! The world heaves a sigh of relief.

▲ Fig. 5.4 Diary of the thirteen days

Source 6

> This government has been observing the Soviet military build-up on Cuba. Unmistakeable evidence has established the fact that a series of missile sites is now established on Cuba. The purpose of these bases can be none other than to provide a nuclear strike capability against America.
>
> I call upon Chairman Khrushchev to remove this threat to world peace by withdrawing those weapons from Cuba.

▲ President Kennedy speaking live on television to the American people, 22 October 1962

> ✔ What was the impact of this television broadcast (source 6)?

Source 7

> In 1961 we increased our military aid to Cuba. We were sure the Americans would never agree to the existence of Castro's Cuba. We had to find an effective deterrent to American interference in Cuba.
>
> We had no desire to start a war. Only a fool would think that we wanted to invade the American continent from Cuba. Our aim was the opposite. We wanted to keep the Americans from invading Cuba.
>
> The Caribbean Crisis was a triumph of Soviet Foreign Policy and a personal triumph in my own career. Today Cuba exists as an independent socialist country right in front of America.

▲ From the memoirs of Khrushchev published in 1971. Khrushchev was forced from power in 1964

Why did Kennedy react as he did?

Kennedy wanted to avoid war although he was under great pressure from his own military leaders to take action. He hoped to avoid Soviet retaliation and the outbreak of a war in which nuclear weapons might be used. At the very least it was likely that West Berlin would be invaded.

Kennedy gave himself time to reach a peaceful resolution, avoiding immediate conflict. He did this by ignoring the second letter. Of his options, a blockade was the only one to offer this.

He wanted to avoid resentment by humiliating Khrushchev and so privately it was agreed that the US missiles in Turkey would be removed. This remained secret for 25 years.

Source 8

▲ A cartoon published on 17 October 1962.

Source 9

This is my proposal. No more weapons to Cuba and those within Cuba withdrawn or destroyed. You respond by ending the blockade and also agree not to invade Cuba.

▲ From a letter sent by Khrushchev to President Kennedy during the crisis, 26 October 1962.

Source 10

Our purpose has been to help Cuba develop as its people desire. You want to relieve your country from danger. Your rockets are stationed in Turkey. You are worried about Cuba. You say that it worries you because it is a distance of 90 miles from America. Turkey is next to us!

I make this proposal. We agree to remove missiles from Cuba. The United States will remove its missiles from Turkey.

▲ From a letter sent by Khrushchev to President Kennedy during the crisis, 27 October 1962.

Who won the Cuban Missile Crisis?

The outcome for Cuba	• Cuba remained communist, becoming a base for other communists in South America. • Castro remained in power, keeping control of the American industries he had nationalised at the time of the revolution. • Castro maintained the support and protection afforded to them by the USSR although he was disappointed with the deal Khrushchev agreed with America. • Unable to trade with America and dependent on the USSR, Cuba remained poor and isolated in the western hemisphere.
The outcome for the USSR and Khrushchev	• Khrushchev was able to say that he had acted responsibly by agreeing to remove the missiles from Cuba. • Cuba was maintained as a communist ally in the western hemisphere. This was a significant achievement in the face of American action. • The USA had agreed to remove NATO missiles from Turkey. Because this was a secret agreement, Khrushchev was unable to take the credit. • Many in the USSR felt humiliated by the fact that Khrushchev had been forced to back down and remove the missiles from Cuba. • Khrushchev's reputation was tarnished and he was replaced as Soviet leader within two years. His critics believed he had not been forceful enough.
The outcome for the USA and Kennedy	• The possibility of nuclear war had been avoided. • Kennedy's prestige in the world increased. He was seen by the West as a tough negotiator as he did not back down over his naval blockade. • Some of Kennedy's military advisers, who were critics of containment, thought he should invade Cuba to turn back communism. He avoided this high-risk strategy by standing up to these hard-liners. • Cuba remained a communist state close to America. Restrictions on trade between Cuba and America remained in force. • The US was criticised by some of its allies including Britain. British newspaper articles were critical of America's "two-faced" attitude, happy to have its missiles in Turkey and at other European bases and yet prepared to complain about Cuba. • Kennedy had agreed concessions, both not to invade Cuba and also to the removal of missiles in Turkey. The issue over Turkey was more difficult as technically they were NATO missiles. This left some NATO members unhappy. The removal of the missiles was kept from the American public.

▲ Table 5.1 The outcome of the Cuban Missile Crisis

The aftermath of the crisis

Relations between the USA and the USSR improved after the crisis. Both sides realised that brinkmanship had to be avoided in the future. The Cuban Missile Crisis was the nearest both sides came to conflict during the whole of the Cold War. They were now prepared to reduce the risk of nuclear conflict.

A "hotline" telephone link was established between the Kremlin and the White House so that problems could be discussed.

A Test Ban Treaty was signed in 1963.

Source 11

> We had to find a way of stopping US interference in the Caribbean. The answer was missiles. I had the idea of installing missiles with nuclear warheads in Cuba without letting the United States find out they were there until it was too late to do anything about them. We had no desire to start a war.
>
> We sent the Americans a note saying we agreed to remove our missiles on the condition that the President promised that there would be no invasion of Cuba by the forces of the United States.
>
> Finally Kennedy gave in and agreed to give us such an assurance. It was a great victory for us, a spectacular success without having to fire a single shot!

▲ Khrushchev's views of the crisis in his autobiography *Khrushchev Remembers*, published in 1971.

Exam-style questions

1. Why was Kennedy concerned by events in Cuba between 1959 and 1961?

2. Did any country win the Cuban Missile Crisis?

3. Study sources 6 and 7. Having read source 7 are you surprised by what Khrushchev is saying in source 7? Explain your answer using details from the sources and your knowledge.

4. Read sources 6 and 8. Having read source 6 and studied the events of the Cuban Missile Crisis, are you surprised by the content of source 8?

5. Study source 8. What is the cartoonist's message? Explain your answer using details of the source and your knowledge.

6. Study sources 9 and 10. Was Khrushchev lying in one of these sources? Use the sources and your knowledge to explain your answer.

7. Study all the sources. How far do these sources support the view that Khrushchev's motive for putting missiles into Cuba was to protect Cuba from the USA? Use the sources to explain your answer.

5.3 American involvement in Vietnam

Background

Before the Second World War, Vietnam (or Indo-China as the French called it) was ruled by France. In 1942 it was occupied by the Japanese. In 1945, following the defeat of Japan the French returned hoping to rule Vietnam.

There was strong opposition to French rule. This was led by the Vietminh. This resistance movement had been set up by Ho Chi Minh. They were determined to rule their own country. In 1954 the Battle of Dien Bien Phu marked the end of French involvement in Vietnam.

Under the Geneva Peace Accords of 1954, agreed by the Vietminh and the French, Indo-China was split into three countries: Laos, Cambodia and Vietnam. Vietnam was temporarily portioned into two parts (north and south) at the 17th parallel. Free elections were to be held in 1956. These elections never took place because America feared the communists would win. The idea of the "domino theory" was introduced by the US, where if one country fell to communism, others nearby would follow.

Vietnam was seen as a battleground against communism and so in 1955 the Americans supported Ngo Dinh Diem to set up the Republic of South Vietnam. Diem was bitterly opposed to communism. He ran a corrupt government, showing little consideration for the Vietnamese.

Soon after the peace conference the South began fighting against the Vietcong. The Vietcong were a communist party based in South Vietnam and supported by the communists of the North. The Vietcong used guerrilla warfare.

The conflict was widening and bringing full-scale war closer.

Why did America become involved in Vietnam?

- Diem's government was weak and needed support.
- US policy was based on the idea of "containment". The French were supported to avoid the spread of communism across Asia.
- President Eisenhower believed in the "domino theory"— if South Vietnam was allowed to become communist, then Laos, Cambodia, Burma, India, Thailand and Pakistan would quickly follow.
- American airforce pilots were sent to support France.
- After France had left, military and economic aid was offered to the South. Additionally 900 military advisers were sent to South Vietnam.
- By 1963, the communist Vietcong controlled 40% of South Vietnam.

▲　Fig. 5.5 The domino effect

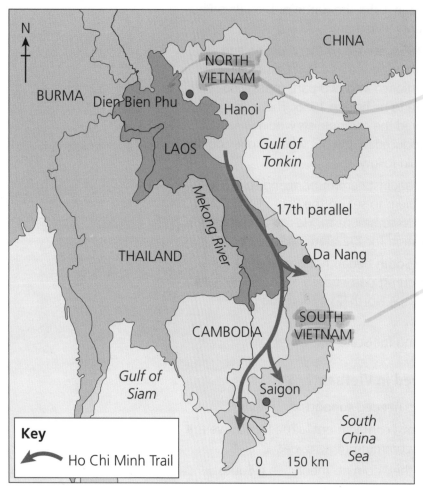

▲　Fig. 5.6 The location of Vietnam

Why did American involvement in Vietnam increase?

President Kennedy decided to increase American military presence. He wanted to look strong after the failed Bay of Pigs invasion and the Cuban Missile Crisis. As well as money to increase the size of the South Vietnamese army he increased the number of advisers sent to Vietnam by 100. The role of the advisers was to train the South Vietnamese army.

Tension between the North and South increased and by the end of 1962 the number of military advisers had reached 12,000. South Vietnam also received 300 helicopters. In 1963 the number of advisers totalled 16,000.

In November 1963, President Diem was overthrown by a military coup and later the same month President Kennedy was assassinated. His successor President Lyndon B Johnson was more prepared to enter into full-scale conflict in Vietnam than Kennedy had been.

In August 1964, two American warships were attacked by North Vietnamese gunboats while in international waters. This confrontation was known as "The Gulf of Tonkin Incident". In response, the American Senate granted Johnson permission to give armed support to South Vietnam.

Main events of the Vietnam War

February 1965	**Operation Rolling Thunder**—bombing of North Vietnam started, with targets that included the Ho Chi Minh Trail.
March 1965	The first American combat troops were sent to Vietnam.
January 1968	The Tet Offensive—a large-scale communist attack on major towns and cities in South Vietnam. Targets included the American embassy in Saigon. Although the communists were defeated, the attacks were a major shock to Americans who thought the war almost won. The American media called it a defeat and public support for the war plummeted. Following the Tet Offensive peace talks started. A ceasefire was not achieved for a further five years.
March 1968	A group of American soldiers were searching for Vietcong. They landed by helicopter close to the village of My Lai. They failed to find any and so rounded up the inhabitants of the village and massacred them all, including infants. When news of the massacre reached the American people there was shock and horror. Numerous anti-war demonstrations followed.
October 1968	Operation Rolling Thunder finished. More bombs have been dropped on North Vietnam than were dropped by the US on Germany and Japan during the Second World War. Also in this month the American policy of **Vietnamisation** started. It was introduced by President Nixon.
1970	President Nixon attacked Cambodia to prevent the Vietcong from using it as a base from which to attack US forces.
1973	A ceasefire agreement was signed.

▲ Table 5.2 Events of the Vietnam War

Operation Rolling Thunder

A US plan to stop North Vietnam supplying the Vietcong. They bombed factories, military bases and the Ho Chi Minh Trail. The idea was to make the bombing so heavy that ground troops would not be required.

Vietnamisation

This was support given by the US to strengthen the South Vietnamese army to allow the gradual withdrawal of American combat troops.

Whose military tactics were the most effective—the USA's or the communists?

Strategy used by the Vietcong during the Vietnam War	
Ho Chi Minh based the Vietcong **guerrilla warfare** strategy on the methods used by the communists to gain power in China.	
Features of Vietcong guerrilla warfare	**Impact**
• Guerrilla fighters did not have a base camp. • They did not wear a uniform, making it difficult to differentiate between villagers and Vietcong. • They used the element of surprise and then just as quickly disappeared into the jungle, taking refuge in villages or their underground tunnels. • They ambushed American troops and set booby traps using trip wires and mines. • The closeness of fighting ("hanging on to American belts") negated the greater strength of American fire power.	• Reduced the morale of the American troops whose average age was only 19. • Increased the number of American casualties.

▲ Table 5.3 The Vietcong's strategy

Guerrilla warfare

A method of fighting employed by the Vietcong. It involved hit-and-run tactics in an attempt to reduce the morale of the opposition.

Source 12

> You never knew who your enemy was or who was your friend. They all looked alike. They were all Vietnamese. Some of them were Vietcong. A woman says her husband isn't Vietcong. She watches your men walk down a trail and get killed by a booby-trap. Maybe she planted it herself. The enemy was all around you.

▲ An account by an American marine captain. This account was given after the end of the war.

Source 13

▲ A Vietnamese poster published in 1968.

✔ Why did the Vietnamese publish the poster in source 13?

Strategies used by the USA during the Vietnam War	
Strategy	**Impact**
Strategic bombing During the war the US bombed Vietcong strongholds, supply lines and key cities. Operation Rolling Thunder started in 1965. Bombing continued after Operation Rolling Thunder stopped in 1968.	• Supply lines were disrupted but not stopped. The system of tunnels and underground passages was not affected by the bombing. • South Vietnamese targets were still attacked. Remember this was the area the US were supposed to be protecting. • Extensive bombing of Hanoi (the North Vietnam capital) encouraged the commencement of peace discussions. • The cost of bombing to the US was huge.
Chemical weapons The Americans developed **Agent Orange** and also used **napalm**.	• Agent Orange was used to carry out defoliation of the jungle in South Vietnam. The chemical was dropped from the air and removed the leaves from the trees in an attempt to prevent the Vietcong hiding in the jungle. The Vietcong underground supply lines were not affected. • Napalm was often dropped on villages to destroy them. Thousands of innocent Vietnamese civilians received terrible burns and often died. This shocked the American people back home, and lost troops on the ground the support of the villagers.

Search and destroy
 	
 In response to the guerrilla tactics of the Vietcong the Americans carried out raids using helicopters. The helicopters would land near Vietnamese villages. The US forces would then kill hiding Vietcong fighters and set fire to the village.
	• Although some Vietcong were killed the impact was minimal.
	 • The raids were often based on incorrect information resulting in:
	   o villages being destroyed and large numbers of innocent villagers killed
	   o US troops becoming unpopular with the peasants who then gave their support to the Vietcong.
	   o Inexperienced US troops walking into traps.

Strategic villages Whole villages were moved to a new site. The new site was enclosed by barbed wire.	• The Americans were able to control and check those who entered and left the village.

▲ Table 5.4 The USA's strategy

Agent Orange

A strong chemical which killed living vegetation, much like a weedkiller does.

Napalm

A fiercely burning form of petroleum jelly which sticks to the skin causing burns that go down to the bone.

▲ Fig. 5.7 American troops on a "search and destroy" mission.
A soldier is setting fire to a Vietnamese peasant's home.

What other problems did the Americans face during the Vietnam War?

The use of inexperienced troops: The average age of American troops was 19. After 1967, they were "drafted" (conscripted) into the army. Many had just left school and just wanted to return home safely. They were often from poorer homes or immigrant backgrounds.

Low morale: The use of guerrilla warfare affected the morale of the troops as they feared what might happen to them.
Troops turned to drugs, thousands deserted and many committed suicide.

Declining support in South Vietnam: The winning of "hearts and minds" was seen as crucial to US success but the use of tactics which killed civilians lost the support of the Vietnamese people. The My Lai massacre was an event that highlighted the failure of this policy.

Aid from Asian countries: Neighbouring countries of Vietnam showed sympathy to the Vietcong by allowing them to access arms and ammunition. America could not, for diplomatic reasons, enter these countries. Cambodia and Laos used the Ho Chi Minh trail to supply necessities to the Vietcong.

Source 14

> There was no way we could stand up to the Americans. When they attacked we just ran away from them. But when they turned round, we followed them. The Americans' way of fighting was to attack, then call for back-up from their planes and artillery. We would disappear if we could, but if we couldn't we would move very close to them, so the planes could not get at us.

▲ A Vietcong soldier remembers how they fought the Americans in 1996.

Why did the USA withdraw from Vietnam?

Tet Offensive	Up to 1967 the war had been going well for the Americans. During the New Year holiday in January 1967, communist troops attacked major Vietnamese towns and cities including the American embassy in Saigon. The hoped-for revolution in South Vietnam did not materialise and the Vietcong were pushed back. The Offensive was widely seen as a turning point for the US in the war as it was realised that without increasing the number of combat troops the war could not be won. Additionally, increased numbers of troops would bring even more casualties.
My Lai	In March 1968 an American troop patrol entered the village of My Lai. They were on a search-and-destroy mission having been informed that members of the Vietcong were hiding there. No Vietcong were found, but nearly 400 civilians, many of whom were women and children, were massacred by the Americans. When details of the brutal massacre become known it shocked the American public, undermining support for the war. The horror of My Lai and the increasing view that the war was unwinnable lead Johnson to decide not to run again for president.
Press and media	In the early years of the war, most American newspapers and news journalists were supportive of the war. The reports they produced were positive as they did not wish to undermine the American government's policy of containment. By 1967 reports from Vietnam were via television programmes which often showed scenes of shocking violence from search-and-destroy raids. At the same time TV reporters were increasingly arguing that the war was unwinnable. One such reporter was CBS' Walter Cronkite. This changing attitude was not just influencing the American public but even President Johnson. US military leaders including General Westmoreland put forward the view that the media reduced support for the war effort in Vietnam. Others put forward the view that attitudes had been changing since the Tet Offensive of 1967.
Protests against the war	Public opinion was changing. As more and more bodies of young servicemen were brought home in body bags the public began asking if America could win the war. To show disapproval, "draft cards" were burnt and President Johnson was taunted by students. American student anti-war protests reached their height towards the end of the 1960s. They held the view that the war was morally wrong and therefore did not wish to receive the draft. Often the protests involved the burning of the American flag and ended in violent clashes with the police. One such clash was at Kent State University where the US national guard fired into a group of unarmed protestors. Four students were killed.
Human and economic cost	In 1967, *Life* magazine calculated that it was costing $400,000 for each Vietcong fighter killed. This meant cutbacks in the spending on social reforms in President Johnson's "Great Reform" programme. By 1968, 300 US troops were dying each week. Over 50,000 US troops eventually lost their lives.

▲ Table 5.5 Reasons for US withdrawal from Vietnam

The end of war in Vietnam

It was left to President Nixon to find a way out of Vietnam. This was a difficult task as from 1965 the American government had argued that the war was just and vital.

Nixon introduced a policy of "Vietnamisation". This meant that America would train and equip the South Vietnamese so that American troops could withdraw.

In February 1973 a ceasefire was agreed.

Results of the war

Within two years of the end of the war, South Vietnam fell to the communists, as did Cambodia and Laos. During 1975 communist troops took South Vietnam including the capital, Saigon. In 1976 North and South Vietnam were reunited as a single communist country ruled by Ho Chi Minh.

Relations between Vietnam and the USA remained hostile until 1993 when trade was resumed.

Over 700,000 war veterans suffered psychological effects from the fighting. Huge areas of land were left ruined by the use of chemicals. The land was littered with unexploded shells and bombs.

The end of the policy of containment was announced by President Nixon.

> ✔ 1. Produce a timeline of important events in relation to the Vietnam War. Start in 1954 and end in 1975.
> 2. What were the consequences of the war in Vietnam. Display these on a spider diagram.

Exam-style questions

1. What was Vietnamisation?
2. Why was television an important aspect of media coverage of the war in Vietnam?
3. 'Search and destroy was the most effective military strategy used by America in Vietnam.' How far do you agree?
4. Read sources 12 and 14. Which of these sources is more useful to explaining military tactics used in Vietnam?

How secure was the USSR's control over Eastern Europe, 1948–c.1989?

Background

The end of the Second World War had brought increasing Soviet control over the countries of Eastern Europe. To some this generated hope based on the significant industrial growth achieved by the Soviet Union prior to the war. However, the reality of Soviet control was very different: the right to democratic government and free speech was lost; newspapers were censored; government critics were put in prison; travel to countries in the West was prohibited.

Eastern bloc factories produced the goods demanded by the Soviet Union rather than those ordinary people wanted. There were shortages of basics including coal, milk and meat. Clothing was very expensive and consumer goods such as electric kettles and radios were unavailable. Wages were even less than those in the Soviet Union. Stalin forbade the countries of Eastern Europe from applying for Marshall Aid.

When Stalin died in 1953 to be replaced by Khrushchev, Khrushchev talked of peaceful co-existence with the West and wanting to improve living standards for the people of Eastern Europe. He indicated to these countries that they would be allowed greater independence to control their own affairs. Khrushchev even went as far as denouncing Stalin. A programme of de-Stalinisation was to follow.

The people of Eastern Europe saw this changing attitude as a positive step towards greater freedom. How was Khrushchev likely to respond to any challenge? The world was soon to find out!

6.1 Why was there opposition to Soviet control in Hungary in 1956 and how did the USSR react?

Reasons for opposition to Soviet control

- The country was run by the Hungarian Communist Party despite them only achieving 17% of the vote.
- The people suffered from repression and strict control. Russian control had brought censorship, secret police and restrictions on education. Religion was banned for being subversive.
- Following the war, Hungary was poor and needed rebuilding yet much of the industrial production was sent to Russia. Food produced ended up on a similar journey, causing the standard of living to drop.
- The Hungarians resented the presence of thousands of Soviet troops and officials in their country, especially as they had to pay for the troops.
- They were unhappy with the hard-line communist leader Rákosi. He was "retired" from office to be replaced by Gerö who was just as unacceptable. The more acceptable Imre Nagy then took over to form a new government.

Actions planned by Nagy's government

When Nagy took over he introduced a plan to change life in Hungary.
- Free elections would be held.
- Law courts would become impartial.
- Farm land was to be restored to private ownership.
- There would be a reduction in the Soviet influence on the daily way of life in Hungary.
- He wanted to ensure the total withdrawal of the Soviet army. (Some troops had already withdrawn.)
- Crucially Nagy intended to withdraw Hungary from the Warsaw Pact.

Why did the Hungarians think they would be successful?

- As already stated there was a feeling that Khrushchev was in favour of reduced control over the satellite countries following Stalin's death.
- When there had been a rising of workers in Poland in June 1956, Russia had given in to some of their demands.
- Hungarians thought they would have support from the United Nations and also the new US President, Eisenhower. He had made supportive comments in speeches.

Source 1

▲ A British cartoon published on 31 October 1956. Khrushchev is shown with a whip, trying to train the 'bears' of Eastern Europe.

How did the USSR react to this opposition?

At first Khrushchev appeared to be prepared to accept some reforms but he was not prepared to accept Hungary leaving the Warsaw Pact. On 28 October, Khrushchev agreed to the demands of Nagy to remove Soviet troops.

But on 4 November thousands of Soviet troops and one thousand tanks moved into Budapest, the capital. Bitter street fighting followed as the Hungarians did not give in. The latest research suggests about 3,000 Hungarians died along with about 8,000 Russians. Another 200,000 fled the country.

Nagy was imprisoned and later executed.

Source 2

> Civilised people of the world! Our ship is sinking. Light is fading. The shadows grow darker over the soil of Hungary. Hungary is dying. Help us!
>
> There is no stopping the wild onslaught of communism. Your turn will come, once we perish. Save our souls! Save our souls! We beg you to help us in the name of justice and freedom.

▲   From a broadcast by Radio Budapest to the West in November 1956.

Source 3

> The Fascist Rebellion in Hungary has been crushed thanks to the strong action of the Hungarian people and Soviet armed forces fighting the counter-revolution. This action was at the request of the Hungarian government.

▲   The Soviet representative speaking at the United Nations, December 1956.

6.2 Why was there opposition to Soviet control in Czechoslovakia in 1968 and how did the USSR react?

Reasons for opposition to Soviet control

- Communism was restrictive. Censorship, lack of freedom of speech and the activities of the secret police were aspects of daily life hated by the people.
- The Czechoslovakian economy was struggling and the standard of living falling during the 1960s.
- Dubcek introduced the idea of the "Prague Spring" of 1968. This became known as "socialism with a human face". Dubcek's proposals for change included:
  - the abolition of censorship, allowing the press to print what they wanted
  - freedom of speech, allowing criticism of the government
  - in industry, the creation of workers' councils and increased rights for trade unions
  - freedom of movement for all people.
- Wary of what happened in Hungary, Dubcek made a clear statement that Czechoslovakia did not wish to leave the Warsaw Pact or end its alliance with the Soviet Union.
- Dubcek, however, planned to cooperate with Romania and Yugoslavia. This increased Soviet concerns.

How secure was the USSR's control over Eastern Europe, 1948–c.1989?

6

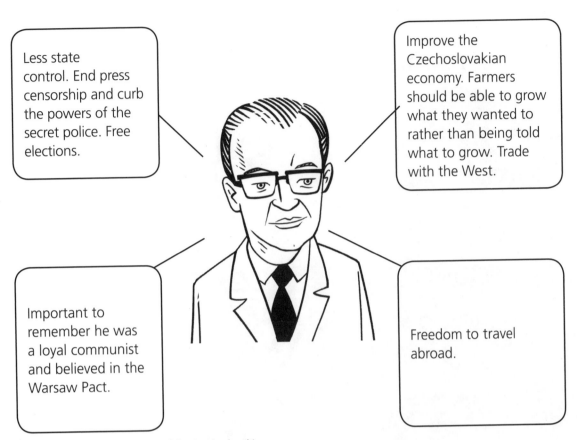

Less state control. End press censorship and curb the powers of the secret police. Free elections.

Improve the Czechoslovakian economy. Farmers should be able to grow what they wanted to rather than being told what to grow. Trade with the West.

Important to remember he was a loyal communist and believed in the Warsaw Pact.

Freedom to travel abroad.

▲ Fig. 6.1 What Dubcek wanted for Czechoslovakia

In 1968 Brezhnev had taken over as leader of the Soviet Union. He was just as determined as his predecessors to maintain Soviet control of Eastern Europe. Czechoslovakia was an important country within the Warsaw Pact because of the strength of its industry. He knew that if Czechoslovakia gained more freedom other Eastern European countries would want the same.

He took action to stop reform in Czechoslovakia:

- Brezhnev instructed Dubcek to stop his reforms.
- Pressure was put on Brezhnev by the East German Leader, Ulbricht.
- Troops from countries within the Warsaw Pact carried out training exercises on the Czech border.

Source 4

> Tass is authorised to state that the Party and Government leaders of the Czechoslovak Socialist Republic have asked the Soviet Union and other allied states to give assistance to the Czechoslovak people, including assistance using armed forces. This action was brought about by the threat from anti-government forces. The troops will be withdrawn as soon as the threat to Czechoslovakia has been eliminated.
>
> These actions serve the purpose of peace. Nobody will ever be allowed to break the chain of Socialist countries.

▲ A report issued by Tass, the official news agency of the Soviet Union, on 21 August 1968.

On 20 August 1968 Soviet tanks moved into Czechoslovakia. While some fighting occurred there was nothing comparable to what happened in Hungary. Generally the Czechs refused to cooperate.

Dubcek was removed from power and taken to Moscow.

Source 5

"She Might Have Invaded Russia"

▲ An American cartoon published in September 1968

The Brezhnev Doctrine

This was introduced in order to stop such events happening again in other countries. It stated that all Warsaw Pact countries should work together to prevent any attempt by a country to leave the Pact. Military force could be used by the USSR if any attempt to leave the Pact was made by a member country.

6.3 How similar were events in Hungary in 1956 and in Czechoslovakia in 1968?

	How were events similar?	How were they different?
Causes	Both countries had a long-term resentment of Soviet rule.	Hungary was affected by issues in other countries: the rebellion in Poland inspired them to act. Czechoslovakia was affected by issues at home: economic depression and a desire for political change.
Aims of the rebels	Both wanted to give their people more rights and lessen the control of the communist state.	In Hungary these changes included withdrawing from the Warsaw Pact and Soviet influence. Czechoslovakia did not want to go that far.
Actions of the people	Both involved groups of people protesting.	In Czechoslovakia, the people's actions were largely started by the role of their leader. It was his changes that encouraged them to protest. In Hungary, it was the people who acted first.
Why the Soviet Union intervened	The Soviet Union was very suspicious and fearful that any form of rebellion/change would spread and lead to a split in its control in other countries.	The political nature of Czechoslovakia was particularly dangerous for the Soviets; they had faced people-led rebellions before like that in Hungary, but the "Prague Spring" was started by people who were meant to be under Soviet control.
How each state responded to Soviet intervention	Both leaders were removed from office. Both resulted in mass emigration.	In Hungary the people armed themselves and fought when the Soviets attacked. In Czechoslovakia, following orders from the government, the people did not fight back. In Czechoslovakia there were several protests after the Russian invasion including suicides.
Reaction of the wider world	Reactions to both were wholly negative to Soviet use of force. The situation in Hungary was discussed at the United Nations; with Czechoslovakia the Soviet actions were condemned by different countries including the USA.	With the Czechoslovakian invasion some members of the communist Warsaw Pact expressed shock at Soviet actions. The Romanian leader complained about Russian intervention.

▲ Table 6.1 Similarities and differences between the events in Hungary (1956) and in Czechoslovakia (1968)

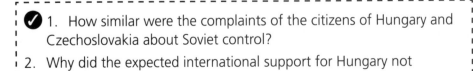

1. How similar were the complaints of the citizens of Hungary and Czechoslovakia about Soviet control?

2. Why did the expected international support for Hungary not materialise?

6.4 Why was the Berlin Wall built in 1961?

What was the Berlin Wall?

At the end of the Second World War, the city of Berlin was split into four zones. A wall was constructed to seal East Berlin from the West.

The Wall was constructed on 13 August 1961. Originally the wall was constructed of barbed wire but over time it became a permanent concrete structure. All crossing points were sealed except one which became known as Checkpoint Charlie.

▲ Fig. 6.2 A photograph taken on 13 August 1961 showing the Berlin Wall under construction.

Berlin was now divided by a wall 87 miles long. The wall was to prevent the movement of people from East to West. Already nearly 2.6 million had left East Germany for the West. Anyone trying to defect to the West was shot.

Why were people leaving East Berlin?

The quality of life was much better in the West. West Germany had been able to use Marshall Aid to rebuild following the devastation of war.

In West Berlin shops were full of a variety of goods and freedom was greater, as was wealth. The attraction of capitalism was significant compared to the harsh regime of East Germany under hard-line communist leader Ulbricht.

What was the impact of this movement on East Germany?

The communists feared a "brain drain" as skilled workers, including engineers, physicians, teachers, and lawyers were all leaving in high numbers.

Negative propaganda was created. In the context of the Cold War the numbers that were leaving a communist country created a feeling of unpopularity for communism. It became good propaganda for the West—the West was attractive while the East had to erect a wall to keep people in.

What were the immediate consequences of the building of the Berlin Wall?

There were two immediate consequences:

- The flow of people from East to West stopped.
- Berlin became a focus of the Cold War.

6.5 What was the significance of "Solidarity" in Poland for the decline of Soviet influence in Eastern Europe?

The rise of Solidarity

From the end of the Second World War, Soviet control of Poland increased in unpopularity. Over the years there had been numerous protests about wages and food prices in an attempt to improve the standard of living but nothing which offered a challenge to the rule of the Soviet Union.

By 1979 the Polish economy was at crisis point. In July of 1980 the government was forced to raise the price of goods, including food, while at the same time blocking any pay increases. People were facing poverty and responded by going on strike. The strikes spread quickly across the country.

One such strike was led by Lech Walesa. The strikers worked at the Lenin Shipyard in Gdansk (Danzig). They went on strike on the 14 August 1980, dismayed with the conditions they were facing. The strikers had a list of 21 demands as well as demanding the right to form a trade union.

By the end of August the right to form a union free from government control was accepted and by mid-September "Solidarity" was formed.

Why did the communist Polish government agree to meet the demands of Solidarity?

Fear of a general strike: The government was afraid of a general strike which would devastate the economy of Poland. They thought there might be a general strike as originally the Solidarity membership came mainly from important areas of shipbuilding and heavy industry.

Popularity: The movement was thought of as trustworthy and represented around 80% of the workers from a wide spectrum of Polish life. Walesa was seen as a folk hero by many. Popularity was helped as the union message was spread through its own newspaper.

Support of the Catholic Church: In Poland the government was unable to crush the church because of the strong faith of the people.

The Polish government hoped that in a relatively short period of time Solidarity would split into splinter groups, just as previous protest movements had.

In his negotiations, Walesa was careful not to provoke the Soviet Union, working to reinforce the view that Solidarity was not an alternative to the Communist Party. Violence was avoided.

The Soviet Union needed to tread carefully. Solidarity had gained support in the West though media support and the charisma of Walesa.

Why was action taken against Solidarity in December 1981?

General Jaruzelski became Prime Minister of Poland in February 1981. He and Walesa tried to work together but their relationship was tense. It finally failed in December.

Solidarity had gone too far. Jaruzelski claimed he had evidence that the Solidarity leaders were planning a coup.

Jaruzelski wanted to avoid the Soviet Union entering Poland to restore communist control. Brezhnev had ordered the Red Army to carry out "training" on the Polish border. Jaruzelski imposed martial law and Solidarity was outlawed. Walesa and most of the Solidarity leaders were put in prison.

Events of 1981 had shown that without military force, communist control was very shaky.

Source 6

> I was summoned three times to the Soviet Union. On the last occasion I was shown army manoeuvres all along the Polish border. The Soviet army leader, Marshall Ustinov, informed me that the USSR would not accept what was happening to Poland.

▲ General Jaruzelski describing the pressure applied on him by the Soviets to deal with Solidarity in late 1981.

How important was Solidarity?

In 1985 Gorbachev became leader of the Soviet Union. He introduced a number of reforms, including the release of political prisoners connected with Solidarity. However, Gorbachev's reforms did not improve Poland's economic situation.

Although Jaruzelski was technically still in power, Solidarity held the real power. It was only a matter of time before communism collapsed in Poland.

By 1988 strikes were again sweeping through Poland as food costs rose by 40%. Walesa negotiated with the Polish government to find a solution.

In April 1989, Solidarity was again legalised, fielding candidates in the upcoming elections. Solidarity won every seat it contested and the first non-communist government of the post-war era was formed with Walesa as President. Solidarity had demonstrated to the rest of the eastern bloc that communist control could be resisted.

How secure was the USSR's control over Eastern Europe, 1948–c.1989?

6

Source 7

"DON'T SAY WE DIDN'T WARN YOU – THIS CRISIS IS ENTIRELY YOUR FAULT!"

▲ A British cartoon published in December 1981.

> ✔ 1. Study source 6. How far do you think that Jaruzelski is telling the truth in this source?
> 2. Study the cartoon in source 7. What is the cartoonist's message?

6.6 How far was Gorbachev personally responsible for the collapse of Soviet control over Eastern Europe?

What was the state of the Soviet Union in 1985 when Gorbachev became leader?

- Soviet citizens had no loyalty to the government, resenting the way their lives were run.
- The controlling of other countries was outdated. The Soviet Union could no longer afford the cost of maintaining a military presence in European satellite states.
- The economy was very weak as too much money was being spent on the arms race and an unwinnable war in Afghanistan. The economy was still run as it was at the time of Stalin. Factories produced cheap, shoddy goods. Food was in short supply.
- The standard of living was low compared to the West.
- There was much corruption in government.

The role of Gorbachev

Gorbachev introduced a policy of "glasnost" (openness). This involved freedom of expression with more freedom for the media, allowing news of government corruption and the criticism of government officials. Citizens became aware of some of Russia's past—details about some of Stalin's brutal excesses were revealed.

The other main Gorbachev policy was "perestroika" (restructuring). This aimed to make the Soviet economy more modern and efficient. It included:

- encouraging private ownership of Soviet industry and agriculture
- reducing state control over imports and exports
- allowing trade with non-eastern bloc countries
- allowing foreign investments in Russian businesses
- an increase in the production and trade in consumer goods.

He realised that Eastern Europe must be allowed to choose its own destiny. He made it clear he would not stand in the way of attempts at democracy in Warsaw Pact countries, and unlike in the past, troops would not be used to keep countries tied to the Soviet Union.

He abandoned the Brezhnev Doctrine, making moves to establish a more friendly relationship with the West. Arms reduction treaties were signed with the USA.

The reforms were introduced too quickly, however, and without proper thought and planning. This plunged the Soviet Union into confusion and economic chaos. Soviet people began to demand an end to communism.

Reforms were introduced too quickly and without proper thought and planning, plunging the Soviet Union into confusion and economic chaos.

Introduced a policy of "glasnost" (openness). This involved freedom of expression.

Arms reduction treaties were signed with the US.

Introduced "perestroika" (restructuring). This aimed to make the Soviet economy more modern and efficient by increasing production and trade in consumer goods.

He abandoned the Brezhnev Doctrine, making moves to establish a more friendly relationship with the West.

Decided Eastern Europe must be allowed to choose its own destiny.

▲ Fig. 6.3 Gorbachev and the collapse of communism

Source 8

▲ A British cartoon published in June 1990. It depicts Soviet President Mikhail Gorbachev sitting on a wall.

> ✓ 1. Look at source 8. How far would the people living in eastern bloc countries agree with the message of this source?
>
> 2. How far would you agree with the view that "Gorbachev cannot be blamed for the collapse of Soviet control over Eastern Europe"?

The role of other countries

Between the spring of 1989 and the spring of 1991 every communist or former communist Eastern European country held democratic parliamentary elections.

In November 1989 the Berlin Wall was dismantled and on the 3 October 1990 Germany became a united country once again.

Many people in Eastern Europe were suffering from poverty. They were affected by food shortages, crime and alcoholism. Gorbachev was unable to shield the public from the fact that eastern bloc countries were much poorer than the majority of people in the capitalist West.

The war in Afghanistan

The war badly overstretched the Soviet economy and demoralised their military. Soviet actions were condemned by other countries who applied pressure to withdraw. The cost was significant, as was the loss of 10,000 Soviet soldiers. Even more important was the impact of the war on the Muslim world.

The role of the USA

US President Ronald Reagan sought to end the Cold War. Reagan and Gorbachev signed treaties to limit nuclear weapons. The Soviet Union found it could not compete with the US in the "arms race" and so had to use diplomacy to secure peace. Additionally its outdated industry was causing environmental problems, such as the explosion at the Chernobyl nuclear power plant in 1986.

Exam-style questions

1. What action did the Soviet Union take against Hungary in 1956?

2. Why was Soviet action in Czechoslovakia different to that in Hungary?

3. 'The Berlin Wall was necessary.' How far do you agree with that statement?

4. How important were Gorbachev's policies in ending Soviet power over countries in Eastern Europe?

5. Study source 1. Why was this cartoon published in October 1956. Explain your answer using details from the cartoon and your knowledge.

6. Study sources 2 and 3. After reading source 2, are you surprised by the comments of the Soviet representatives (source 3)? Use the sources and your knowledge to explain your answer.

7. Study source 4. How reliable is this source as evidence of the reasons for Soviet involvement in Czechoslovakian in 1968? Use the source and your knowledge to explain your answer.

8. Study source 5. What is the cartoonist's message? Use details of the cartoon and your knowledge to explain your answer.

9. Study all the sources. How far do these sources provide convincing evidence that the Soviet Union wanted to help the citizens of Hungary and Czechoslovakia? Use the sources to explain your answer.

Why did events in the Gulf matter, c.1970–2000?

Background

By the final third of the twentieth century oil was a vital commodity for industrialised nations of the world. The states located around the Persian Gulf (Iran, Iraq, Kuwait, Saudi Arabia, Bahrain, Qatar, United Arab Emirates and Oman) collectively housed around one half of the world's known oil reserves. It was therefore of vital importance that countries followed diplomatic and foreign policies which promoted peace and stability in this part of the world. Events in the Gulf were therefore of prime importance to the rest of the world to ensure steady supplies at stable prices. Yet throughout this period the Gulf region was one of instability and volatility.

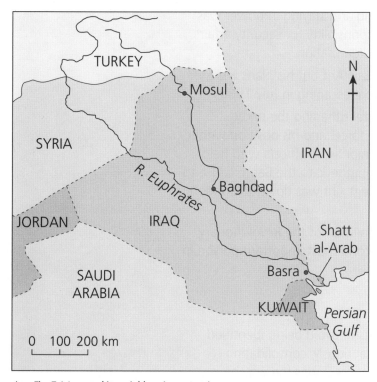

▲ Fig. 7.1 Iraq and its neighbouring countries.

7.1 Why was Saddam Hussein able to come to power in Iraq?

Early life

Saddam, politically influenced by his uncle Khairallah Tulfah, developed an appreciation of Arab nationalism. Inspired by these political views he joined the Baath party in 1957 becoming involved in violent anti-government activities. In these early years Saddam established his credentials as a ruthless operator and man of action.

In July 1958 the Hashemite monarchy was overthrown by General Qassem and Iraq became a republic. Saddam was selected by the Baath party to participate in an attempted assassination of General Qassem in October 1959. The attempt failed but Saddam emerged as one of Iraq's most wanted men. Saddam had to go into exile and spent the time extending his education in Egypt.

In February 1963 Qassem was overthrown and died. He was replaced by a government consisting of army officers and the Baath Party. Saddam held a minor position in this government.

Building up a power base

Saddam gave his support to the new Prime Minister, Ahmad Hasan al-Bakr, and set out to prove he was indispensable. Following infighting in the Baath Party they were ousted from power. While the extremist wings of the party were discredited, Bakr's position as leader of the moderates strengthened. This helped Saddam, as his support was rewarded with a position within the Regional Command. This was the decision-making body of the Baath Party within Iraq.

Saddam soon realised that the key to acquiring and staying in power was an armed force. He now aimed to acquire responsibility for security affairs and was put in charge of the Party's military organisation.

He immediately plotted a coup against President Arif but his plans were uncovered and he spent two years in jail before escaping in July 1966.

Upon his escape, Saddam concentrated on strengthening the party, including the establishment of a new military force, and his position within the party. He collaborated with a group of senior army officers who held key government positions and who were sympathetic to the Baath cause to carry out a bloodless coup (July 1968). President Arif was flown to London and Bakr became President.

Saddam's reward was to be made Deputy Chairman of the Revolutionary Command Council. Saddam was now the second most important person in the government.

The road to presidency

In his position as Deputy, Saddam was anxious to avoid being identified as having presidential ambitions. He moved cautiously, consolidating his political relationship with Bakr. His key to success was the way he outwitted, outmanoeuvred and eliminated those who might pose a threat to him. This was often through the uncovering, or invention, of plots and conspiracies. His targets included civilian politicians as well as high-ranking military personnel.

He appointed individuals friendly to himself to the Revolutionary Command Council. He was the master of political cunning, keeping a low profile and maintaining the dignity of the presidency.

Saddam was extremely adept at foreign issues. He ensured Iraq had a superpower ally by negotiating a Treaty of Friendship and Cooperation with Soviet Russia.

Using money from the nationalised oil industry he improved the lives of the ordinary people by building schools and hospitals, in addition to improving transport facilities.

In 1979 an aging, ailing President Bakr was "encouraged" to resign in favour of Saddam. At the age of 42, Saddam Hussein had achieved the position of leader of Iraq.

✔ Discuss in groups the reasons for Saddam coming to power in Iraq. Classify the reasons under the headings of "Long-term" and "Short-term". Within each of these two groups place the reasons in order of importance. Present your findings to the whole class.

7.2 What was the nature of Saddam Hussein's rule in Iraq?

Saddam Hussein ruled Iraq as a dictator. As President he was Commander-in-Chief of the armed forces. Saddam's political hero was Joseph Stalin, the leader of Soviet Russia. He closely followed many aspects of Stalin's method of governing.

Purges and terror

Once in power Saddam began to deal with those who questioned the way he had gained power.

One high-profile incident involved Mashhadi, the Secretary General of the Revolutionary Command Council, who questioned the validity of Saddam's appointment. He was relieved of his duties and brought before the senior Baath Party members. He gave a detailed fabricated confession of crimes against the state and naming 66 alleged co-conspirators. At a special court, 55 were found guilty and either sentenced to death or given prison sentences.

The purging continued. Hundreds of party members and military officers were removed from their positions, with many being executed.

False accusations, arrests, torture and trials became a regular feature of Saddam's rule by terror. In most instances the accused received lengthy prison sentences or were executed.

Waging war on his own people

Saddam aimed to unify the state of Iraq but this was difficult because of the differences within the population with 20% being Kurds and 60% Shiites. The Shiites were hostile to the Sunni-dominated regime.

Saddam's brutal campaign against the Kurds, who wanted independence, was at its height between 1987 and 1988 and again in 1991. He destroyed half of Kurdistan's villages and towns, killed thousands of Kurds using mustard gas and cyanide, and displaced more than a million people. Many fled to Iran or Turkey while others were housed in concentration camps in the Iraqi desert.

In 1991 Saddam took action against the Shiites. The Republican Guard carried out arrests and summary executions. Civilians were used as human shields, fastened to the front of tanks. Women and children were shot on sight.

In the south-east of Iraq Saddam wanted to destroy the marshes to enable a new waterway to be constructed. The Marsh Arabs were victims of chemical weapon attacks or were starved to death.

Personality cult

Saddam realised that to survive long-term he needed to move away from fear and terror. To sustain his dictatorship, he needed to cultivate popularity and make the Iraqi people love him. Saddam set out to cultivate an image of a father-style leader. This was achieved by:

- establishing a permanent exhibition about himself in Baghdad
- featuring his life story through the press
- glorifying himself though articles in newspapers and on television
- hanging portraits on street corners and in party and government offices
- having songs written in praise of him
- renaming roads after himself
- commissioning statues, murals and paintings

Modernisation

From Iraq's massive oil revenues he carried out an extensive modernisation programme. Wages rose, taxes were cut and basic foodstuffs were subsidised. Modernisation included:

- supplying electricity to even remote villages
- developing heavy industry including, steel, petrochemicals and coal
- building a countrywide network of oil pipelines
- establishing a new radio and television network to enable the spreading of government propaganda
- starting major building programmes for schools, houses and hospitals
- introducing a major campaign to end adult illiteracy
- making hospital treatment free.

Military expansion

Iraq became a major military power, with Soviet Russia providing most supplies. Additional supplies came from many European states. Saddam purchased tanks, planes, helicopters, surface-to-air missiles and electronic equipment.

 1. How important was the cult of personality for Saddam in maintaining his position as President of Iraq?

2. In what ways was Iraq under Saddam a totalitarian state?

By the middle of 1979 he had constructed his first chemical warfare plant and was soon producing chemical weapons, including agents such as anthrax.

Totalitarianism

Saddam aspired to, and ultimately achieved, absolute power in Iraq. He and the Baath Party controlled virtually every aspect of life.

At school, children were brainwashed as were young adults in the Baath youth organisations as they introduced the idea of a glorious leader. Censorship ensured critical views of Saddam were never heard or read. It was a capital offence to criticise government. The law courts were under Saddam's influence, and all economic production was geared to the needs of the state.

Membership of the Baath Party was essential if a career in public office was to be followed.

7.3 Why was there a revolution in Iran in 1979?

The Shah of Iran left the country in January 1979, never to return. He had upset almost every sector of society and the last year of his rule was one of demonstrations, violent deaths and widespread strikes. The pressures for the Shah to go had been building for over 25 years.

Opposition to foreign influence

The Iranian Prime Minister Mohammed Mussadeq was popular with the people as he did not want foreign domination. He nationalised Iran's oil industry thereby upsetting the British who controlled it. The Shah, supported by the CIA and MI6, overthrew Mussadeq in 1953.

This coup resulted in the Shah being associated with the British and Americans whose main interest was the safeguarding of oil supplies to the West. The influence of the USA was even more noticeable when the Shah began importing large quantities of American foodstuffs. This affected local farmers. The Shah even attempted to introduce local shopping malls, damaging the interests of the bazaar merchants.

Dissatisfaction with the Shah's modernisation programme

In the 1960s the Shah introduced the "White Revolution". Many reforms were soon regarded as inadequate.

- Land reform was supposed to redistribute land among the peasantry but in fact most peasants ended up with holdings barely sufficient to support their families.
- The programme failed to ensure that villages all had piped water, electricity and roads.
- Health reforms increased the number of doctors, nurses and hospital beds but failed to reduce infant mortality rates.
- Education reforms failed to impact on the high levels of adult illiteracy.

By the end of the 1970s the distribution of income was becoming more unequal. The rich were living in palaces while the poor were condemned to shanty towns without proper roads and other essential facilities. The actions of the Shah showed insensitivity to the plight of many citizens.

The vast sums of money from oil were used to build up military capability while the majority of the population saw little improvement in their living standards.

Resentment at autocratic and repressive government

Members of the government had to be prepared to accept the Shah's leadership. The cabinet and parliament were packed with supporters.

In March 1975 the Shah established a one-party state. The new Resurgence Party immediately made enemies by waging an anti-profiteering campaign in the bazaars, attacking the clerical establishment and introducing a new calendar.

Established in 1957, the secret police (SAVAK) rooted out opposition to the Shah's rule. It became known for its brutal tactics, including torture, forced confessions and summary execution.

In 1977 there was some relaxation of police controls. This was largely because of international criticism of human rights violations. The Red Cross was allowed into prisons and measures to ensure fair trials were introduced.

The leadership of Ayatollah Khomeini

By the mid-1970s there was widespread opposition to the leadership of the Shah. What was needed was an inspirational person to lead the disparate opposition groups.

Ayatollah Khomeini, a political activist, fulfilled this role. He had been forced into exile in 1964 for undermining the Shah. He clarified the issues to be fought for, particularly the Shah's readiness to agree to foreign influences and supporting Israel against the Muslim world.

He made it clear that he would not return until the Shah had left the country. He returned on 1 February to be met by crowds of over three million. Thousands of civilians celebrated the popular revolution on the streets.

> ✔ Discuss in groups the reasons why the Iranian revolution was successful. Place the reasons in order of importance.

7.4 What were the causes and consequences of the Iran–Iraq War, 1980–88?

In September 1980 Iraq's land and air invasion marked the beginning of war which destabilised the region. The causes were both long-term and also more immediate. On the face of it Saddam was the undoubted aggressor, but it could also be argued he was launching a pre-emptive strike. He wanted to destroy Khomeini before Khomeini destroyed him.

Territorial disputes

Iraq and Iran shared a land border of 1,400 kilometres so it is hardly surprising that there was friction related to territorial issues.

One area of particular dispute was the Shatt al-Arab waterway. This waterway was important for both countries for their oil exports as it provided a link to the Persian Gulf. It was Iraq's only outlet to the sea. In 1937 an agreement, favourable to Iraq, had been signed which placed the boundary between the two countries on the eastern bank of the river. In 1969, the Shah of Iran rejected this treaty and refused to pay any further shipping tolls.

Saddam claimed the right to control the south-western Iranian province of Khuzestan and encouraged the Arabs who lived there to revolt against the Shah's rule. Khuzestan was an oil-rich province. In retaliation Iran began encouraging the Kurds in the north of Iraq to take up arms against Saddam's regime. The Shah provided training bases and military equipment.

The signing of the Algiers Agreement between the two countries in 1975 was regarded as a setback by Saddam and he was determined to regain lost ground. Under the agreement Iran ended its support for the Kurds and in return Iraq dropped its claims to Khuzestan. It was also agreed that the border along the Shatt al-Arab was to be more equitable. Saddam renounced this agreement shortly before invading Iran in September 1980.

Domination of the Gulf

Saddam was looking for a shift in power which would give him dominance of the Gulf. Iraq and Iran were the only serious contenders to be the dominant country as they alone had the necessary financial and military resources. The war between the countries can be regarded as part of the age-old contest for power between the Persians and the Arabs going back to the ancient civilisations.

Saddam believed that with the annexation of Khuzestan and control of the Shatt al-Arab waterway, his oil reserves would expand at the expense of his main rival.

Gaining power was seen by Saddam as an aid to being made leader of the Arab world following Egypt's expulsion as a result of their peace accords with Israel.

The opportunity provided by the Islamic Revolution

Saddam was keen to exploit the impact of the Islamic Revolution of 1979. The overthrow of the Shah brought to an end the alliance between the USA and Iran thus depriving the Iranian army of much needed spare parts for its military weapons. The revolution also brought a major purge of senior officers in the Iranian army thus reducing its effectiveness.

Saddam saw Iran as being politically unstable, in diplomatic isolation and with its military disintegrating. It was a unique opportunity for him.

Delaying would provide Iran with an opportunity to recover but Saddam had miscalculated. Iran was not as weak as anticipated.

Ayatollah Khomeini's opposition to Saddam Hussein

Ayatollah Khomeini regarded Saddam's regime with contempt. This was partly because of its religious composition and partly because he was expelled from Iraq in 1977. Iran was a Shiite Muslim state governed in accordance with Muslim law. By contrast Iraq was a secular state where the leading politicians were Sunni Muslims.

From June 1979 Khomeini encouraged the Iraqi Shiites to overthrow the Baath regime and establish another Islamic republic. Anti-Baath riots broke out and Saddam became convinced that Khomeini was deliberately trying to undermine his government. In Saddam's view the best form of defence was attack.

The course of the war

- Iraq invaded Iran on 22 September 1980, triggering a bitter eight-year war which destabilised the region and devastated both countries.

- Saddam Hussein claimed the reason for invasion was a dispute over the Shatt-al-Arab waterway. This waterway formed the boundary between the two countries. In addition there was regional rivalry.

- Saddam Hussein felt threatened by the Islam Revolution that had brought the Shah to power in 1979.

- The Khomeini saw Saddam as a brutal Sunni tyrant who was oppressing his country's Shia majority.

- By 1982 Iranian forces had regained the territory they had lost but Khomeini rejected an offer of a ceasefire.

The conflict turned into a war of attrition with each side disregarding the human cost:

- Thousands of young Iranians were sent to their death in 'human wave attacks';

- Chemical weapons were used against the Iranians by Saddam and against the Kurds of Halabja – his own people;

- The civilian population of both sides was constantly bombarded from the air;

- Both sides attacked opposition oil tankers in the Gulf in an attempt to prevent trade.

The 'tanker war' changed the war into an international one:

- Both the US and Soviet Union became involved in response to Kuwait's appeal for protection;

- Faced with this opposition Iran became exhausted and isolated. A ceasefire was accepted by Khomeini in July 1988.

Western involvement in the war

The Western powers' interest was two-fold. Firstly they wanted to preserve the balance of power in the Middle East. Secondly they wanted to ensure the uninterrupted flow of oil supplies.

The greatest fear was instability and volatility in the region that would result from an Iranian victory and the installation of Islamic revolutionary governments in the Gulf states. The USA's aim was to ensure that at the very least Iraq did not lose the war. They supplied Iraq with arms, intelligence and finance. Britain, France and West Germany supplied military equipment.

The USA became involved more from May 1984, sending warships to the Gulf to help guarantee oil supplies as each side was attacking the other's tankers and merchant shipping.

Partly as a result of Western assistance Iraq ended the war with a clear military advantage over Iran. It was partly this military superiority that convinced Khomeini to agree to a ceasefire in August 1988.

The consequences of the war

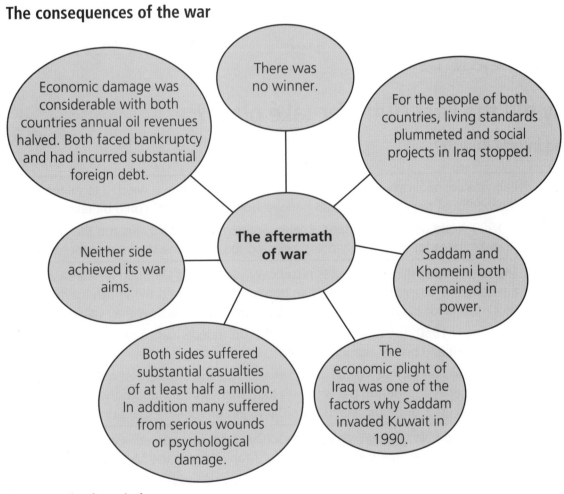

▲ Fig. 7.2 The aftermath of war

The view of Saddam

Saddam claimed a glorious victory for Iraq. He had halted the spread of the Islamic Revolution and prevented the toppling of his regime.

An imposing monument to this achievement appeared in Baghdad, yet Saddam recognised that the people would not be bought off by extravagant symbols. He needed to increase the wealth of his country.

Source 1

"NEARLY THERE..."

Wed 5 Aug 1990

▲ A British cartoon published in August 1990

> ✔ Study source 1.
> What is the cartoonist's message?

7.5 Why did the First Gulf War take place?

Why did Iraq invade Kuwait?

Economic reasons	Iraq was economically weak following the Iran–Iraq War and needed to increase the wealth of the country. Kuwait had valuable oil wells that could be taken over.
	In 1990 world oil prices dropped steeply. Saddam blamed Kuwait and the United Arab Emirates for deliberately overproducing to undermine the Iraqi economy.
Historical relationship with Kuwait	Saddam claimed that Kuwait was historically part of Iraq although it had existed as a separate territory much longer than Iraq had. Iraq blamed the British for it being an almost landlocked state—meddling by imperialists was how they viewed it.
	In the early 1960s the British recognised the full independence of Kuwait. At first Iraq did not and border tensions existed.
	Saddam was angry that Kuwait was demanding the repayment of a $14 billion loan of money lent during the war with Iran. Many Iraqis thought the Kuwaitis ungrateful after being protected from the threat of Iranian expansion.
Standing in the world	Saddam had failed to gain regional leadership from the war—this was another opportunity to become the most powerful Arab leader in the Middle East.
	Iraq was militarily the strongest country in the area and Saddam did not believe the USA or Europe would take any action. After all they had supported the overthrowing of the Shah, an American ally, and had supplied Saddam with arms during the Iranian war.
	Saddam was valued as a stabilising influence in the region. The USA had taken no action when he crushed the Kurds and suppressed the Shiites.
Problems within Iraq	Saddam needed to divert attention away from the problems he was considered to have caused. After the war with Iran, the Iraqi economy was in tatters and yet Saddam continued to strengthen his military machine. There was to be no post-war economic recovery. Saddam was held to blame by factions within society and there were several attempts to overthrow him between 1988 and 1990.

▲ Table 7.1 Reasons for Iraq's invasion of Kuwait

The wider-world reaction to the invasion of Kuwait

The interests of the West were at risk as Saddam was threatening their oil supplies.

As in the case of Iran, Saddam had miscalculated. If he had known in advance that his invasion would have created such a storm he would have taken diplomatic means to achieve his objective.

The United Nations (UN) took the following actions.

- Trade sanctions were placed on Iraq—no country was to trade with Iraq, effectively preventing their oil exports.

- Saddam was ordered to remove his troops by 15 January. If troops were not removed the UN would use "all necessary means" to remove them.

- Saudi Arabia, Syria and Egypt were concerned about what Saddam's next move might be and therefore supported the UN action.

- British Prime Minister Margaret Thatcher and American President Bush decided that Saddam's power should be curbed.

The course of the war

Saddam's Iraqi troops invaded and occupied Kuwait in August 1990.

An international force of over 600,000 troops assembled in Saudi Arabia. A coalition of 34 nations contributed troops, armaments and cash. The involvement of troops from Arab countries such as Egypt and Syria as well as from Muslim countries such as Pakistan and Bangladesh meant Saddam could not claim that this was the West against Arabs and Islam.

Operation Desert Storm, the liberation of Kuwait, began on 17 January 1991.

Air war	• Bombing attacks were carried out on Baghdad (the Iraqi capital) causing many civilian casualties. • Military targets, bridges and roads were also attacked. • Iraq launched SCUD missile attacks on Israel hoping to provoke a split between the West and their Arab allies. This did not happen.
Ground war	• Kuwaiti oil wells were set on fire and blown up by Iraq. Millions of gallons of crude oil poured into the Persian Gulf. • Iraq carried out a brief invasion of Khafji in Saudi Arabia but was driven out by coalition forces. • Within four days the Iraqis had been routed and driven out of Kuwait. Estimates put the Iraqi dead at 90,000 compared to less than 400 of the coalition. Around 10,000 were killed on the "Highway of Death", the six-lane motorway from Kuwait to Basra. • The retreating Iraqis were at the mercy of the coalition but Bush called a ceasefire as he feared the Allies would lose the support of the Arab nations.

▲ Table 7.2 The liberation of Kuwait

◀ Fig. 7.4 The road from Kuwait City to Iraq, the "Highway of Death", showing the aftermath of an American attack, February 1991.

What were the consequences of the First Gulf War?

Following the ceasefire, peace terms were imposed on Iraq by the UN. These terms were:

- recognition of Kuwait's sovereignty

- payment of reparations

- Iraqi cooperation with the UN to uncover and destroy all biological, chemical or nuclear "weapons of mass destruction" (WMD)

- trade sanctions which virtually cut off Iraq from the rest of the world

- "No-fly" zones to be established and policed by American planes flying out of Saudi Arabia as it was feared that Saddam would carry out further atrocities against his own people in the southern and northern areas of the country.

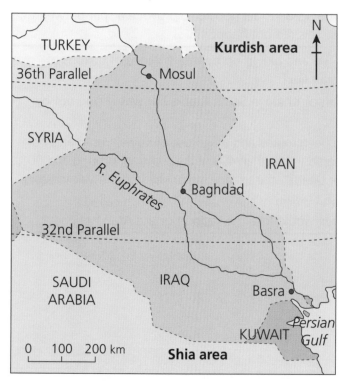

◀ Fig. 7.3 "No-fly" zones of the northern and southern sectors of Iraq

Saddam had suffered a massive, humiliating defeat. His forces had been removed from Iraq within 100 hours of the start of the ground war. Much of Iraq's infrastructure had been destroyed by coalition air attacks. This included power stations, oil refineries, water purification plants, roads and bridges.

Civilian fatalities were estimated at around 100,000. Civilians were facing shortages of food, clean drinking water and medical supplies.

The war and resultant sanctions meant financial disaster for the country.

The future

Saddam had lost the trust of most of the international community through his actions against Kuwait. Major countries whose main concern was the stability of the region began to wonder if Saddam should be removed from power.

> ✔ 1. Produce a diagram to show the main features of the "cult of Saddam".
> 2. Why was Saddam's regime considered brutal?
> 3. What was the significance of oil to the unrest in the Middle East?

Exam-style questions

1. Describe how Saddam treated his own people.
2. What was Saddam's 'personality cult'?
3. Why were the people of Iran unhappy with the Shah's rule?
4. 'The Iran-Iraq War failed to change anything.' How far do you agree with that statement?
5. How significant were the roles of Thatcher and Bush in the First Gulf War? Explain your answer.

8 The First World War, 1914–18

Background

On 28 July 1914 Austria declared war on Serbia. Two days later Russia began the mobilisation of its armed forces despite warnings from Germany. On 1 August Germany declared war on Russia and on 3 August on France. The following day the Schlieffen Plan was put into operation with Germany invading Belgium. This action brought Britain into conflict with Germany.

The First World War, between two rival groups of countries, had started although tensions in Europe had been increasing throughout the early years of the new century. As far back as 1905 General Count Alfred von Schlieffen had created a military plan for Germany.

Source 1

HE WONT BE HAPPY TILL HE GETS IT

▲ A postcard published in Britain in 1914. It shows the Kaiser reaching for the soap.

✔ Study source 1. Are you surprised that this source was published in Britain in 1914?

8.1 Why was the war not over by December 1914?

How was the Schlieffen Plan intended to work?

The plan was designed to ensure a quick, decisive victory for Germany. It was based on the assumption that it would take Russia six weeks to become fully mobilised. During these six weeks, France was to be defeated. This was essential if Germany was not to fight a war on two fronts.

Around 90% of Germany's armed forces were to move through Holland, Belgium and Luxembourg, encircling Paris from the west, and forcing the French to surrender. The remainder of the German army would be sent east to stop the Russian advance.

It was anticipated that Britain would not enter the war at this stage and that Belgium would not resist.

The plan depended on France anticipating the German attack to come through Alsace-Lorraine.

Why did the Schlieffen Plan fail?

1. The German high command thought the plan too daring and changed the route of attack, avoiding Holland and taking the more direct but narrower route through Belgium. On 4 August an army of over one million German soldiers marched into Belgium. The Germans were not expecting the fierce Belgium resistance they encountered. This resistance seriously delayed them.

2. The British Expeditionary Force of 100,000 professional soldiers was sent to France and slowed the German advance at Mons. The Belgian resistance and the BEF slowed down the Germans. They failed to reach Paris in six weeks.

3. The Russians mobilised more quickly than expected and continued to engage with part of the German army. The Germans had to send a further 100,000 troops out of the army advancing on Paris.

4. German forces moved south rather than encircle Paris. This allowed the British to continue to send troops ashore as the Channel ports were not attacked.

5. The French followed "Plan 17" but had to regroup after being heavily defeated in Alsace-Lorraine. They moved their forces to defend Paris from the advancing Germans. By that time the Germans were finding it difficult to keep their army supplied with food and ammunition. Long marches in the August heat were also causing exhaustion.

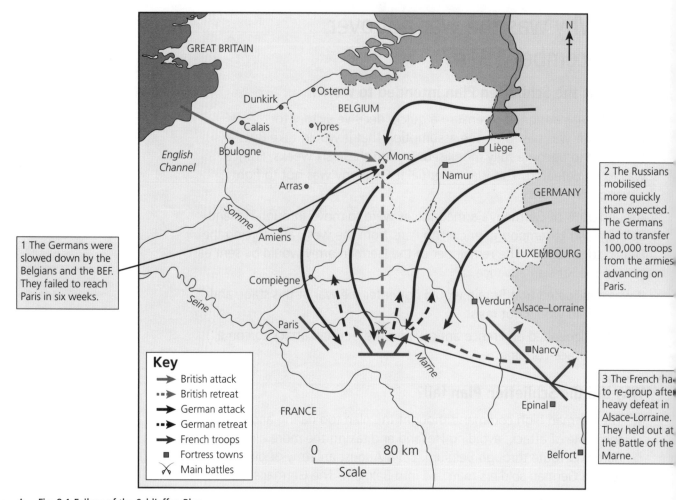

The map contains the following labelled annotations:

1 The Germans were slowed down by the Belgians and the BEF. They failed to reach Paris in six weeks.

2 The Russians mobilised more quickly than expected. The Germans had to transfer 100,000 troops from the armies advancing on Paris.

3 The French had to re-group after heavy defeat in Alsace-Lorraine. They held out at the Battle of the Marne.

Key
- → British attack
- ··▶ British retreat
- → German attack
- ··▶ German retreat
- → French troops
- ■ Fortress towns
- ✗ Main battles

0 ——— 80 km
Scale

▲ Fig. 8.1 Failure of the Schlieffen Plan.

How successful was the British Expeditionary Force (BEF)?

On 23 August the BEF encountered the Germans near to the Belgian town of Mons, fighting heroically and slowing the German advance.

The Germans thought they were facing machine guns, so fast and accurate was British rifle fire. However, the BEF was outnumbered and had to retreat.

The Battle of the Marne

The French and British were on the defensive but things were not going to plan for the Germans. The loss of 100,000 troops to the Russian front had weakened them. Troops were hungry, exhausted and short of ammunition.

The German commander deviated from the original plan by marching to the east of Paris.

The combined strength of the British and the French successfully stopped the German advance along the line of the River Marne. They then counter-attacked, forcing the Germans back to the River Aisne.

Neither side was able to push the other back, resulting in stalemate. For protection from **snipers**, both sides dug trenches.

The race to the sea

The Battle of Marne was a turning point. Germany was now at war on two fronts; the Schlieffen Plan had failed. They realised they were incapable of breaking through enemy lines.

Sniper

A highly-trained marksman who used a rifle to shoot any soldier putting his head above the parapet of the trench.

The Germans took the decision to try to outflank the enemy and the race to the sea began on 12 October 1914.

The first Battle of Ypres (Belgium)

This was a key battle lasting from October to November 1914.

The British lost around 50,000 men with Germany losing twice as many. The British held important ground, preventing the Germans from breaking through. They were able to keep the English Channel ports open, ensuring they were supplied with equipment and reinforcements.

Ypres was the end of the BEF, however. The heavy losses suffered had virtually destroyed the force. Britain would now have to rely on volunteers.

Deadlock

By November 1914 a deadlock had been reached which was to last until 1918. The BEF had been decimated and the French had suffered over one million dead or wounded.

Millions of troops were in trenches which stretched from the sea in the west to the Alps in the east. What had started as a war of rapid movement was now a war of attrition.

This became known as the Western Front.

Exam-style questions

1. Describe the part played by the BEF in the early part of the war.
2. What was the Schlieffen Plan?
3. Why was the failure of the Schlieffen Plan significant?
4. How significant was the role of Belgium in the failure of the Schlieffen Plan?

8.2 Why was there stalemate on the Western Front?

What was living and fighting in the trenches like?

Trench warfare was defensive rather than offensive. The two armies were evenly matched and had to resort to defensive formations to avoid significant losses.

▲ Fig. 8.2 German engineers laying barbed wire in front of a trench.

Infantry men spent much of their time repairing trenches or digging new ones. Supplies and equipment had to be carried along the communication trenches. Some men spent time on sentry duties or in secret listening posts close to the enemy lines. **Sappers** dug tunnels under enemy trenches, placing huge mines there.

There were many dangers to life in the trenches.

Military attacks	• There was a constant risk of being hit by a sniper's bullet. • Infantry charges had replaced cavalry charges. Soldiers were ordered "over the top" and across no man's land to attack the enemy's trenches. In doing this they had to get through barbed wire. • Machine guns were used to repel infantry charges. Millions died well before they reached the enemy trenches. • There was the risk of being hit by shrapnel from the artillery shells fired at enemy lines. • Occasionally there was danger from misdirected shells fired by their own artillery.
Other dangers	• Rats and lice lived on the discarded food, decomposing bodies and other waste. These rats spread infections and contaminated food. The smell in the heat of summer was appalling. • Diseases such as dysentery were rife. Men rarely washed for days or weeks; there were limited toilet facilities and a shortage of fresh water. • Trenches often flooded after heavy rain. This caused a condition called trench foot, an infection causing the flesh to waste and the feet to go numb. It could result in amputation. Duckboards were placed at the bottom of trenches in an attempt to solve the problem of waterlogged trenches.
Other effects	• Many men suffered from "shell shock" due to the constant noise of exploding shells. This caused mental breakdowns. • Due to the awful conditions and fear of death, many soldiers refused to obey orders. This insubordination often resulted in a court martial followed by execution. • Life was tedious and boring.

▲ Table 8.1 Dangers faced by soldiers living in the trenches

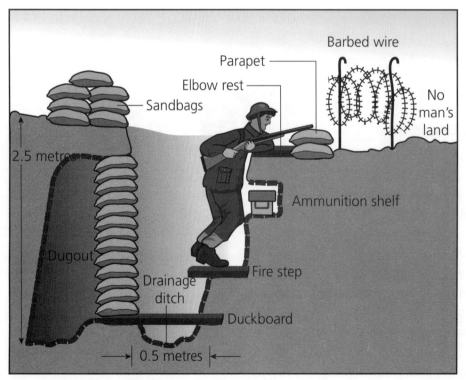

▲ Fig. 8.3 Cross-section of a trench.

Sapper

A member of the British army who dug tunnels and trenches. It was an extremely dangerous job.

Attempts at breakthrough, 1915

Attempts at making a breakthrough were made mostly by the Allies. The Germans were content to remain mainly defensive. They generally held the higher ground.

January	The French attacked at Champagne, but lost over 100,000 soldiers who died or were wounded by German machine guns. No more than eight kilometres was gained.
March	At Neuve Chapelle a breakthrough almost happened but the Allies did not have the necessary equipment. Thirteen thousand British were wounded or killed.
April	The Germans attacked at Ypres and used poison gas for the first time.
May	The advancing British, at Ypres, were mown down by German machine gunners. Again they did not have enough shells to make an impact.
September	At Champagne the French drove the Germans back three kilometres.

▲ Table 8.2 The Allies' attempts at breakthrough

By the end of the year there was still stalemate.

The Battle of Verdun

Why was this battle fought?	To win the war Germany believed they had to force the French to surrender, hoping that at the same time Britain would withdraw. Verdun was important to the French. It was a heavily fortified town and a symbol of French military pride. Germany hoped that success here would be a devastating blow to French morale.
Events	In February 1916 the Germans subjected Verdun to an intense bombardment. This was followed by an attempt to break through and open up the French line. The French were unprepared for such a devastating assault. At one point a French army of 200,000 faced over one million German soldiers. The French were close to breaking point. The Germans failed to break through against the dogged determination of the French and the battle finally ended in December.
Why was this battle significant?	It was the longest battle fought in the entire war. It crucially led to the Battle of the Somme as the French persuaded the British to develop a new offensive elsewhere to make the Germans withdraw some of their troops from Verdun. Despite vast numbers of men and large numbers of casualties it demonstrated that there was little chance of a breakthrough with trench warfare.

▲ Table 8.3 The Battle of Verdun

The Battle of the Somme, July 1916–November 1916
The plan

Phase 1	Phase 2	Phase 3
Action	**Action**	**Action**
1. Heavy artillery shelling of enemy lines for seven days and ending on 1 July. 2. Planting of large mines in tunnels below the enemy trenches.	1. Infantry to advance across no man's land towards enemy front line trenches. 2. The infantry would walk, rather than run, as they were to carry heavy packs.	A second wave of attacks including cavalry to sweep through the seized trenches and onwards.
Purpose	**Purpose**	**Purpose**
1. To damage German defences, inflict heavy casualties and clear barbed wire from no man's land. 2. To cause maximum damage to German front line trenches.	1. To clear German front line trenches of any personnel remaining after shelling. 2. The infantry would carry the heavy repair equipment needed to rebuild and defend the trenches taken from the Germans.	To attack the fleeing German forces and complete the rout.

▲ Fig. 8.4 The plan of attack

Why did the battle take place?	The war had been raging for nearly two years and since the end of 1914 (winter) there had been stalemate. This battle was launched to break through the German lines, killing as many German soldiers as possible (war of attrition). It was also an attempt to relieve pressure on the French at Verdun by getting the Germans to move some of their troops. A victory would have the effect of weakening the German army and reducing their morale. The Commander-in-Chief of the British army Field Marshall Sir Douglas Haig was convinced that the enemy could be overwhelmed by sheer weight of numbers.
Did Haig overestimate the ability of the artillery?	• The Germans were on higher ground, giving a good view of attacking forces. Most of their machines were undamaged by the shelling. • The Germans had taken opportunities to strengthen their defences. Their dugouts were deep underground and fortified with concrete. They had all the food they needed so they were largely unaffected. • The wire in front of the German trenches was almost impossible to penetrate. • Many of the shells supplied to the artillery were of poor quality and not powerful enough to destroy the defences of the enemy. Many shells failed to explode. • The barbed wire in no man's land was not destroyed. Exploding shells lifted it into the air causing an even greater tangle.
The first day of the Battle of the Somme	Intelligence, plus the heavy bombardment, warned the Germans that an attack was imminent. The infantry attack began at 7.30am on 1 July when 200,000 Allied soldiers attacked German trenches. Commanders were confident there would be little resistance.

	The slow walking pace of the British infantry gave the Germans time to emerge from their dugouts and set up their machine guns.
	The wire remained undamaged in some places, making British troops funnel into areas where there were gaps. They were sitting targets for German machine gunners.
	It was the worst military disaster in the history of the British army with 20,000 Allied troops killed and 40,000 wounded.

▲ Table 8.4 The Battle of Somme

Source 2

> How did the military planners imagine that British soldiers, having survived all the other hazards, and there were plenty crossing No Man's Land, would get through the German wire? Who told them that artillery fire would pound the wire to pieces? Any British soldier serving in the trenches could have told them that shell fire lifts wire up and drops it down, often in a worse tangle than before.

▲ George Coppard, a British machine gunner, remembers the first day of the Somme

Significance of the Battle of the Somme

Significance of the battle	The battle continued until November 1916. It became a battle of attrition.
	When it ended it had claimed a million casualties on all sides.
	Around 12 to 15 kilometres of land had been gained by the Allies at a cost of 600,000 casualties.
	There was a realisation of how long the war might last. The soldiers were heavily demoralised.
	Machine guns were effective in dealing with attacks across no man's land but the use of tanks was less effective. Used for the first time in war they struggled in the mud and over half broke down.

▲ Table 8.5 Significance of the Somme

Source 3

> ✓ Look at source 3. Discuss in groups the message of the British illustration.

◄ After the battle of the Somme, one English soldier asks: 'Have we taken much ground?' 'Not even enough to bury our dead in.'

How far was Haig deserving of the title "Butcher of the Somme"?

Questions asked about Haig's approach	Did Haig sacrifice thousands of mainly young males in an unwinnable battle? Did he understand what trench warfare was about? Were the disastrous consequences of the battle the result of his sheer incompetence?
	Did he overestimate the value of the artillery bombardment? Was he let down by British intelligence which failed to realised that the Germans were dug in much more deeply than thought?
	Why was Haig not advised as to the possible outcome of the bombardment on the barbed wire? Would a running attack, rather than a measured one, have been more successful?
Details of his approach	Haig was not capable of changing. When he realised the British full-frontal attacks were not working he did not stop men going over the top. He did not stop using the artillery bombardment which warned the Germans that an attack was imminent. He did not use tanks in the early days as he doubted their value.
	The issue about the poor weather, which increased the mud that the infantry had to contend with, was another example of his intransigent approach.
	He was fully in control. He had warned the politicians that to win the war they had to be prepared for heavy losses.
	Haig believed that the objective of the Somme had been achieved. It saved Verdun. A bonus was that many of Germany's best troops were killed and injured and overall their losses were greater.

▲ Table 8.6 Haig's approach to the battle of the Somme

Source 4

1 JULY 1916

Very successful attack this morning. All went like clockwork. The battle is going very well for us and already Germans are surrendering. The enemy is so short of men they are having to bring them from different parts of the Front Line. Our troops are in wonderful spirits and full of confidence.

▲ From Haig's official report about the Battle of the Somme.

1. Study sources 3 and 4. Does source 3 prove that Haig was lying in source 4?

2. In class, discuss how the Battle of the Somme should be remembered. Produce a presentation which suggests how the British people should remember the Battle of the Somme. Here are some headings you may wish to use:
   - A great victory
   - A campaign which achieved its objectives
   - A campaign blighted by incompetence
   - A disaster
   - A brutal campaign
   - An unnecessary loss of life.

How important were technological developments for the war on the Western Front?

The tank	The tank was first used in July 1916 on the Somme. While they were successful, more were needed to break the deadlock on the Western Front. Early tanks were unreliable and often broke down. Of the first 50 tanks used, 17 broke down before engaging the enemy. The successful ones often moved too quickly for the supporting troops to keep up and were captured by the enemy. At the Battle of Cambrai 400 British tanks were used to great effect.
The machine gun	The machine gun was one of the most devastating weapons used in the First World War. It was used to good effect by both sides. The machine gun was particularly effective as troops advanced across open land cutting down hundreds of men.
Gas	Gas was used by the Germans at the Second Battle of Ypres in April 1914. It accounted for 4% of war deaths. Mustard gas was the most lethal, destroying flesh. Chlorine gas destroyed the lungs. By 1917 effective gas masks were in use.

Aircraft	Aircraft had little impact on the outcome of war. They were mainly used for observation and reconnaissance, allowing troop movements and battlefield tactics to be observed from the air.
	The greatest problem was communication between land and air as they did not have radios.
	The German invention of a plane firing a machine gun in 1915 was copied by the British and the French and "dogfights" between rival aircraft took place.
	By 1917 bombers were being used but their range was limited.
Artillery	Artillery caused the greatest number of deaths, estimated at around 75%.
	By 1914 single guns were being organised into batteries. This increased the density of the bombardment.

▲ Table 8.7 Technological developments used on the Western Front

The offensives of 1917

The Nivelle Offensive (named after the French General)	The French troops were decimated by machine-gun fire having been trapped against uncut barbed wire. By the end of April many French troops were refusing to obey orders. The ring leaders were executed.
Battle of Vimy Ridge	In April at Vimy Ridge near the town of Arras, troops mainly from the British Empire went over the top in heavy sleet and snow. They were successful in taking the Ridge from the Germans. They used an accurate, "creeping barrage" artillery bombardment. The planned attack was kept a secret, with thousands of troops hidden around the town.
The Third Battle of Ypres (the Battle of Passchendaele)	Haig launched this offensive to: • take pressure off the French at Messines • inflict heavy losses on the Germans; Haig was convinced they were exhausted and ready to collapse • capture the Belgian ports of Zeebrugge and Ostende; these ports were important bases for the German submarines which were creating problems for British shipping. Was Passchendaele a success? • The British had lost 30,000 men and 67,000 by the end of August. • Passchendaele was finally captured by the Canadians in early November. The attempt to achieve a breakthrough failed because: • the Germans were aware of the imminent attack and strengthened their defences • the Allies had no protection against mustard gas which was used for the first time • the battleground was a sea of mud, making it impossible for artillery and tanks.

Battle of Cambrai	At Cambrai in November an unexpected attack was made against a heavily fortified stretch of trenches. Tanks were used but the attack could not be sustained as many broke down. Others had to turn back as there was a shortage of infantry support after the losses at Passchendaele.

▲ Table 8.8 The offensives of 1917

Despite the various successes, stalemate remained on the Western Front.

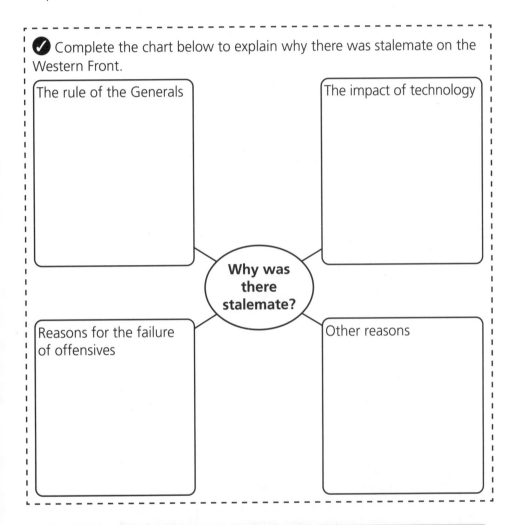

✔ Complete the chart below to explain why there was stalemate on the Western Front.

The rule of the Generals

The impact of technology

Why was there stalemate?

Reasons for the failure of offensives

Other reasons

Exam-style questions

1. What dangers faced soldiers fighting in the trenches on the Somme?
2. Why were attempts to break the stalemate on the Somme unsuccessful?
3. Why was the battle of Verdun important?
4. 'The use of the tank on the Somme had greater impact than did any other technical development.' How far do you agree with this statement?
5. How important was the development of the machine gun in reducing the impact of the attritional nature of trench warfare?

8.3 How important were other fronts?

Who won the war at sea?

Even though the Anglo–German naval race of the early twentieth century increased the size of the navies and created tension between the two countries, surprisingly there were relatively few major naval engagements during the First World War. Generally the German navy remained in their ports.

The aim of the British navy was to:

* preserve the supply lines between Britain and its major trading partners, and between Britain and northern France

* choke Germany into submission through the implementation of a blockade. Soon after the outbreak of war in August 1914 the North Sea was declared a British military area. All neutral merchant shipping was searched for materials which could help Germany's war effort. This resulted in Germany having difficulty feeding its population and producing armaments.

Germany's navy aimed to:

* deter rather than fight, by for example laying mines in the North Sea

* deploy its developing submarine force to help gain control of the North Sea.

Early events	
29 August 1914	Germany lost six ships at the Battle of Heligoland Bight in the North Sea.
1 November 1914	At the Battle of Coronal, off the coast of Chile, two British cruisers were lost. This was the first British naval defeat since 1812.
November and December 1914	The German High Seas Fleet attacked the east Yorkshire coastal towns of Hartlepool, Whitby and Scarborough, resulting in 137 fatalities.
24 January 1915	At the Battle of Dogger Bank, two German battle cruisers were destroyed. The remaining German ships escaped because one of the British battle cruisers was damaged.

▲ Table 8.9 Early events of the Anglo-German war at sea

The Battle of Jutland, May–June 1916

Admiral von Scheer aimed to lure the British Grand Fleet from its base at Rosyth. However, the British had decoded all the German messages and were aware of the trap. The British Admiral Jellicoe set sail much earlier than expected and was lying in wait for Scheer.

On the evening of 31 May the two fleets battled of the coast of Jutland in Denmark.

Who won the Battle of Jutland?	
Was it Germany?	**Was it Great Britain?**
Lost 11 ships, including 1 battle cruiser	Lost 14 ships, including 3 battle cruisers
Lost 3,058 dead and wounded	Lost 6,784 dead, wounded and captured
Able to deploy 10 large ships immediately after the battle	Able to deploy 24 large ships immediately after the battle
Never risked a major sea battle again	Maintained its control of the North Sea
	Able to sustain its blockade of the north German coast.

▲   Table 8.10 Who won the Battle of Jutland?

The battle failed to achieve the important German objective of lifting of the blockade. It showed that the German surface fleet was in no position to challenge the Royal Navy in the North Sea. Indeed the German fleet returned to port never to venture out again.

Any attacks on the Royal Navy or Allied merchant shipping would have to be carried out by submarines.

Source 5

> The Kaiser has addressed the crews of the German High Seas Fleet and congratulated them. The British Fleet was beaten. The first great hammer blow has been struck, and the great British world naval supremacy has disappeared.

▲   From an official German statement issued in June 1916

Source 6

THE GERMAN NAVY TAKING ROOT!

STIKPHASTZ

"AND THE GREEN GRASS GREW ALL ROUND ME BOYS!"

▲   A British postcard published after the Battle of Jutland

✔ Study sources 5 and 6. Having looked at source 6, are you surprised by what is being said in source 5?

Submarine warfare

Britain was vulnerable with 60% of its food being imported. In 1915 Germany launched a campaign of unrestricted submarine warfare. Under this strategy, ships heading towards Britain were targeted.

7 May 1915	The Germans sank the passenger liner *Lusitania* which was sailing from New York to Liverpool. The liner was just off the Irish coast. It sank within twenty minutes with 1,098 lives lost, including over 100 Americans. This caused great tension between the US and German governments.
1916	After the sinking of the *Lusitania* the Germans called off their unrestricted submarine warfare, but started again in 1916.
June 1917	By now Britain had lost 500,000 tonnes of shipping to U-boats. It was estimated that by this time only six weeks' supply of grain remained. Food rationing was introduced. Tactics against U-boats needed improving.
1917 onwards	From 1917 merchant ships crossed the Atlantic in larger, tight groups. They were escorted by fast warships. This made it more difficult for U-boats to pick off isolated ships. The warships dropped depth charges if a submarine was thought to be in the area. The reduction in losses was significant.

▲ Table 8.11 Submarine warfare

In retaliation to the U-boats, the Q ship was first used in 1915. Its powerful guns were disguised as freight. Its aim was to lure U-boats to the surface where they could be attacked and sunk.

Also thousands of mines were laid in the North Sea in an attempt to destroy German submarines.

Source 7

The *Lusitania* was naturally armed with guns as were most English steamers. Moreover it is well known here that she had large quantities of war material in her cargo. Her owners knew the dangers to which the passengers were exposed on the journey from America to England. The owners alone bear all responsibility for what has happened.

▲ From an official German communication made public in Berlin soon after the sinking of the *Lusitania* in 1915.

✔ Study source 7. How reliable is this source? Discuss your views in class groups.

Why did the Gallipoli campaign of 1915 fail?

There was deadlock on the Western Front. One possible way to achieve a breakthrough was to attack one of Germany's allies.

Turkey was one of Germany's more vulnerable allies. If Constantinople was captured, Turkey might surrender.

This would also open up a sea route to the Eastern Front, so that the allies could get supplies to the Russians and reduce pressure on other fronts. By defeating Turkey the allies could attack Austria–Hungary through the Balkans.

Events in Gallipoli	
18 March 1915	The naval attack began but three battleships were blown up by mines in the water. The rest of the fleet retreated. This attempt to knock out the guns on the Gallipoli shoreline had failed and any element of surprise for the April landings had been lost, enabling the Turks to strengthen their position.
25 April 1915	British, French, Australian and New Zealand troops launched an invasion of Turkey. The landing was a disaster. Out-of-date maps were used and landings had not been practised. The Turks were ready and killed thousands of troops as they advanced up the beaches. Those who were able dug trenches on the beach.
Summer 1915	In summer the heat and dust was horrendous. Water was in very limited supply. Flies covered all the food causing dysentery. Corpses littered the fighting area, rotting in the very hot weather. The stench this caused was unbearable. Temporary ceasefires allowed for the dead to be buried.
Winter 1915	In winter there was mud, snow and freezing conditions. Troops were without overcoats and many died of exposure.
December 1915	The attack was called off. Men were secretly and quietly led down the beaches to waiting boats. Tactics, such as firing shots from different trench positions, were used to convince the Turks that there were still men in what were empty trenches.

▲ Table 8.12 Events in Gallipoli

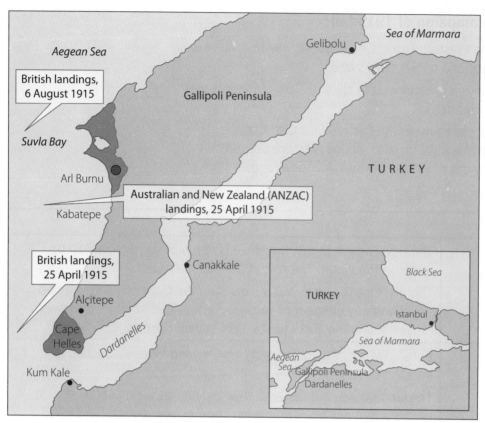

▲   Fig. 8.5 The Gallipoli campaign

Results of the campaign	
Successes	• The evacuation from the beaches was successful. Thousands of Allied soldiers were saved. • The campaign diverted the Turks from the fighting in the Middle East and Egypt. • British submarines managed to destroy seven Turkish naval vessels.
Failures	• The naval campaign and the landings failed. • Turkey was not knocked out of the war. • Just over half of the 410,000 Allied troops lost their lives. Only a quarter of these died actually fighting.

▲   Table 8.13 Results of the Gallipoli campaign

The campaign failed for a number of reasons.

- Lack of support: there was little support for the Gallipoli campaign as commanders would not release armed forces from the Western Front. It was believed that the war would be won on the Western Front.

- Poor organisation: landings were not practised and out-of-date maps were used. The navy failed to remove Turkish mines. No account was taken of the impact of the extremes of weather. The only realistic opportunity for success required the army and navy operations to be combined. In practice they were independent.

- The Turkish army: the fighting power of the Turkish army was seriously underestimated; it was believed to pose little threat. However, the Germans had supported the Turks to increase their defensive forces in strategic positions above the beaches. Vital training was also given.

- A lack of surprise: the earlier naval attempt lost the element of surprise. The Turks were waiting for the armed forces to land.
- The plan was too ambitious: the plan had little chance of success as it was highly unlikely that Turkey and then Austria would be knocked out of the war.

Why did Russia leave the war in 1918?

Events on the Eastern Front	
August 1914	Russia entered the war in August 1914. The war started well with Russia enjoying early successes against Austria–Hungary and Germany. The Germans soon recovered and heavily defeated the Russians at Tannenberg, however. The Russians suffered 30,000 casualties.
September 1914	Another heavy defeat was suffered at Masurian Lakes against Hindenburg's German forces, losing around 100,000 men.
1915	Tsar Nicholas took the role of Commander-in-Chief of the Russian forces. During 1915 Russia retreated in the face of German advances. Warsaw was abandoned and by the end of the year the Russians had been forced out of Poland.
June 1916	Russia, under General Brusilov, mounted a successful counter-offensive against the Austrian and German troops. However, Russian forces became exposed to poison gas attacks when the artillery support ceased. A Russian retreat followed with more than 500,000 Russians killed, wounded or taken prisoner.
March 1917	Tsar Nicholas was forced to abdicate and a Provisional Government was established in Russia.
November 1917	The Provisional Government was overthrown by the Bolsheviks. The Bolsheviks took the decision to end the war. Russia and Germany signed the Treaty of Brest Litovsk in March 1918. Russian troops had in fact stopped fighting at the end of 1917. This treaty was extremely harsh on Russia. The British and French were horrified as the signing of the treaty meant that thousands of German troops would return to fight on the Western Front.

▲ Table 8.14 Events on the Eastern Front

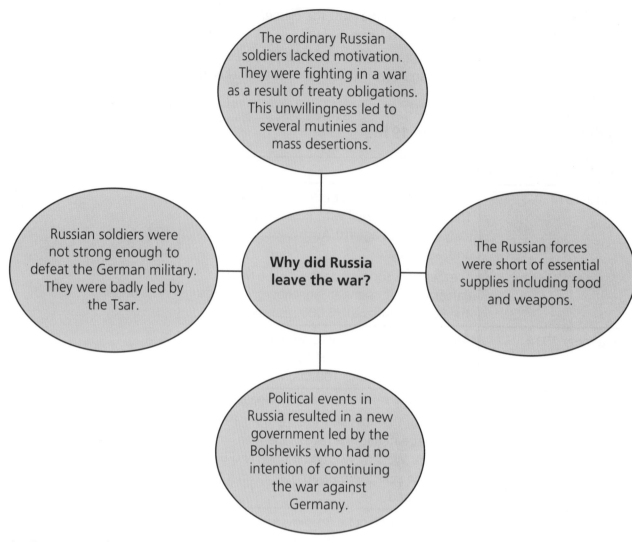

The ordinary Russian soldiers lacked motivation. They were fighting in a war as a result of treaty obligations. This unwillingness led to several mutinies and mass desertions.

Russian soldiers were not strong enough to defeat the German military. They were badly led by the Tsar.

Why did Russia leave the war?

The Russian forces were short of essential supplies including food and weapons.

Political events in Russia resulted in a new government led by the Bolsheviks who had no intention of continuing the war against Germany.

▲ Fig. 8.6 Reasons for Russia's leaving the war

Was Russia's participation in the war of any value to the Triple Entente?

- The Battle of Tannenburg succeeded in halting the German advance on Paris as it diverted resources away from the Western Front.
- Brusilov's offensive relieved the pressure on Verdun.
- The Allies needed Russia in the war. Russia's withdrawal at the end of 1917 could well have been a disaster for the Allies had the Americans not entered the war.

What was the impact of war on civilian populations?	
Civil liberties	The outbreak of war brought many restrictions to the lives of civilians.
	The British government introduced the Defence of the Realm Act (DORA). This gave the government wide powers to ensure "public safety". The new powers included the introduction of press censorship, imprisonment without trial, reducing hours for the selling of alcohol and the introduction of British Summer Time.
	The USA passed major legislation to ensure that the war effort was not threatened. Measures passed included making it illegal to release classified information or to interfere with the recruitment of troops.
Conscription	Each of the major combatants introduced conscription, although Britain relied on a volunteer army for the first two years. Some men refused to be conscripted and were known as conscientious objectors. Around half of these accepted a non-combatant role in the armed forces. Others were imprisoned or sent to a military unit in France.
Food shortages	Most combatant nations suffered from food shortages. Common causes were a loss of farm workers to the military and blockades. Britain was vulnerable to blockade, with the German campaign of unrestricted submarine warfare having a devastating effect on the import of essential food. Germany's civilians suffered similarly as a result of the Royal Navy blockade. Food shortages in Russia were mainly caused by the poor quality of the railway network and the backward agricultural system. The consequence of food shortages was a sharp rise in inflation with average food costs rising by nearly 90%.
	France was less affected as it was able to feed its population from agricultural land unaffected by war. The USA was also self-sufficient and also able to provide essential supplies for its allies.
	Rationing of food was introduced in both Britain and Germany.
Employment for women	The need to produce more food gave opportunities for the employment of women on the land. Britain created the Women's Land Army in 1915.
	Another area where opportunities for women increased was within the industrial workforce, often in munitions factories. In Britain women accounted for 37% of the workforce by 1918. Once the war was over, considerable public pressure forced women out of their new jobs.
Civilian deaths	It is thought around 940,000 civilians lost their life as a result of military action. Almost six million died from disease, malnutrition and accidents.

▲ Table 8.15 What was the impact of the war on civilian population?

Exam-style questions

1. What was the impact of the war at sea?

2. Why did both sides claim a victory at the Battle of Jutland?

3. Why was Russia leaving the war significant?

4. 'Submarine warfare was the most important aspect of the war at sea.' How far do you agree with this statement?

5. How significant was the part played by the weather in the failure of the Gallipoli campaign of 1915?

8.4 Why did Germany ask for an armistice in 1918?

Why did the United States enter the war?

The United States formally joined the war in 1917, having maintained a policy of isolation since the nineteenth century. While the United States was officially neutral it was giving loans and supplying equipment to the Allies.

The United States, having developed closer links with Europe, had no wish to see one single dominant power, particularly if the dominant power was at odds with the American belief in democracy.

The policies of Germany during the war pushed the United States closer to the Entente powers. The use of unrestricted submarine warfare highlighted the aggressive nature of the Central Powers. President Wilson reacted furiously to the American fatalities on the *Lusitania* in 1915.

Wilson had unsuccessfully spent 1915 and 1916 trying to broker peace between the two sides. In February 1917, Germany resumed unrestricted submarine warfare which hardened American public opinion for war.

Public support for war was further increased by the publication of a telegram, intercepted by the British, sent by the German Foreign Minister to the German ambassador to Mexico offering United States territory to Mexico in return for joining the war on Germany's side.

On 6 April 1917 Wilson declared war on Germany.

What was the initial impact of America entering the war?

Initially America was not geared for war and the troops were slow to arrive. When they did the first ones were short of uniforms and equipment.

Destroyers and merchant ships were sent to increase anti-submarine capabilities. Additional support aided the destruction of mines in the North Sea.

US forces reached France in small numbers. By March 1918 300,000 men had arrived. By July a further 800,000 were in position. These soldiers provided valuable support in combating the German offensives of June and July.

The arrival of the Americans provided a tremendous morale boost following the disasters of 1917 when the effects of the submarine campaign, the Battle of Passchendaele and Russia's withdrawal threatened victory.

Source 8

◄ A cartoon published in Britain in 1917.

Why was the German offensive of 1918 unsuccessful?

In January 1918, German war prospects were not good. They were still fighting on the Eastern Front, the submarine campaign had failed to achieve its target and recruits for the army were drying up. Furthermore, the United States was expected to send large numbers of fighting men.

On 21 March 1918, Germany launched the German Spring Offensive (Operation Michael) conceived by General Ludendorff. The offensive was initially a success, with German forces, including many transferred from the Eastern Front, breaking through the Allied lines and advancing 56 kilometres in the first three weeks. The German army was now 8 kilometres from Paris.

This German push was stopped by an Allied counter-offensive but at great cost. Britain suffered 178,000 casualties and France 77,000. German casualties numbered over one million during the offensives of 1918.

German troops of 1918 were not as good as those of 1914. Their discipline was poor and they were badly fed and supplied. Crucially they did not have reserves to call upon. The numerical advantage of the well-equipped Allies was beginning to make an impact and between May and August the Germans made no further progress.

The failure of Ludendorff's plan can be firmly placed within its initial success. By breaking out from the heavily fortified Hindenburg Line, the Germans changed the war from one of attrition into one of movement.

This transformation played into the hands of the Allies who had more tanks, men and aircraft. On 8 August the Allies launched a counter-attack along the Western Front and by late September, they had reached the Hindenburg Line. September saw the Germans in full retreat.

A serious influenza epidemic within the German army left only 2 of its 13 divisions fit for action. Low morale, alcohol abuse and desertion were now features of what had been a highly disciplined fighting force.

By the end of September it had become of question of when, rather than if, Germany would surrender.

Source 9

THE SANDS RUN OUT.

◄ A cartoon published in 1918.

> ✔ Study sources 8 and 9. How similar are the messages of these two cartoons?

Conditions in Germany towards the end of the war

Why did the revolution break out in Germany in October 1918?

The war effort	Generals Hindenburg and Ludendorff began to interfere in domestic affairs under the pretext of directing the country's war effort. At the same time, the Reichstag started to question the war effort. The long-term cause of the German revolution was war weariness and by July 1917 the Reichstag was unsuccessfully demanding peace.
New government	The first stage of the revolution in October 1918 occurred following the formation of a new government under the newly appointed chancellor von Baden. He asked US President Wilson for an armistice. This was refused until Germany agreed to allow "true representatives of the German people" to negotiate. On 26 November, the Kaiser introduced the October reforms which transferred power to the Reichstag.
Mutiny	The second stage was triggered by the mutiny of sailors at the naval bases of Kiel and Wilhelmshaven. Not wanting to partake in a planned large naval assault on the British High Seas Fleet the sailors either refused to return from leave or refused to set sail.
Riots	Riots broke out across Germany and the Kaiser abdicated, fleeing to the Netherlands. Friedrich Ebert was appointed as the new chancellor.

▲ Table 8.16 Reasons for the revolution in Germany in October 1918

Why did Germany sign the armistice?

- To avoid revolution: revolutions were threatened across Germany and Ebert feared a Bolshevik (communist) revolution.
- Conditions in Germany: the blockade had brought terrible shortages of food, causing ill health.
- To take advantage of Wilson's Fourteen Points.
- Fear of invasion: on 28 September, Ludendorff and Hindenburg agreed that Germany had no choice but surrender. Failure to do so would result in the destruction of the army and the invasion of Germany.
- Morale: by early November the morale of German forces was at an all time low and the troops were in a state of permanent retreat.
- The Central Powers were defeated: Bulgaria called for an armistice following defeat at Monastir-Doiron. Turkey agreed a peace deal on 30 October and four days later Austria did the same.

The armistice was signed on 11th November.

The terms included:
- German troops to withdraw from France, Belgium and Alsace-Lorraine in the west.
- In the east the withdrawal was to be to the original territorial boundaries.
- The immediate surrender of equipment including weapons and warships.
- The Treaty of Brest-Litovsk to be repudiated.

▲ Fig. 8.7 Terms of the armistice

Exam-style questions

1. What actions by Germany resulted in America entering the war?
2. Why did revolution break out in Germany in 1918?
3. Why was an armistice signed in November 1918?
4. Why did America declare war on Germany?
5. How significant was the German defeat at Amiens to the failure of the German Offensive of 1918?
6. How important was America's entry into the war to Germany's defeat?

Germany, 1918–45

KEY IDEAS

This section will:

→ Look at politics and society in Germany at the end of the First World War.

→ Raise understanding of the German reaction to the Treaty of Versailles.

→ Examine the Weimar Republic to evaluate the reasons for its problems and achievements.

→ Consider the reasons for the collapse of the German economy in 1923, the effects of this crisis, and how the crisis was overcome.

→ Examine the reasons for the Nazis coming to power.

→ Raise understanding of the impact of Nazi rule.

→ Consider the Nazi economic policy and war economy, and the different experiences of people living in Germany.

Background

The armistice bringing the First World War to an end was signed on 11 November 1918. Shortly before the signing, Kaiser Wilhelm II of Germany abdicated and a democratic government, the Weimar Republic, was set up. This democracy lasted 14 years before it was destroyed by the establishment of Hitler's dictatorship.

The new Weimar Republic, led by Friedrich Ebert, was facing many problems. The war had been most severe on Germany and its people. The blockade of Germany by the Allies had contributed to the difficulties faced by creating severe food shortages. The new government became immediately unpopular by signing the Treaty of Versailles in 1919.

9.1 Was the Weimar Republic doomed from the start?

How did Germany emerge from defeat at the end of the First World War?

Germany was on the edge of revolution. German sailors at the port of Kiel had mutinied and councils, similar to soviets in Russia, were being set up around the country. There were severe food shortages because of the naval blockade by the British.

The Kaiser abdicated on 9 November 1918. This raised German hopes of a more lenient peace.

Germany was declared a republic on the day the Kaiser abdicated. Ebert, leader of the Social Democrat Party (SDP), became the first President. His first tasks were to restore law and order but he faced a number of challenges.

Challenges faced by the new government

Anger at the Treaty of Versailles	It was the Republicans who made peace with the Allies. They became known as the "November Criminals". Most Germans were furious at the Weimar Republic for accepting the terms of the Treaty of Versailles. They thought their treatment was too harsh, especially as most did not believe that Germany had lost the war.
Weak coalition governments	The new government had a president as head of state and a chancellor. Elections to the Reichstag were decided by proportional representation. This made it unlikely that any party would form a government of its own.
The threat from extreme political groups	The communists in Germany, known as Spartacists, wanted a revolution similar to the one that occurred in Russia in 1917. In January 1919, the left-wing activists led by Rosa Luxemburg and Karl Liebknecht seized power in Berlin. They were crushed by the Freikorps, who were ex-soldiers and bitter enemies of the communists. This showed the weakness of the new government as it had to rely on a military group outside its control. In March 1920, Wolfgang Kapp, an extreme nationalist, together with some Freikorps units, seized power in Berlin. This was known as the Kapp Putsch. The nationalists wanted a strong government. The army refused to intervene. Kapp was not supported by the Berlin workers who went on strike, refusing to cooperate. After four days Kapp and his supporters fled Berlin.

▲ Table 9.1 Challenges faced by the Weimar Republic

Source 1

> The German nation is in grave danger. Law and order is in danger of collapsing. Hardship is increasing and starvation threatens. We are threatened by Bolshevism. We shall get rid of this weak republic and replace it with a strong government.

▲ Wolfgang Kapp speaking in 1920

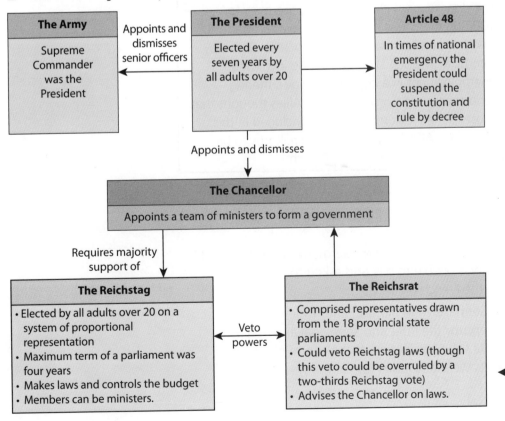

▶ Fig. 9.1 Constitutional organisation of the new government

The Army — Supreme Commander was the President

Appoints and dismisses senior officers

The President — Elected every seven years by all adults over 20

Article 48 — In times of national emergency the President could suspend the constitution and rule by decree

Appoints and dismisses

The Chancellor — Appoints a team of ministers to form a government

Requires majority support of

The Reichstag
- Elected by all adults over 20 on a system of proportional representation
- Maximum term of a parliament was four years
- Makes laws and controls the budget
- Members can be ministers.

Veto powers

The Reichsrat
- Comprised representatives drawn from the 18 provincial state parliaments
- Could veto Reichstag laws (though this veto could be overruled by a two-thirds Reichstag vote)
- Advises the Chancellor on laws.

Disadvantages of the new constitution.

- Through proportional representation some extremist parties were represented in the Reichstag, giving them a voice and publicity.
- Proportional representation prevented overall control by one party. This meant coalition governments made up of representatives from a number of different political parties.
- Article 48 gave too much power to the President giving the opportunity for him to act undemocratically.

What was the impact of the Treaty of Versailles on the Weimar Republic?

Terms of the treaty	
Blame for the war	The Germans were furious at the harsh terms of the Treaty. They had believed the Treaty was to be based on Wilson's Fourteen Points.
	The Treaty was regarded as a "diktat", a dictated peace. The Germans were not allowed to attend the Conference to discuss the terms.
	Germany had to accept the blame for starting the war (War Guilt Clause) and therefore pay reparations. The reparations figure was fixed in 1921 at £6,600 million. This figure was about 2% of Germany's annual output.
Loss of territory	Germany lost a lot of territory including the industrial areas of the Saar and Upper Silesia, making it more difficult for them to pay the reparations.
The army	The disarmament clause, limiting the army to 100,000 men, was resented as it was argued that this number was too small to keep Germany safe from invasion. The clause also increased unemployment in a country already suffering serious economic problems. The Allies thought that those in the Freikorps should be included in this figure. An Allied request for the Freikorps to be disbanded caused the Kapp Putsch.

▲ Table 9.2 Terms of the Treaty of Versailles

Crisis in the Ruhr

The first instalment of reparations was paid by Germany in 1921. In 1922 the German government was unable to pay and asked for more time. While the British agreed, the French did not.

The French thought the Germans were bluffing and, together with the Belgians, decided to occupy the Ruhr and seize coal and iron as reparations. In January 1923 the occupation of the centre of German industry began. The results were disastrous for Germany.

The German workers used "passive resistance". This meant the German workers would not work in the mines or accept orders from the occupiers. The result was that there would be nothing to take away.

Source 2

> The greatest fraud in the history of the world is now being carried out in Germany, with the full support of its population. Germany is full of wealth. She is humming like a beehive. Poverty is almost non-existent. Yet this is a country that is determined not to pay its debts. Germany is a nation of actors. If it were not for the fact that the German has no humour, one might imagine the whole German nation was carrying out a great practical joke.

▲ A letter to a British newspaper, from a businessman who had just returned from Germany, published in 1922.

✔ Discuss in class. How far would the cartoonist in source 3 agree with what was published in the British newspaper in source 2?

Source 3

A TRANSPARENT DODGE.

GERMANY. "HELP! HELP! I DROWN! THROW ME THE LIFE-BELT!"
MR. LLOYD GEORGE. }
M. BRIAND   . . .} "TRY STANDING UP ON YOUR FEET."

▲ A cartoon published in Britain in 1921

The French reacted harshly, killing over 100 workers and expelling over 100,000 protesters.

The halt in production caused the collapse of the German currency. The government decided to print money. This caused prices to rise out of control and resulted in hyperinflation. The German currency was virtually worthless.

People's savings became valueless and pensioners suffered as they were on fixed incomes. Prices rose faster than incomes. Shop prices were increasing almost every hour. People could not afford food and heating. The Weimar government was in danger of collapse.

In August 1923 Gustav Stresemann became chancellor. He introduced a rescue plan which:

- ended passive resistance in the Ruhr
- stopped the printing of money in November 1923
- stabilised the currency by introducing the temporary Rentenmark
- resumed reparation payments to the Allies
- resumed production in the Ruhr.

To what extent did the Republic recover after 1923 under Stresemann?

The next six years were characterised by economic recovery.

- Stresemann introduced a temporary currency, the Rentenmark, and the Ruhr industries restarted production. In 1924 this temporary currency was replaced by the permanent Reichmark.
- In 1924 Stresemann agreed the Dawes Plan with the USA. This linked Germany's reparations payments to economic performance. In addition US loans of 800 million gold marks helped to kick-start the German economy. German industry benefited from this investment, inflation and unemployment fell, industry expanded and exports increased. By 1928 German industrial production was greater than pre-war levels.
- The Young Plan of 1929, which reduced reparations, further helped Germany's economic recovery.

However:

- Some groups, including shopkeepers, farmers and small businessmen still struggled.
- Unemployment still remained too high.
- The economic recovery was based on American loans.

Stresemann aimed to get Germany accepted back into the international community

- As part of the Locarno Treaties of 1925, Germany agreed to accept the terms of the Treaty of Versailles and as a result Germany was accepted internationally being admitted into the League of Nations the following year.

What were the achievements of the Weimar period?

Political:

- In 1923 Germany was still regarded with distrust and suspicion. By the time of his death in 1929, Germany was engaging on equal terms with the major powers of the world.
- France left the Ruhr by 1925.
- The Locarno Treaties placed Germany on an equal level with signatories, providing guarantees for the frontiers of Germany, France and Belgium.
- In 1926 Germany was admitted to the League of Nations as a responsible member of the international community.

Cultural:

- The 1920s was a decade of cultural revival in Germany, especially Berlin.
- The new democratic republic was committed to civil liberties. It lifted censorship, encouraged artists, writers, film and theatre directors and designers. The rejection of traditional approaches resulted in the favouring of expressionism.
- At a popular level, night clubs, dance halls, cafes and restaurants increased, affording opportunities for cabaret artists, singers and dance bands.

However:

- Many of these developments were regarded with shock and disgust by the right-wing of German politics. Artistic development was seen a sign of decadence, corruption and moral decay.
- Under the Nazis many artists, writers and thinkers were forced to take refuge abroad.

Literature	Bertolt Brecht and Kurt Weill, *The Threepenny Opera* (1928)
	Thomas Mann, *The Magic Mountain* (1924)
	Herman Hesse, *Steppenwolf* (1927)
	Erich Remarque, *All Quiet on the Western Front* (1924)
Art	George Grosz, *Grey Day* (1921)
	Otto Dix, *Big City* (1928)
Film	*Metropolis*, directed by Fritz Lang (1927)
	The Blue Angel, directed by Josef von Sternberg (1930)
Architecture	The Bauhaus style founded by Walter Gropius

▲ Fig. 9.2 Examples of Germany's cultural revival, 1921–30.

Renewed economic crisis

- Following the Wall Street Crash of October 1929, the American economy went into recession and many of the loans offered to Germany since 1924 were recalled.
- The German economy suffered a double blow. It had to cope with a world depression and the consequent reduction in export orders but they had to repay substantial amounts of money to the USA. Unemployment rose to alarming levels. By 1932 the German unemployment figure stood at 6 million, one third of the workforce.

Political instability

- Support for the moderate parties that made up the coalitions of the Weimar governments began to decline.
- Support for the two extreme parties, the Nazis and the communists, rose from 13% in 1928 to 52% in 1932.

Exam-style questions

1. What problems faced Germany immediately following the end of the war in 1918?
2. Why was the Weimar constitution considered a weakness?
3. To what extent did Germany recover after 1923?
4. How important was the work of Stresemann to the recovery of Germany after 1923?

9.2 Why was Hitler able to dominate Germany by 1934?

What did the Nazi Party stand for in the 1920s?

The German Workers' Party (DAP, the forerunner of the Nazi Party) was established by Anton Drexler in January 1919. It was an extremist national party.

At the end of the war Hitler had stayed in the army working for the intelligence services. This is how he came across the DAP. In September 1919, he joined the Party. Soon he was taking responsibility for publicity, propaganda and public speaking.

In 1920 the Party published its 25-Point Programme and renamed itself the National Socialist German Workers' Party (Nazis). The Programme showed strong nationalist and anti-Semitic features. They used the swastika as the party badge.

In July 1921, Hitler replaced Drexler as leader. In August 1921, he founded the SA (Storm Troopers), who were noted for their violence against any opposition.

Key points from the Nazi Party objectives published in 1920
• The union of all Germans in a Greater Germany.
• The destruction of the Treaties of Versailles and St Germain (which would then allow the union of Germany and Austria).
• German citizenship exclusive to those of German blood (thereby excluding Jews).
• No more immigration of non-Germans.
• A strong central government in Germany.
• Generous provision for old age pensioners.

The Munich Putsch, 1923	
Chances of success	Hitler wanted to achieve the violent overthrow of the unpopular Weimar Republic and replace it with a Nazi government. He thought this attempt would be successful as the Weimar government was unpopular for the following reasons: • the ending of passive resistance in the Ruhr gave the impression of giving in to the French • hyperinflation was at its height • Germany had resumed paying reparations (the hated treaty). Hitler was supported by the wartime leader General Ludendorff. It was thought he would increase the support for the putsch.
Events	On 8 November Storm Troopers forced their way into a political meeting in a Munich beer hall. They planned to take over Munich and march into Berlin. Kahr, the Prime Minister of Bavaria, was forced at gunpoint to give support to the revolution. On 9 November Kahr went back on his promise. Hitler marched through the streets of Munich to gain support. Armed police opened fire killing 16 Nazis.

Reasons for failure	The army remained loyal to the Weimar government.
	Hitler and Ludendorff were arrested and charged with high treason. This was an offence punishable with a death sentence.
	The loyalty of Bavarian politicians had been underestimated.
	Hitler miscalculated the mood of the German people. They did not rise to support him.
Outcomes	Hitler was sentenced to five years in prison. Ludendorff was acquitted.
	The trial gave Hitler the opportunity to gain publicity for his ideas.
	Hitler used his time in prison to write *Mein Kampf* (My Struggle). This emphasised the superiority of the German (Aryan) race, especially in comparison with Jews and Slavs; the dangers of communism; the need for "lebensraum" or living space; Germany's rise to be the dominant state in Europe. He realised that power could not be achieved by the use of violence.
	Hitler had sympathisers within the judiciary. He only served nine months and this was in great comfort at Landsberg Castle.
	The Nazi Party was banned but this restriction was lifted in 1925.

▲ Table 9.3 The Munich Putsch, 1923

What was the status of the Nazi Party by the end of the 1920s?

In the general election of May 1928 the Nazis only won 12 seats in the Reichstag, polling 2.6% of the votes.

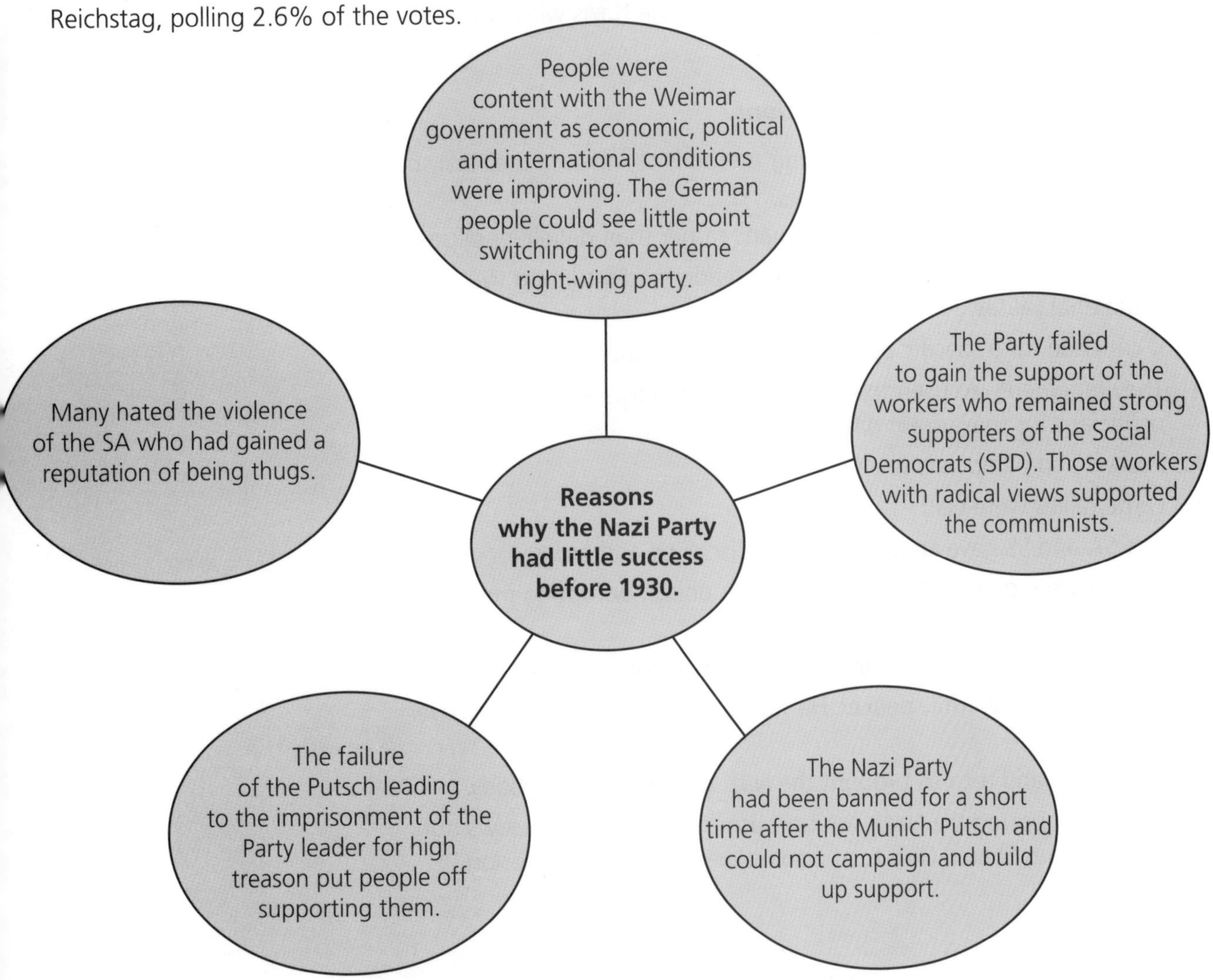

People were content with the Weimar government as economic, political and international conditions were improving. The German people could see little point switching to an extreme right-wing party.

The Party failed to gain the support of the workers who remained strong supporters of the Social Democrats (SPD). Those workers with radical views supported the communists.

Many hated the violence of the SA who had gained a reputation of being thugs.

Reasons why the Nazi Party had little success before 1930.

The failure of the Putsch leading to the imprisonment of the Party leader for high treason put people off supporting them.

The Nazi Party had been banned for a short time after the Munich Putsch and could not campaign and build up support.

▲ Fig. 9.3 Reasons why the Nazi Party had little success before 1930

Why was Hitler able to become Chancellor by 1933?

In October 1929, Stresemann died. The economy he had built up was fragile, being dependent on German loans. In the same month disaster struck as the Wall Street Crash in America started the Great Depression.

As a result many US banks recalled their loans. German businesses began to close. Millions became unemployed. By 1930, unemployment had reached four million.

As unemployment increased many Germans felt let down by the Weimar Republic and turned to extremist parties. Support for the Nazis and communists increased. In the 1930 elections, the communists (KPD) gained 77 seats, the Nazis 107.

Why did the Nazis benefit from the Depression?

Germany was thrown into economic chaos and no government could solve the problems. President Hindenburg ruled by decree.

Unemployment had reached six million by 1932. Hitler and the Nazis promised to get these people back to work and provide food. They gained support from all areas of German society, including powerful industrialists.

There was fear of a communist revolution as some workers. This worried many industrialists and farmers. They turned to the Nazis who opposed the communists.

Why did the Nazis succeed in elections?

Goebbels introduced new campaigning methods to increase the Nazi share of the vote.

- The Nazis relied on generalised slogans rather than detailed policies.
- They talked about uniting behind one leader and returning to traditional values.
- If criticised for a specific policy, it would be dropped.
- They repeatedly accused the Jews, the communists and the Weimar politicians for the current difficulties.
- Posters and pamphlets were everywhere.
- Large rallies were held.
- The SA and SS gave an impression of discipline and order.
- The SA were prepared to fight the communists, disrupting meetings and rallies.
- The Nazis provided soup kitchens and hostels for the unemployed.
- Hitler was a powerful speaker. He travelled by plane to rallies all over Germany.
- Film, radio and records brought the Nazi message to everybody.
- People supported the Nazis not because they shared Nazi views but because they shared Nazi fears and dislikes ("negative cohesion").

✓ In small groups discuss the reasons for the success of the Nazis in elections. Place the reasons in order of importance with the most important first.

Make a presentation to the rest of your teaching group to argue your choice of rank order.

What happened in the elections of 1932?

Presidential election	In 1932, Hitler opposed the elderly President Hindenburg. In his speeches he blamed the "November Criminals" and the Jews for Germany's problems. He promised to build a better Germany. This was not enough to get him the support he needed and despite going to a second vote, Hitler was unsuccessful.
Elections for the Reichstag, July 1932	As a result of the 1932 elections the Nazi Party was the largest party in the Reichstag with 230 seats. It did not, however, have an overall majority. The election campaign had been a violent one with street battles between Nazis and communists. Nearly 100 people were killed. As the leader of the largest party, Hitler demanded the Presidency. Hindenburg was suspicious of Hitler and appointed von Papen.
Elections for the Reichstag, November 1932	Von Papen lacked support and called another election. The support for the Nazis dropped to 192 seats but still they remained the largest party.

▲ Table 9.4 The elections of 1932

	July 1932	**November 1932**	**March 1933**
Social Democrats	133	121	120
Centre Party	75	70	73
KPD (left wing)	89	100	81
Nazis (right wing)	230	196	288
Nationalists (right wing)	40	51	52

▲ Fig. 9.4 Results of elections for the Reichstag, 1932–33

How did Hitler become Chancellor in January 1933?

Von Papen found that it was still impossible to form a stable government and von Schleicher became Chancellor in early December. He experienced similar problems to von Papen.

Towards the end of January 1933, von Papen managed to persuade Hindenburg to agree a political deal. Hitler would become Chancellor with von Papen Vice-Chancellor. With only a few Nazis in the Cabinet they were confident that Hitler could be controlled. How wrong they were!

How did Hitler consolidate his power in 1933–34?

The Reichstag Fire, 27 February 1933	On the evening of 27 February 1933 the Reichstag building burnt down. A Dutch communist, van der Lubbe, was arrested and charged with starting the fire.
	Hitler claimed it was proof of a communist plot against the state. Hitler took the opportunity to whip up public fear against the supposed communist threat.
	There were many theories as to how the fire started including that the Nazis might have started the fire themselves.
	President Hindenburg was persuaded by Hitler to issue an emergency decree.
Hitler's use of the emergency decree	The decree gave Hitler wide-ranging powers, including the power to deal with the "state of emergency" that had arisen following the Reichstag Fire.
	The decree curbed freedom of speech and the right of assembly. It gave the police an excuse to arrest communists. In Prussia over 4,000 were arrested in the days immediately after the fire.
	Hitler was now out of control.
The general election, 5 March 1933	Hitler aimed for full control of Germany. He banned the Communist Party and shut down their newspapers. The SA were used to intimidate political opponents.
	The Nazis won 288 seats.

The Enabling Act, 23 March 1933	Hitler still did not have enough elected support to have complete control of Germany. He needed to pass an Enabling Act, but to gain this required two-thirds of the votes of the Reichstag members. To gain this level of votes he expelled the 81 communist members from the Reichstag and ordered the SA to continue their intimidation of the opposition. Only the Social Democrats dared oppose the measure. The Act was passed by 441 votes to 94.
Consequences of the Enabling Act	Hitler was now dictator of all Germany. He could now pass laws for four years without consulting the Reichstag. He was able to ban all other political parties (which he did in July 1933). Germany was now a one-party state. In May 1933 the trade unions were abolished, their leaders arrested and funds confiscated. Strike action was made illegal. All workers had to belong to the German Labour Front. The civil service was purged of all Jews. The democratic Weimar Republic had been destroyed.

▲   Table 9.5 Hitler's steps to power

Source 4

VOX POPULI
THE GERMAN ELECTION TAKES PLACE TO-MORROW

▲   A cartoon published 4 March 1933

> ✅ Study source 4. Why was this cartoon published in Britain at that time? Explain your answer.

The Night of the Long Knives, June 1934

By the early months of 1934 Hitler's power was nearly complete. Hitler was worried about the growing independence of Ernst Röhm, the leader of the SA. He decided to take action at the end of June.

Reasons	• If Hitler did not send a clear signal to the army that they were to remain a special, highly-trained, professional body, central to his plans, then there was the danger that they would launch a coup against him. • Senior army generals had heard that Röhm was in favour of merging the army with the SA under his leadership. These generals were upset by such rumours and unsure as to how Hitler regarded the idea. • Hitler was beginning to see Röhm as a threat because he was expressing disappointment with Nazi achievements and arguing in favour of a "second revolution". This would have involved introducing radical policies such as nationalisation, upsetting business leaders. • Hitler needed to reassure the army and show the SA leadership who was in control.
Events	• On the night of 30 June 1934, Röhm and other SA leaders were arrested and shot. During the next two weeks several hundred senior SA men, other rivals and potential enemies, including von Schleicher, were also murdered by the SS.
Effects	• The army could no longer be in any doubt that Hitler favoured them in preference to the SA. • The SA were brought firmly under the control of Hitler's leadership. • When President Hindenburg died on 2 August 1934, Hitler proclaimed himself Chancellor and Reich Führer. As such he was Head of State and Commander-in-Chief of the Army. Every soldier was required to swear an oath of personal loyalty to Adolf Hitler. Hitler's dictatorship was now a matter of fact as well as a matter of law. Hitler had achieved total power.

▲   Table 9.6 The Night of the Long Knives, June 1934

Exam-style questions

1. Describe the Munich Putsch of 1923.
2. Why was the Munich Putsch important for Hitler and the Nazi Party?
3. Why were the achievements of the Nazi Party limited before 1929?
4. 'Hitler was able to become Chancellor of Germany because of the work of Goebbels.' How far do you agree?
5. How important was the Reichstag fire as a reason for Hitler being able to establish a dictatorship?

9.3 The Nazi regime

How effectively did the Nazis control Germany, 1933–45?

It is difficult to assess fully the nature and strength of opposition to the
Nazi state because of its secretive nature.

How much opposition was there to the Nazi regime?	
Religious opposition	At first the Catholic Church agreed not to interfere in Nazi policies (Concordat of 1933). This was in return for the Nazis agreeing not to interfere in religion. However, Hitler broke his promise and the Nazis were denounced as anti-Christian by the Pope. Many churchmen spoke out against the Nazis including Pastor Niemöller who spent eight years in a concentration camp for forming a rival church to the Nazi Reich Church. Bishop Galen spoke out strongly against euthanasia, forced sterilisation and concentration camps.
Opposition among the young	Although many young people joined the Hitler Youth there were some who rejected this influence. Members of the "Swing" movement were condemned by the Nazis because they were interested in British and American popular music and dance, including banned jazz music. They also accepted Jews into their groups. The Edelweiss Pirates mocked the Nazis through song, attacked members of the Hitler Youth, distributed broadsheets and scrawled graffiti on walls. During the war they spread anti-Nazi propaganda and, in 1944, took part in an attack on the Gestapo during which an officer was killed. Twelve Pirates were publicly hanged in November 1944. The White Rose Group formed by university students in Munich was another group of young opponents. The leaders Hans and Sophie Scholl were executed in 1943 for anti-Nazi activities.
Military opposition	In 1944, a group of senior army officers planned to assassinate Hitler. This "July Bomb Plot" failed and led to 5,000 executions.
Political opposition	The Enabling Act had given Hitler power to ban all political parties. Many socialists and communists fled the country.

▲   Table 9.7 How much opposition was there to the Nazi regime?

How effectively did the Nazis deal with their opponents?

To ensure absolute obedience to Nazi rule the favoured methods were
persuasion and indoctrination. For persistent opponents the Nazis relied
upon force and terror.

The Nazi police state enforced Nazi laws and dispensed Nazi justice in
several ways.

- The SS led by Heinrich Himmler: the SS had extensive powers to arrest, detain without charge, interrogate, search and confiscate property. They were responsible for running the concentration camps and implementing Nazi racial policies including the Final Solution.

- The Gestapo: the Gestapo was under the general control of the SS. They were feared by the ordinary citizens as they had sweeping powers. They spied on Germans by tapping telephones, intercepting mail and accessing information through a network of informers which made it unsafe for anyone to express anti-Nazi views.

- Concentration camps: enemies of the Nazis were sent to the camps as well as gypsies, beggars and tramps. Camps were run by SS Death's Head units. Discipline was harsh with many deaths from beatings and torture. During the Final Solution these camps were used for the extermination of the Jewish population.

- The courts and judges: judges had to take an oath of loyalty to Hitler. Jewish judges and lawyers were sacked. Capital offences were increased to make, for example, telling anti-Nazi jokes and listening to a foreign radio station, punishable by the death sentence.

How did the Nazis use culture and the mass media to control people?

The Nazis believed in complete loyalty and obedience. One of the tools for this was propaganda.

Hitler appointed Josef Goebbels as Minister for Propaganda and Enlightenment. Goebbels' job was to spread Nazi ideas, creating loyal followers of Hitler. The ministry controlled the mass media, press and films.

> ✔ Study source 5. How useful is this poster to an historian studying the effectiveness of Nazi propaganda?

Source 5

▲ A German poster from the 1930s.

All newspapers were under Nazi control and only allowed to print stories favourable to the Nazis.

All radio stations were brought under Nazi control. Cheap radios were made available. These were unable to receive foreign broadcasts. Radios were installed in cafés, bars and factories, while loudspeakers were positioned in the streets so that important announcements and Hitler's speeches could be heard by everyone.

Nazi flags and posters were everywhere. Goebbels arranged mass rallies which included marches, torchlit processions, speeches and pageantry. The most spectacular was the annual rally at Nuremberg. These rallies emphasised power, control and order. They also brought colour and excitement into people's lives. At these rallies people could hear the extraordinary speaking abilities of Hitler.

The Nazis took control of the German film industry ensuring that what was presented reflected Nazi ideals and values.

All areas of culture were Nazified. This made it impossible to hear and read non-Nazi views. Literature, art and the theatre were affected. Public book burnings occurred to destroy unacceptable views and the work of Jews.

The 1936 Berlin Olympics presented Goebbels with the perfect propaganda opportunity to advertise the achievements of the Nazis including the superiority of the Aryan race. The Germans topped the medals table, however the black American Jesse Owens was the star athlete.

Why did the Nazis persecute many groups in German society?

In Hitler's view the German people constituted the Aryan race. They were the master race, superior in terms of intelligence, physique and work ethic. Eventually they would rule the world. To preserve the purity of the Aryan race, it was essential to maintain its separateness.

Hitler also believed that Germany was overburdened with undesirables. He regarded these as a drain on the resources of the state.

Nazi propaganda blamed the Jews for everything.

- This blame related to losing the First World War and the signing of the Treaty of Versailles.
- From 1933 Jews were banned from the professions and government employment.
- Boycotts of Jewish shops were put in place and those who dared to shop in them were intimidated. "Jews not wanted" signs were displayed in cafés and public places.
- The 1935 Nuremberg Laws removed German citizenship from Jews and forbade marriage between Jews and non-Jews.
- In November 1938, as a reprisal for the shooting of a German diplomat by a Jew, the Nazis organised Kristallnacht (Night of Broken Glass). Nazi mobs attacked and burnt Jewish shops, homes, businesses and synagogues. Over one hundred Jews were murdered.
- After Kristallnacht, Jews were forbidden to attend German schools and banned from theatres and concert halls.

The Nazis persecuted many other groups who were thought to be inferior.

- Gypsies violated the racial and efficiency requirements and were sent to concentration camps. Other undesirable groups suffered the same fate.
- Following the Sterilisation Law of 1933, mentally ill people were compulsorily sterilised. In 1939 such people were killed in euthanasia programmes.

Was Nazi Germany a totalitarian state?

In a totalitarian state the government controls all aspects of public and private life through propaganda and terror. This includes the political system, the economy, and social, cultural and religious activities.

Political system	Nazi Germany was a one-party state with a charismatic leader. Political opponents posed no threat. Virtually all aspects of political life in Germany were controlled.
Economy	Overall, Nazi control was far from complete as the economy was largely in the hands of private enterprise which enjoyed a measure of independence.
Society	Nazi control over German society was extensive but not complete. A significant minority of teenagers rebelled against conformity.
Mass media and culture	In this aspect Nazi control was more or less complete through the use of censorship.
Religion	The Nazis never managed to control the Catholic Church. Attempts to form the Reich Church were not successful.
Government machinery	Nazi government was defined by power struggles, inefficiency, inconsistency and improvisation. Hitler used "divide and rule" to protect his position and prevent alliances rising against him. Hitler was not hardworking, disliking paperwork.

▲   Table 9.8 Was Nazi Germany a totalitarian state?

What was it like to live in Nazi Germany?

How did young people react to the Nazi regime?

The Nazi regime affected the lives of young people through formal education and the youth movement. This combination would ensure future generations of loyal Nazis.

Schools	• Schools in Germany were controlled by the Nazi Ministry of Education.
	• Teachers had to take an oath of loyalty to Hitler and join the Nazi Teachers' League.
	• Jewish teachers were sacked.
	• All schools were to give a uniform message.
	• The curriculum was changed to ensure that Nazi ideas and racial beliefs were reflected in the teaching of subjects like biology, history and mathematics.
	• Religious education was scrapped.
	• Emphasis was placed on sport and physical education.
	• Girls were taught "home making" skills.
Youth movements	• The Hitler Youth was available outside of school. It was founded as a voluntary organisation in 1926. The Hitler Youth Law of 1936 made it compulsory. Other youth groups were banned.
	• There were separate sections for boys and girls and for different age groups.
	• Children were indoctrinated with Nazi ideas, learning about the evils of the Jews and the injustice of the peace settlement.
	• Boys were given basic military training and discipline including drill, camp-craft, map reading and looking after a rifle. Running, hiking and tracking enhanced physical fitness.
	• Girls were prepared for motherhood, learning domestic skills such as cooking, sewing and managing the household budget.
	• Not all young Germans enjoyed the opportunities offered by the Hitler Youth. Some expressed themselves through the "Swing" movement and the Edelweiss Pirates. These groups believed in freedom of expression and values that often conflicted with those of the Nazis.

▲ Table 9.9 Education under the Nazi regime

Source 6

Source 7

▲ A photograph of the Hitler Youth on parade

▲ A drawing of anti-Jewish studies in the classroom. It is taken from a youth magazine published by the Nazis.

✅ Look at sources 6 and 7. Which of these two sources would be the more useful to a historian studying the youth of Nazi Germany?

How successful were Nazi policies towards women and the family?

The Nazis believed in traditional Aryan family values including the important role of women as wives and mothers.

This belief was partly because it gave stability but more importantly it provided the best prospect of raising the birth rate. The birth rate needed to be boosted to provide men to fight for the military and to occupy defeated countries. Measures were introduced to encourage marriage and childbearing including loans, awards and family allowance welfare benefits. The birth rate had increased by 1939.

Women were forced out of work. They were expected to remain at home, raise children and provide for their husband. Not all women were happy at losing their job in a profession.

After 1937, there was a reversal in this policy as women were needed to work in the armaments factories as demand could not be met from the pool of unemployed men.

Source 8

▲ A poster published by the Nazis.

✅ Study source 8. Why did the Nazis publish this poster?

Did most people in Germany benefit from Nazi rule?

The recovery of the German economy	When Hitler came to power unemployment was at almost six million.
	By 1938 there was almost no unemployment.
	The Nazis introduced public works schemes, building autobahns, schools hospitals and houses.
	Rearmament created jobs as did the introduction of conscription to the armed forces. Increased opportunities came from an attempt at introducing self-sufficiency to reduce the need for imports of raw materials and food.
Workers' rights and conditions	Workers had to join the Nazi Labour Front.
	Wages were low while working hours increased.
	The availability of consumer goods was limited.
	The "Beauty of Labour" movement improved working conditions by introducing washing facilities and low-cost canteens.
Free time activities	Schemes such as "Strength Through Joy" gave workers cheap theatre and cinema tickets.
	Workers were offered cut price cruises on the latest luxury liners.
	Workers saved in a state scheme to buy a Volkswagen Beetle, although no worker ever received a car.

How did the coming of war change life in Nazi Germany?

- Food rationing began in September 1939. Clothes rationing followed in November.

- Propaganda encouraged support of the war effort. The Gestapo watched for people who did not give their support.

- The gamble of invading the Soviet Union in 1941 resulted in civilians facing cutbacks, shortages and longer working hours. Labour shortages saw increasing numbers of women in the factories.

- From 1942 Albert Speer began to direct the war economy. Everything was focused on the armaments industry.

- In 1944 Germany directed all its resources in a "Total War".

- The cinemas remained open and were the only entertainment on offer. They showed propaganda films.

- There were massive bombing raids on German cities, undermining morale. One of the most significant was the bombing of Dresden.

- By the end of the war, three million civilians had died and people were short of food.

The Final Solution

As the German army captured huge areas of Eastern Europe millions of Jews came under Nazi control. The SS were responsible for shooting around 800,000 Jews.

At the Wansee Conference in January 1942, the decision was taken to eliminate all European Jews. Captured Jews were taken to remote extermination camps in Poland. The death camps were equipped with gas chambers and crematoria.

The Nazis killed around six million Jews through gassing, shooting, working to death and starvation. They tried to cover up their murderous activities.

Exam-style questions

1. Describe the religious opposition to the Nazi regime.
2. Describe the education provided by Nazi schools.
3. Why did the Nazis persecute many groups in German society?
4. How successful was the Hitler Youth Movement?
5. 'Most people benefited from Nazi control of Germany.' How far do you agree with this statement?
6. How significant was the contribution of culture and mass media to the control of the German people?

10 The USA, 1919–41

KEY IDEAS

This section will:

→ Examine the factors on which the US economic boom was based and its impact.

→ Consider American attitudes in the 1920s.

→ Evaluate the reasons for the Wall Street Crash and its social and economic consequences.

→ Raise awareness of the reasons for a change from a Republican to a Democrat President.

→ Evaluate the success of the New Deal.

Background

America's industry, based on huge natural resources of coal, timber, iron and oil as well as farming had grown steadily since the mid-nineteenth century.

Although only involved in fighting towards the end of the First World War, American businesses made money supplying arms and equipment as well as loaning money.

Whereas Britain, France and Germany were, in 1918, exhausted by war, the American economy emerged stronger. The war gave Americans confidence and wealth. It allowed them to withdraw from international politics.

10.1 How far did the US economy boom in the 1920s?

On what factors was the economic boom based?

The USA at the end of the First World War was the world's greatest economic power. Its industry had been boosted by wartime production. The 1920s became the boom years in the USA. However, not everyone shared in the boom with many, notably black, Americans continuing to suffer poverty.

Factors on which the economic boom was based	
Invention and innovation	Advances in chemicals and synthetics brought rayon, Bakelite (a form of plastic) and cellophane into common use.
	The widespread availability of electricity meant consumer goods including radios, washing machines, vacuum cleaners and refrigerators became widely available.
Republican policies	The Republican governments of the 1920s followed financial policies favourable to industry. The policy was known as laissez-faire where the government favoured non-intervention. Taxation was kept low and to protect against imports and prevent competition, high import tariffs were introduced.

Mass production	Assembly-line production was used by Henry Ford in the manufacture of cars. This method of production was used to make many other items. Its use led to a fall in prices.
The motor industry	The automobile industry was central to America's economic success. With the cost of a car reducing in price, one in five Americans owned one by 1929.
	The car industry boosted a whole range of associated industries including glass, rubber, steel and leather. The number of roads increased as did roadside filling stations, hotels and restaurants.
Mass marketing	Advertising for radio and the cinema was developed, while giant billboards displayed posters alongside highways. New merchandise was advertised in magazines, newspapers and mail order catalogues.
Hire purchase credit	Customers who could not afford to buy a product outright were able to pay by instalments under a hire purchase agreement.

▲ Table 10.1 Factors on which the economic boom was based

Source 1

> Work is planned on the drawing board and the operations sub-divided so that each man and each machine only do one thing. The thing is to take the work to the man, not the man to the work.

▲ Henry Ford, in 1925, describes assembly-line production.

Why did some industries prosper while others did not?

The boom was based mainly on new industries. As these industries boomed the number of jobs increased. Wages for many Americans rose as did a feeling of confidence. Increased wealth meant that people could afford the new consumer goods.

The 1920s was a golden age for building and construction. New businesses required offices and showrooms which had to be connected by new roads. Many public buildings, including schools, were constructed as were skyscrapers.

Although an established industry, steel production did not suffer because of the demands of the car and building industries.

While there was an increased demand for clothes there was less demand for cotton and woollen textiles. The demand was for clothes manufactured using synthetic materials such as rayon.

The coal industry suffered from the increased use of cleaner, more efficient oil, gas and electricity alternatives.

Why did agriculture not share in the prosperity?

There were a number of factors affecting agriculture at this time.

- During the First World War agriculture had boomed with exports to Europe. These exports were no longer needed once the war had ended.
- One of the problems was overproduction. The USA could not eat all the food that was produced; neither could the surplus be exported. As a result prices fell.
- American agriculture was facing competition from Canada and Argentina.

- Many farmers borrowed from banks but as prices fell they were unable to repay the loans. The banks seized their farms.
- The south was worst affected as there was a reliance on single crops making it more vulnerable.
- Many European countries would not take American farm products as America had placed high tariffs on imports.
- Crops were lost to pests such as the boll weevil.

Source 2

 A photograph of a black family and their home in Virginia, in the 1920s.

Did all Americans benefit from the boom?

The increase in wealth was not shared equally. By 1929 around 60% of families lived below the poverty line.

Many black Americans worked as sharecroppers. With the agricultural slump many moved north to work in the lowest paid sectors such as domestic service. They were segregated into slum areas such as Harlem in New York.

Native Americans lived in reservations where growing land was poor quality. Those who remained in the reservations suffered from poverty, poor education and ill health.

New immigrants found that only the lowest-paid jobs were available to them. Many suffered religious discrimination and had a lack of education.

✅ Study source 2.
1. Why was this photograph published?
2. Is this photograph of any use to an historian studying 1920s America?

Exam-style questions

1. What was the main development in the motor car industry during the 1920s?
2. What problems did farmers face in the 1920s?
3. Why did some industries prosper more than others?
4. How far did all Americans benefit from the boom?
5. How significant were Republican policies in causing the 'boom' in America in the 1920s?
6. How significant was the impact of the economic boom on the people of America?

10.2 How far did US society change in the 1920s?

What were the "Roaring Twenties"?

Following the end of the First World War, Americans benefited from increased prosperity. Some spent their new wealth on entertainment.

For some young women life was much freer. This was the decade of shorter skirts, make-up, bobbed hair, smoking in public and going out without a chaperone. Many went to night clubs and danced to jazz music. A new dance, the Charleston, became popular.

The car gave Americans the freedom of movement to visit clubs, cinemas and restaurants.

For the majority of the population, however, the "Roaring Twenties" was more an image than a reality.

Entertainment opportunities	
The cinema	Cinema provided an opportunity for escapism from the daily grind. Audiences more than doubled, reaching 95 million in 1929.
	Many new stars were created by Hollywood including Charlie Chaplin, Mary Pickford and Rudolph Valentino.
	"Talkies" arrived in 1927 with the release of the film *The Jazz Singer* starring Al Jolson.
	Some Americans expressed concern that films corrupted public morals.
Jazz	Jazz music originated in the African–American community of the south.
	Jazz was linked to dance music and led to the formation of many night clubs. One well-known jazz performer was Duke Ellington.
	Jazz appealed to young whites who found it exciting, dynamic and modern.
Radio	Radio broadcast light musical entertainment to a mass audience producing the age of the great dance bands.
	As variety theatres declined, radio provided a fresh start for many artists.
Sport	Sport became a form of mass entertainment. Huge crowds attended baseball games.

▲ Table 10.2 Entertainment opportunities during the "Roaring Twenties"

How widespread was intolerance in US society?

Many established Americans wanted to maintain traditions and were fearful of those who threatened the American way of life. Many saw a threat coming from new immigrants: communists, anarchists, blacks, Jews and Catholics. It was the ambition of many to maintain the supremacy of the white, Anglo-Saxon, Protestant community (WASPs).

The Red Scare	The "Red Scare" was caused by the large number of immigrants arriving from southern and eastern Europe. It was thought that they might be infected with communist and anarchist ideas following the Bolshevik Revolution in Russia in 1917. Suspected agitators were arrested and deported. A series of bomb blasts in 1919 offered evidence of a supposed conspiracy against the state. In one extreme case, two Italian radicals, Vanzetti and Sacco, faced a charge of murder despite the evidence being flawed. As they were immigrants, and they were anarchists, they were found guilty and executed for murder. The Red Scare was stoked up by hysteria in the press and no evidence of a serious threat to the state was uncovered.
Religious intolerance	Fundamentalist Christians in rural areas of the south believed in a literal interpretation of the Bible. Urban Christians accepted Darwin's theory of evolution. The fundamentalists succeeded in outlawing the teaching of evolution in six states. In Tennessee, one of the six states, biology teacher John Scopes deliberately broke the law by teaching evolution. The so-called "monkey trial" of 1925 was a national sensation. Scopes was found guilty but the fundamentalists lost the argument and were ridiculed.
Jim Crow laws	In the south, black people suffered from segregation under the Jim Crow laws. Most lived in poverty and permanent fear of lynch mobs. In the northern cities many black people found it hard to get a good job and had to endure the worst housing.
Immigration policy	This law restricted entry to the United States of certain national groups. This affected immigrants from southern and eastern Europe. Immigrants from China and Japan were completely barred. The law resulted in 85% of immigrants to the US coming from northern Europe.
The Ku Klux Klan	The Klan was the most extreme example of intolerance and racism during the 1920s. The Klan claimed to have a membership of five million in 1925. Membership included high-ranking politicians and government officials. Many supporters were from areas that had largely been excluded from the new prosperity. The Klan's hatred went wider than just black people. Catholics, Jews, foreigners, liberals and homosexuals were also targets. The most extreme forms of persecution included beating, mutilation and lynching.

▲ Table 10.3 Intolerance in US society

Source 3

I have known Judge Thayer all my life. I say that he is a narrow-minded man; he is an unintelligent man; he is full of prejudice; he has been carried away with the fear of the Reds. This fear of Reds has raised strong emotions in about ninety per cent of American people.

▲ A leading American lawyer speaking about Judge Webster Thayer in 1921 following the trial of Sacco and Vanzetti. Judge Thayer was the judge at that trial.

Source 4

Southern trees bear strange fruit,
Blood on the leaves and blood on the root,
Black bodies swinging in the Southern breeze,
Strange fruit hanging from the poplar trees,
Here is the fruit for the crows to pluck,
For the rain to gather, for the wind to suck
For the sun to root
For the tree to drop
Here is a strange and bitter crop.

▲ Lyrics of an anti-racist song written in 1939 by Lewis Allen for a black singer called Billie Holliday.

Why was Prohibition introduced and later repealed?

The 18th Amendment to the American Constitution was passed through Congress in 1919. This prohibited the manufacture, transport and sale of alcohol.

The Volstead Act of 1920 gave the Federal government the power to enforce prohibition. From January 1920 the US was officially "dry".

Why was Prohibition introduced?	• Prohibition was supposed to make the US consistent nationwide with regards to its laws on alcohol. Eighteen states, mainly in rural areas of the South and Midwest, already had their own prohibition laws. • It was claimed that alcohol caused social problems such as poverty, crime, violence and ill health. The Anti-Saloon League and the Women's Temperance Union were strong campaigners for abolition, suggesting the USA would become a better place. • The Protestant Church supported the cause, believing alcohol brought a decline in moral standards and family life in the big cities. • Many American brewers were of German descent. The First World War had created strong anti-German feelings and it was seen by some as unpatriotic to consume alcohol. • Some believed that grain used for alcohol could be better used for making bread. • It was seen as an opportunity to pick up votes by some politicians. • Some industrialists, including Nelson Rockefeller, argued that Prohibition would be good for the economy as it would reduce absenteeism and promote hard work.
Why was Prohibition repealed?	• Consumption of alcohol went up as Prohibition had the undesired effect of making alcohol more attractive. Illegal bars, called "speakeasies", became common. Here drinking continued behind closed doors. • It is believed that by 1929 New York had 32,000 illegal drinking bars. • Drinking continued at home, with private deliveries of wines and spirits being made to the homes of the rich. • Some people tried to make their own alcohol. This was called "moonshine". Deaths were caused by drinking moonshine. • It was impossible to prevent alcohol being smuggled into America. Many of those involved in this illegal trade made large amounts of money. "Bootleg" rum was smuggled from the West Indies and whisky from Canada. • Prohibition boosted crime. Organised gangs controlled the manufacture and sale of alcohol. They bribed policemen and government officials. There was much feuding between the gangs leading to incidents like the Valentine's Day Massacre of 1929 when rival gang members were murdered by Al Capone's gang. • The government appointed several thousand enforcement agents. However, this was not enough and as they were poorly paid they were open to threats and bribes made by the criminal gangs. • State officials, judges, senior police officers and jury members were often bought off with bribes.

▲ Table 10.4 Reasons for the introduction and repeal of the Prohibition

It was clear by the early 1930s that Prohibition had failed. The Depression increased this view. It was daft to spend public money trying to enforce the law. This money would be better used in creating jobs for the unemployed. Money could also be made from imposing taxes and duties on alcohol.

When Roosevelt came to power he supported the proposal to repeal Prohibition. This was done under the 18th Amendment. Prohibition ended in December 1933.

Source 5

THE NATIONAL GESTURE

▲ An American cartoon published in 1926 during Prohibition.

 1. Read source 4. How useful is this source to an historian studying intolerance in America in the 1920s?

2. Look at source 5. What is the cartoonist's message?

How far did the roles of women change during the 1920s?

The First World War saw women performing men's work in the war industries while men were in the armed forces. After the war women went back to traditional types of work.

The 1920s brought a revolution in the role of some women. Some became known as "flappers". These were often young, wealthy, middle and upper class women from the larger towns and cities. These were the "showy and noisy" minority.

Women from rural areas were less affected by the changes, continuing their traditional roles and restricted lives. Many of these women actually opposed the changes.

Politics	In 1920 women got the vote in all states. They now made up 50% or more of the electorate.
Work	The number of women in employment increased by 25% to 10 million by 1929, although women continued to be paid less than men for precisely the same work.
	Office work and manufacturing accounted for much of the increase and in some new industries, such as electronics, women were preferred to men.
Dress	Corsets were abandoned and women began wearing shorter, lighter, skirts and dresses that were often sleeveless. The new fashions and materials, such as rayon, permitted greater movement and self-expression.
Lifestyle	Women began smoking, drinking, and kissing in public. Chaperones were no longer required.
	Women also drove cars. It has been suggested that Henry Ford introduced coloured cars in 1925 as a response to the female market. Previously all Ford cars had been black.
	Short hair and make-up became symbols of the new freedom.
	Women were acting with more independence. The divorce rate increased from 100,000 in 1914 to 205,000 in 1929.
	Labour-saving devices affected the lives of a minority with only 30% of households owning a vacuum cleaner and 24% a washing machine.

▲ Table 10.5 The role of women in the 1920s

Exam-style questions

1. What was Prohibition?
2. Describe the activities of the Ku Klux Klan.
3. Why Was Prohibition repeated?
4. 'The roles of women changed little during the 1920s.' How far do you agree with this statement?
5. To what extent was intolerance a feature of US society in the 1920s? Explain your answer.
6. 'The significance of the impact of the Ku Klux Klan on American society was greater than that of Prohibition'. How far do you agree with this statement?

10.3 What were the causes and consequences of the Wall Street Crash?

How far was speculation responsible for the Wall Street Crash?

During the 1920s the American stock market on Wall Street shared in the economic boom. Prices of shares rose sharply and people got used to the idea that share prices would always go up. Speculators bought shares in a growth company, selling them soon afterwards at a higher price in order to pocket the profit.

People began to borrow money to buy shares often "on the margin". This meant paying only a small percentage of the share's worth on purchase, reselling at a profit and then paying the balance out of the profit. The banks were often prepared to lend up to 90% of the share price.

On the stock market everything depended on confidence in the share prices rising. By the end of the 1920s the US economy was slowing down. Confidence in the economy was starting to decline.

On "Black Thursday", 24 October 1929, the fall in share prices turned into panic. Prices plunged and desperate investors sold their shares to try to cut their losses.

Thousands were bankrupted as the stock market went into free fall.

Source 6

> There is a surge of women investors: secretaries, heiresses, business women and housewives. In the last ten years the number of women speculators has increased from 2 per cent to 35 per cent of the total number who gamble daily on the stock market. Of course, a woman who wants to take part in the stock market must have money to invest. And she has certainly got that as never before.

▲ From an article in an American magazine published in 1925.

Speculation was just one of a number of causes of the Wall Street Crash and the Great Depression that followed, but it certainly contributed.

Source 7

Exports
• America had limited opportunities for exporting its products.
• Its European customers were impoverished and had still not recovered fully from the financial strains of the First World War.
• American tariffs led to tariffs being set up by potential customers which made it difficult for American exporters to operate in foreign markets.

The action of speculators

Overproduction
• By 1929 American industry was producing more consumer goods than there were consumers to buy.
• The market had become saturated as Americans with money had now bought their cars, fridges, and other domestic appliances.

The Wall Street Crash

Uneven distribution of income
• Estimates suggest that between 50 and 60 per cent of Americans were too poor to take part in the consumer boom of the 1920s.
• Low wages and unemployment especially in the farming sector, the traditional industries, and among blacks and new immigrants reduced the potential of the home market.
• By contrast just 5 per cent of the population was receiving 33 per cent of the income in 1929.
• Too much money was in too few hands. Mass production required mass consumption and that meant higher wages.

Signs of an economic slow-down
• There were signs that the 1920s boom was coming to an end well before October 1929.
• By 1927 fewer new houses were being built, sales of cars were beginning to decline, and wage increases were levelling off.
• Financial exports were aware that stock levels in warehouses were beginning to increase suggesting that the economy was slowing down.
• All this made investors nervous and anxious to sell their shares at the first sign of serious trouble.

▲ Causes of the Wall Street Crash

✔ Look at the reasons given for the Wall Street Crash in source 7. Working as a group, write each of the reasons on a separate piece of card. After a group discussion, place each card in order of importance of its contribution to the crash. Discuss the reasons for making your choice and present these reasons.

What impact did the Wall Street Crash have on the economy?

The stock market crash was an economic disaster. The share prices did not stop falling for three years.

- Businesses and banks went bust. Around 11,000 banks had stopped trading.
- The economy had to adjust to a general reduction in trade and demand for American goods both at home and abroad.
- Businesses had to reduce their operations by cutting production. Workers were sacked or had their wages reduced.

- Less money in the economy meant that people could not afford to buy goods and business confidence collapsed. Any thought of expansion had to be abandoned.
- By 1933 the economy was producing only 20% of what it had in 1929.

What were the social consequences of the crash?

By 1933, nearly one in four of the workforce was out of a job. There were no welfare benefits for those without an income, but rents and mortgages still had to be paid.

Many faced eviction from their home, often being reduced to begging, scavenging in rubbish dumps for food scraps and sleeping on park benches. Shanty towns of tents and makeshift huts, constructed from scrap metal and cardboard boxes, grew up on the edges of towns and cities. These "towns" became known as "Hoovervilles" after the President.

The unemployed queuing for food from charities or soup kitchens became a common sight.

In 1932 the government lost support as a result of the way they dealt with the "Bonus Marchers", a group of thousands of destitute army veterans who had been promised a war service bonus to be paid in 1945. In view of the economic situation they demanded payment in 1932.

Congress refused and the marchers began a peaceful protest camped in a Hooverville opposite the White House. President Hoover thought they were a threat to the government and used the army to clear the camp. The camp was destroyed with the aid of tanks, machine guns and tear gas. Two veterans were killed and nearly one thousand injured.

Source 8

> The troops came with their gas bombs and their bayonets. They set fire to the wooden shacks on the edge of the camp. Men and women were trying to gather what they could and flee. Tanks and soldiers guarded the bridge back into the city so that none of the marchers could escape into Washington and disturb the sleep of a few government officials.
>
> The jeers and cries of the evicted men and women rose above the crackling of the flames. The flames were mirrored in the drawn bayonets of the infantry as they advanced through the camp.
>
> On the evening after the crime against the Bonus Marchers, General MacArthur said, "That mob was motivated by a belief in revolution. In my opinion the President was right to act."

▲ An account of events in Washington in 1932 by one of the Bonus Marchers.

▲ Fig. 10.1 A "Hooverville" in Seattle, 1934.

✔ Read source 8. How useful is this source as evidence of American attitudes?

Why did Roosevelt win the election of 1932?

Hoover's weaknesses	Hoover incorrectly interpreted the early stages of the depression as a normal business downturn. Consequently his approach was to "sit it out" until prosperity returned. When he took action it was regarded as too little, too late. • He took some half-hearted measures including asking employers not to sack people and giving loans to businesses in trouble. • He was against the government providing welfare support as he thought it would undermine America's rugged individualism. This gave the impression of being unsympathetic. This was confirmed by his actions against the Bonus Marchers. • He failed to project himself as a man of vision, giving an impression of being grim-faced and conservative in his approach.
Roosevelt's strengths	• He gained a reputation for helping those in need when he was Governor of New York State where he organised schemes to help the elderly and the unemployed. • Roosevelt had an upbeat personality and appeared warm, charming and optimistic when on the campaign trail. This approach gave confidence to Americans that they would be helped. • Many Americans admired the way he had fought against polio. • His election campaign was about giving Americans a "new deal". Although he was not specific about how it would be achieved, he caught the imagination of the American people. • He went on a train tour of America to meet the people. At these meetings he mercilessly attacked Hoover and the Republicans.

▲ Table 10.6 Reasons for Roosevelt's success in the election of 1932

What had Hoover done to try to combat the Great Depression?

- In 1930 taxes were cut by $130 million to inject more purchasing power into the economy.

- Tariffs were increased by the Hawley-Smoot Act (1930) to protect American-produced food and goods.

- Money was provided to finance a building programme to create more jobs. The most famous project was the Hoover Dam on the Colorado River.

- Employers were encouraged to make voluntary agreements with their employees to maintain wages and production.

- The Reconstruction Finance Corporation (1932) was set up to provide loans, amounting to $1,500 million, to businesses facing hard times.

- The Federal Farm Board was set up to buy surplus produce in an attempt to stabilise prices.

Source 9

THE NEW CHAUFFEUR

▲ An American cartoon published in 1933.

Source 10

▲ An American cartoon published in March 1933.

> ✓ Look at sources 9 and 10. How far do these two sources have the same message?

Exam-style questions

1. What was 'speculation' in relation to the Wall Street Crash?
2. Describe a 'Hooverville'.
3. Why was the US economy showing signs of weakness by 1929?
4. Why did the government deal harshly with the Bonus marchers?
5. 'Hoover could only blame himself for losing the presidential election of 1932.' How far do you agree with this statement?
6. How significant was speculation as a cause of the Wall Street Crash?
7. How important was Roosevelt's promise of a 'new deal' in him being elected President in 1932?

10.4 How successful was the New Deal?

What was the New Deal as introduced in 1933?

The term "New Deal" was applied to various measures introduced by Roosevelt between 1933 and 1938 to rescue America from the Great Depression. The first phase, introduced between March and June 1933, is referred to as Roosevelt's "Hundred Days".

To explain to the public what he was doing, Roosevelt spoke to the country via radio broadcasts. He explained his policies as though he was chatting to friends.

His first action was to deal with the banking crisis. A main feature of this first phase was the creation of "alphabet agencies".

The First Hundred Days	
Banks	• The banking system was close to collapse as customers were panicking and withdrawing their savings, making further bank closures more likely. • Roosevelt ordered a four-day national bank holiday while the Emergency Banking Act was passed through Congress. • Unsound banks, about 5% of the total, were then closed down while the remainder were helped with government grants and advice. • Roosevelt explained what he was doing to the American people through a national radio broadcast, the first of his fireside chats. Those with savings were asked to return their money to the banks when they reopened. Public confidence was restored and the banking system survived.
Unemployed	• Unemployment stood at nearly 13 million in 1933, approximately 25% of the workforce. • The Civilian Conservation Corps (CCC) was set up to provide voluntary employment for young men aged 18 to 25. • Living in government camps, they carried out conservation work, planting new forests, strengthening river banks for flood control, and clearing scrubland. • Wages were low but the scheme provided work for over two million men during the nine years of its existence. • The Public Works Administration (PWA) provided jobs by initiating major construction projects such as dams, bridges, railways, schools, hospitals, and houses. • The PWA spent $7 billion between 1933 and 1939 creating millions of jobs for skilled workers. • The Civil Works Administration (CWA) aimed to provide temporary work over the winter of 1933–4. • Four million jobs were created building roads, airports, and schools before the scheme ended in April 1934.

Farmers	• The collapse of food prices after 1929 had left the farming industry in crisis.
	• The Agricultural Adjustment Agency (AAA) paid farmers to take part of their land out of cultivation and reduce their livestock.
	• Millions of acres of sown land were ploughed up and six million piglets were slaughtered.
	• Prices rose, and between 1933 and 1939 farmers' incomes doubled.
	• Farm labourers were not helped by this measure, however, and many found themselves unemployed.
Industry	• The National Industrial Recovery Act set up the National Recovery Administration (NRA) aiming to stabilise production and prices, and to improve working conditions and pay.
	• In an attempt to achieve this, voluntary codes were drawn up for each industry that enabled employers to regulate prices, output, hours, and wages.
	• Businesses that signed up to their industry code were able to display the NRA badge, a Blue Eagle with the motto "We Do Our Part". The public were encouraged to buy products and services from companies displaying the badge.
	• The scheme definitely led to an improvement in working conditions and reduced the incidence of child labour. It also put an end to price-cutting wars. But it tended to favour the large firms who sometimes forced the smaller firms out of business. When the scheme was declared unconstitutional by the Supreme Court in 1935 Roosevelt made no attempt to revive the idea.
The Poor	• The Federal Emergency Relief Administration (FERA) had a budget of $500 million to assist those in desperate need.
	• The money was used to fund soup kitchens, provide clothing and bedding, and set up work schemes and nursery schools.

▲ Table 10.7 The First Hundred Days of Roosevelt's New Deal

The Tennessee Valley Authority (TVA)

The Tennessee Valley was a vast, depressed region. Agriculture had been badly affected by floods and soil erosion. In wet weather the river would flood. The farming land was a dust bowl. The soil was eroding and turning the land into desert.

Unemployment was high and people were living in poverty. The majority of homes had no electricity.

The Tennessee Valley Authority (TVA) was a showcase for the New Deal. It was an independent organisation which cut across the powers of seven states. It aimed to restore the prosperity of the area. Hydroelectric dams were built and flood prevention schemes introduced. To prevent erosion tree planting took place. New industries were attracted.

 Discuss in groups. Why was the work carried out in the Tennessee Valley so successful?

How far did the character of the New Deal change after 1933?

During 1935, Roosevelt introduced a new phase of reforms which became known as the "Second New Deal". The reforms concentrated more on labour rights and improved welfare.

The Wagner Act, 1935	This replaced part of the National Industrial Recovery Act which the Supreme Court had declared unconstitutional. It confirmed the right of workers to join a trade union.
The Social Security Act, 1935	This set up a scheme to provide old age pensions, unemployment benefit and help for the sick and disabled. It was based on a national insurance scheme.
	This was a landmark piece of legislation contradicting the belief that individuals should provide for their own welfare.
The Works Progress Administration (WPA), 1935	This addressed the persistent problem of unemployment. It supported efforts to find jobs for the unemployed through a broad range of projects and work programmes.
The Resettlement Administration (RA), 1935	This focused on the plight of farm labourers, sharecroppers and tenant farmers. It aimed to move 500,000 families to areas of better land.
	While some families benefited, many farm workers remained in poverty.

▲   Table 10.8 The "Second New Deal"

Why did the New Deal encounter opposition?

There were people who thought that Roosevelt did not go far enough in his reforms while others thought he was too radical.

Radical opposition came from critics like the following individuals:

- Father Coughlin became disillusioned as he felt Roosevelt was failing to tackle the problems of the poor. He broadcast his ideas on radio every Sunday evening to an enormous national audience.
- Dr Francis Townshend campaigned for pension reform through his "Townshend Clubs". They claimed that Roosevelt was more interested in preserving society than changing it.
- Huey Long planned a major redistribution of wealth to stimulate the economy. He planned to take money from the very rich and redistribute it among the less affluent.

Conservative opposition came from the following groups:

- Republicans believed that there should be minimal government intervention and low taxation. The New Deal was seen to undermine what were regarded as core American values. They thought that Roosevelt was becoming too powerful and was acting like a dictator.
- Businessmen resented the level of government interference. They thought it was a form of socialism and un-American. They were unhappy with Roosevelt's support for trade unions.
- The rich thought that it was unfair that they had to pay to help the less fortunate. America had always believed in self-help. They said it would encourage people to be lazy.

- Some state governors argued that aspects of the New Deal conflicted with the rights of state governments to manage their own affairs.

There was also opposition from the Supreme Court.

- The main role of the Supreme Court was to ensure that any measures introduced were consistent with the American Constitution.

- There were nine judges who were Republicans and elderly. They had a natural political dislike for the New Deal.

- They declared the National Recovery Administration (NRA) and the Agricultural Adjustment Act (AAA) unconstitutional.

- Following the Presidential election of 1936, when Roosevelt was re-elected, he wanted to appoint six additional judges sympathetic to his policies.

- He was accused of trying to overthrow the Constitution and acting like a dictator.

- Roosevelt backed down.

Source 11

▲ An American cartoon published in 1937.

Source 12

> The New Deal is an attempt to take money away from those who have been careful with it. This is money that they have been able to save over many years. Once taken away it would be given to those people who have not been as careful with their earnings. The New Deal will destroy any thoughts of the need to save money for times of difficulty. This will discourage people from working hard and give money to those who do nothing.

▲ A Republican opponent of the New Deal speaking in 1935.

Source 13

> A resident of Park Avenue, a wealthy area of New York, was sentenced to a term of imprisonment for threatening to commit violence against President Roosevelt.
>
> This Act was significant as an example of the fanatical hatred of the President which today obsesses thousands of men and woman among the American upper class.

▲ From an article entitled "They hate Roosevelt" published in *Harper's Magazine* in 1936. Harper's was an American pro-Democratic magazine read by the wealthier sections of the community.

 1. Look at source 11. Why was this cartoon published in 1937? How would Roosevelt have reacted to this cartoon?

2. Read sources 12 and 13. How similar are these two sources? Which of these two sources provides the more reliable evidence about American attitudes towards the New Deal?

Why did unemployment persist despite the New Deal?

In 1933, when Roosevelt became President, unemployment stood at 12.8 million. By 1941, it had fallen to 5.6 million. The problem of unemployment was only solved when America entered the Second World War. During the years of the New Deal, unemployment never fell below 5 million. What were the reasons for this?

- The New Deal found work for millions but in jobs that were not permanent.
- Incomes for many Americans remained low, reducing the money available to spend on American goods.
- There was a worldwide depression so the foreign market was not purchasing American goods. Import tariffs were common practice in Europe as well as America.
- Changes in manufacturing required fewer labourers.
- Improvements were frustratingly slow and only with the demands of war came the transformation into economic recovery.

Did the fact that the New Deal failed to solve unemployment mean that it was a failure?

The New Deal as a success	
Unemployment	Unemployment fell by over 30% between 1933 and 1939.
Trade unions	Trade union membership increased to over seven million following the Wagner Act.
	Many strikes were settled in the workers' favour.
	Working conditions generally improved as did workers' pay.
Farmers	Large-scale farmers benefited from the reductions in acreage and livestock, and the increase in prices.
The poor	Millions of Americans were protected from the worst effects of the depression by the introduction of welfare payments and other emergency benefits such as food, clothing and shelter.
	America became a more compassionate society.
Industry	Much business was saved by Roosevelt's speedy action to save the banking system.
	Future industrial development and prosperity was stimulated by the construction of schools, roads, railways, bridges, and hydro-electric dams.
Morale	Roosevelt's policies gave many Americans new hope, new confidence, and a sense of purpose.
	The New Deal ensured that America survived the Great Depression without resorting to extreme solutions. Neither communism nor fascism had much support in America during the 1930s.

The New Deal as a failure	
Unemployment	Unemployment never fell below 14% of the workforce between 1933 and 1939.
Trade unions	Businessmen and industrialists strongly disliked the encouragement given to unions under the Wagner Act.
	Some companies were prepared to use violence to break up strikes and sit-ins. In 1937, ten Chicago steel workers were shot dead by police while taking part in a strike march.
Small farmers	Tenant farmers, labourers, and sharecroppers were forced off the land by government plans to reduce agricultural production.

Black Americans	The New Deal did not end racial discrimination in American society.
	Roosevelt needed the support of Democrats in the south and this prevented him from introducing civil rights laws which they would have opposed.
	Although some black people made gains in employment and housing they did not benefit as much as white people.
Industry	Industrial recovery may have been held back by the increase in rules and regulations, the increases in taxation, and the encouragement given to trade unions.
Second World War	Well before America entered the Second World War in December 1941 it had increased defence spending and begun supplying armaments and other goods to Britain and France.
	These actions clearly had a stimulating impact on the American economy. Arguably it was rearmament rather than the New Deal that was primarily responsible for the economic revival of 1939 and 1941.

Exam-style questions

1. What was Roosevelt's New Deal of 1933?
2. Why did Roosevelt feel it was important to deal with the banking crisis?
3. Why was the New Deal criticised?
4. 'The New Deal was a failure.' How far do you agree with this statement?
5. How significant was the opposition of the Supreme Court in limiting the impact of Roosevelt's New Deal?
6. How important were 'alphabet agencies' to the success of the New Deal?

Israelis and Palestinians since 1945

Background

Conflict between Israelis and Palestinians comes from historical claims which both groups have on land in the Middle East.

The Jews can trace their occupation of Palestine back at least until 1000 BCE where they lived until being expelled by their Roman rulers around 135 CE. The Jews settled in almost every part of the Roman Empire until the Middle Ages when they were expelled, settling in Russia and Poland. In the nineteenth century, facing persecution, many Jews fled to Western Europe and the USA.

For many centuries, the Arabs lived in the lands we now call the Middle East. The Arabs all spoke Arabic and were converted to Islam, becoming Muslims.

By the end of the nineteenth century the Arab Empire, which from the seventh century had spread across the Middle East and North Africa, was in gradual decline under the control of the Turks. With the persecution of Jews in Europe increasing, both groups developed plans to create a homeland in Palestine.

A form of Jewish nationalism, Zionism, gained support with 60,000 Zionists settling in Palestine by 1914.

The First World War was a turning point in the Arab struggle for independence as well as the Jewish struggle for a homeland.

11.1 How was the Jewish state of Israel established?

What were the causes of conflict between Jews and Arabs in Palestine?

British involvement in the First World War gave hope to both Jews and Arabs. The British offered to create an Arab homeland in return for assistance in the war against the Turks. At the same time they offered to create a Jewish homeland in Palestine in return for Jews in America encouraging the USA to enter the war against Germany. What this did was to create further potential for conflict.

At the end of the war, control over the region was passed to Britain under the terms of a League of Nations mandate. For the next 30 years the British government ruled Palestine.

The Arabs were resentful of the British betrayal and were even more angered by increasing Jewish immigration. The Zionists, meanwhile, feared the British were aiming for the creation of an Arab state in Palestine.

The British government was unable to satisfy either Arabs or Jews resulting in violence breaking out throughout the 1920s and early 1930s.

From 1933, Nazi anti-Semitism drove many Jews to flee to Palestine. This left Britain in an impossible position. If they restricted immigration they were accused of not helping Jews avoid Nazi persecution. If they allowed unrestricted immigration, Arab fears of losing their country would increase.

In 1937, the British government set up an inquiry. The Peel Commission recommended the partition of Palestine into two separate states. The Arabs rejected this and continued fighting.

With war in Europe looming, the British government attempted to pacify the Arabs so that oil supplies from the Middle East would continue. The terms of the White Paper, published in May 1939, made no reference to partition, thus outraging the Jews.

During the Second World War both the British government and Jewish leaders made plans for the future of the Middle East after the war. The British plan included proposals for Jewish and Arab states. The Jewish plan demanded the creation of a Jewish state in Palestine and unlimited Jewish immigration.

What was the significance of the end of the Second World War for Palestine?

After the war ended, the newly elected British Labour Government was unsympathetic towards Zionism.

- In October 1945, militant Zionists, the Haganah, joined forces with Irgun and Lehi in a guerrilla war against the British authorities. Acts of terrorism against the British increased. Two British soldiers were hanged by members of Irgun. This was in revenge for the execution of three Irgun members.

- By 1948, 220 British soldiers had been killed by Jewish terrorists under the banner of the Hebrew Resistance Movement in an attempt to force the British out.

- On 22 July 1946, the most notorious act against the British occurred. The Irgun bombed the King David Hotel, a base for the British authorities, killing over 90 people.

- The British government wanted an independent Palestine in which Arabs and Jews would share power and began blocking the mass immigration of Jews to Palestine. The refusal by the British to allow the entry of survivors of the Holocaust was widely criticised. The British prevented boatloads of illegal Jewish immigrants from landing in Palestine. In July 1947 one ship, the Exodus, carrying 4,000 Holocaust survivors was sent back to Europe. US President Truman began to put pressure on Britain to allow Jewish refugees to enter Palestine. Many Americans now supported a state of Israel.

Source 1

▲   A photograph of the damaged King David Hotel in Jerusalem after the Jewish bomb attack.

✔ 1.   Carry out individual research to find out more about the actions of the British towards Jews coming from Europe to escape the Holocaust.
2.   Were the actions of Palestinian Arabs in response to British actions justifiable?
3.   Identify and discuss in small groups the reasons for Britain ending their Palestinian mandate. Categorise your reasons in order of importance.

Why did the British hand Palestine over to the United Nations (UN)?

Britain had emerged from the Second World War exhausted and financially weak, and could not afford to keep 100,000 troops in Palestine to deal with the Zionist campaign of violence. The finances Britain had were being used to deal with food and housing shortages at home.

US President Truman was putting increasing pressure on the British. The British actions in preventing Jewish immigrants to enter Palestine were meeting with worldwide criticism.

Why did the Arabs reject UN plans to partition Palestine?

In February 1947, the British announced that it would hand Palestine over to the UN and that its mandate would end on 15 May 1948.

In November 1947, the UN decided that Palestine would be divided into two states, one Jewish and one Arab.

- The Arab territories would consist of three geographically separate areas.
- The Jews were to be given over half of the land, but only had a third of the population.

- Jerusalem would be governed by an international trusteeship.
- The two new states would form one economic union, with a single currency and customs area.

On 10 October, the USA announced support for partition as President Truman was anxious not to lose access to oil supplies. Surprisingly, three days later the USSR announced their support.

However, the plan was rejected by both the Arabs and Jews.

- The Jews were given a larger area of Arab land, which the Arabs did not want to relinquish.
- The Arabs thought the western powers should find a home for the Jews elsewhere.
- Some Jews were not happy as many Jewish settlements were included within the Arab state.
- Jews did not like the idea of the city of Jerusalem being controlled by an international force.
- The Arab state would be divided into three zones. It would have no direct access to the sea as Jaffa, the main Arab port, would be cut off from the rest of the Arab land. Its land was mostly desert country, making it difficult to farm.

Responsibility for implementation of the plan was given to a new body, the UN Palestine Commission. Britain refused access to Palestine for the new body. With the British setting 1 May 1948 as the date of their withdrawal, Jews and Arabs prepared themselves for a military solution to the future of Palestine.

Why was Israel able to win the war of 1948–49?

Civil war in Palestine

In December 1947, following the publication of the Partition Plan, violence between Jews and Arabs intensified. This violence included a fierce struggle to control the roads leading to Jerusalem.

Soldiers from Iraq and Syria came to Palestine to aid the Arabs. In the meantime, Haganah, using its experience of fighting the British in the Second World War, organised Jewish defence forces.

Immediately before the British withdrawal, some of the bloodiest fighting took place in and around Jerusalem.

The actions of the Irgun and Lehi fighters helped to create terror in the minds of Arab villagers. In one incident on 10 April 1948, the village of Deir Yassin was attacked by Irgun fighters who claimed it was an Arab headquarters. Over 250 of the men, women and children from the village were killed.

By May 1948, when the British withdrew, 300,000 Arabs had fled from what was to become the new Jewish state. Their departure demoralised those Palestinians who remained.

In April 1948, the Jews captured the city of Haifa and attacked Jaffa. Over 100,000 Palestinians fled from these two towns. Neighbouring Arab governments were unhappy about the news of large numbers of Palestinian refugees, fearing they would have to support them.

Source 2

> The partition of the homeland is illegal. It will never be recognised. It will not bind the Jewish people. Jerusalem was and will for ever be our capital.

▲ Menachem Begin, Leader of Irgun.

Source 3

> Arabs throughout the country, induced to believe wild tales of "Irgun Butchery", were seized with limitless panic and started to flee for their lives. This mass flight soon developed into a maddened, uncontrollable stampede.

▲ Menachem Begin writing in 1951 about the massacre at Deir Yassin in April 1948.

Source 4

> The affair of Deir Yassin had immense repercussions. The press and radio spread the news among Arabs as well as the Jews. In this way a general terror was built up among the Arabs. Driven by fear, the Arabs left their homes.

▲ A French Red Cross worker writing in 1950. He had visited Deir Yassin the day after the massacre.

> ✔ Look at sources 3 and 4. Do these sources provide reliable evidence of the impact of events at Deir Yassin in 1948?

The war of independence

On 14 May 1948, the new state of Israel was proclaimed by David Ben-Gurion, the new leader of the Israeli government. On the following day armies from five Arab states (Egypt, Syria, Jordan, Lebanon and Iraq) invaded Israel.

By the first ceasefire in June, ordered by the UN, the Arabs had occupied approximately one-third of Israel's territory, including the Jewish quarter of Jerusalem.

The second phase proved more successful for the Israelis. They were able to recapture the parts of Jerusalem previously lost, push the Syrians back and completely remove the Egyptian forces from Israeli land.

In the third phase of fighting Israel consolidated its earlier gains and even crossed into southern Lebanon.

An armistice was agreed between Israel and Egypt on 24 February 1949 and with other Arab combatants between March and July.

Why was Israel successful in the 1948–49 war?

Israeli strengths	Weaknesses of the Arab forces
The determination of the Israeli people: <ul><li>fighting for their survival, they were determined to win</li><li>they had a desire to protect what they had been fighting for since 1945</li><li>helped by morale boosting support from the USA</li><li>helped by finance from Jews in Europe and America.</li></ul> The armed forces: <ul><li>used the experience gained in the Second World War and the guerrilla campaign against the British</li><li>were better equipped than the Arab forces</li><li>had total air superiority</li><li>had strong military leadership.</li></ul>	Inexperienced military forces with weak military leadership. Communications were unreliable impacting on medical supplies. Forces outnumbered – 7,000 less than the 30,000 Israelis.

▲ Table 11.1 Reasons for Israel's success in the war of 1948–49

What was the significance of the war?

Significance for Israel	Israel was able to increase its territory by 21%.
	Britain, France and the USA agreed to protect Israel against future incursions.
	Israel suffered heavy losses, with 4,000 soldiers and 2,000 civilians losing their lives.
Significance for the Arabs	The Arab states failed in their bid to destroy Israel.
	Any hope the Palestinians had of creating their own state had been destroyed.
	For the Palestinian Arabs it was "the catastrophe". The entire population was now divided between the five Arab nations and two areas of Palestine not taken over by Israel; the West Bank and Gaza.
	Around 700,000 Arabs had fled their homes and many were now living in refugee camps.
	There was now a reason for future Palestinian freedom fighters to take up the fight.

▲ Table 11.2 Significance of the war

Source 5

As long as we don't make peace with the Zionists the war is not over. And as long as the war is not over there is neither winner nor loser. As soon as we recognise the existence of Israel, we admit, by this act, that we are defeated.

▲ The Secretary of the Arab League speaking in 1949 soon after fighting had ended. The Arab League represented all Arab states.

✔ Read this section of the chapter again. Produce a mind map to show the issues which exist over Palestine and which have brought Israelis and Palestinian Arabs to a state of conflict.

Exam-style questions

1. What proposals were made for Palestine by the UN in 1947?
2. Describe events between 1946 and 1948 leading to Britain's leaving Palestine.
3. Why did the Arabs reject the UN plans for partition?
4. How far was the war of 1948–9 avoidable? Explain your answer.
5. How significant was the desire to survive a reason for Israel's success in the war of 1948–9?
6. How important was the attack on the King David Hotel in the decision to withdraw British troops from Palestine?

11.2 How was Israel able to survive despite the hostility of its Arab neighbours?

Why was Israel able to win the wars of 1956, 1967 and 1973?

There was an uneasy peace in the Middle East following the events of 1948 and 1949.

By 1956, the Arab–Israeli conflict was to raise its head again as Arab nations refused to accept the new nation of Israel.

The Israeli victory showed the Arab states to be weak and divided. They became bitterly anti-western, feeling the United States had forced the UN into creating the new state of Israel. They thought Israel would be used by western powers to keep an eye on them.

The West still had influence over Arab governments. In Egypt there were 70,000 British troops. The Suez Canal was owned and run by the British and French. The Canal provided a vital route for oil supplies to the West. In 1954, Colonel Gamal Nasser became President of Egypt. He persuaded the British to remove their troops from Egypt. It was the early years of the Cold War and Britain and the USA wanted to keep on good terms with Nasser as they needed Arab support against the USSR.

The Arab states, apart from Jordan, had refused to give permanent homes to the Palestinian refugees. As a result they had to remain in their camps. In the camps young fighters formed guerrilla groups to attack Israel. These fighters, called Fedayeen, wanted to expel the Jews and regain their homeland. The attacks carried out by Fedayeen were met with reprisals from the Israeli army which resulted in high numbers of casualties.

The Arab League boycotted all goods made by Israelis in Palestine. Israeli ships were stopped using the Suez Canal.

The Suez Crisis, 1956	
Events leading to war	The USA and Britain wanted to maintain an ally in the Middle East. They offered to help Nasser build the Aswan Dam. They thought this would help to control him.
	Nasser requested weapons to defend Egypt from Israeli reprisal raids but, because he recognised the new communist government in China, funding was withdrawn.
	In September 1955, Nasser shocked the West by agreeing to buy Russian arms from Czechoslovakia, a communist ally of the Russians.
	On 26 July 1956, Nasser announced the nationalisation of the Suez Canal and the blockading of the Straits of Tiran, at the entrance to Gulf of Aqaba. This latter action would prevent Israeli ships from reaching the Port of Eilat.
	The cross-border attacks by the Fedayeen were becoming more violent, resulting in the deaths of many Israeli soldiers.
	Between 22 and 24 October 1956, the British and French Foreign Ministers met with Israeli Prime Minister David Ben-Gurion in France for secret talks. They agreed:
	• to teach Nasser a lesson;
	• to destroy the Fedayeen;
	• to break the blockade of the Tiran Straits.

	Israel would invade the Sinai Peninsula. Britain and France would then call on Israeli and Egyptian forces to withdraw. Britain and France, acting as peacemakers, would then invade Suez to stop the fighting and remove Nasser.
Events of the war	Israel invaded Egypt on 29 October 1956, advancing deep into Sinai.
	The next day France and Britain ordered both Israel and Egypt to withdraw.
	Egypt refused. Britain and France responded with military action. There were worldwide protests at this action.
	The UN voted for an immediate ceasefire and the US refused to support the invasion. The Arab countries stopped supplying oil to Britain. The Russians threatened to use military force.
	The Americans refused to supply oil and so Britain and France had no choice but to agree to a humiliating ceasefire.
Results of the war	For Israel:
	• It demonstrated that it was able to inflict heavy military defeats on its Arab rivals. This was helped by the benefit of surprise and the British and French air forces destroying Egyptian aircrafts on the ground.
	• The bases of the Fedayeen had been destroyed.
	• All Sinai had been occupied. (Israel withdrew in 1957.)
	• The blockade of the Tiran Straits had been removed.
	• It was able to secure its relationship with America.
	For the Arab world:
	• This was a heavy defeat.
	• Nasser became the hero of the Arab world for standing up to Britain and France.
	• Nasser had gained complete control of the Canal.
	• Many Arab states became more anti-western and willing to seek Russian aid.
	• They were united in opposition to the state of Israel.
	• They acquired funding for the Aswan Dam and supplies of weapons from the USSR.
	For Britain and France:
	• In the eyes of the international community their credibility was severely damaged.
	• They had not achieved any of their aims.
	• Nasser remained in power.
	• The Canal was closed.
	• They had to introduce petrol rationing.

▲ Table 11.3 The Suez Crisis, 1956

Source 6

> Defying the United Nations' Charter and international law, the Anglo-French imperialists have attacked the independent Egyptian Republic. They are trying to seize the Suez Canal and to occupy Egypt. The Israeli attack on Egypt was just the first step in the plot by England, France and Israel to spread their control to all Arab states.

▲ From the Russian newspaper, Pravda, 2 November 1956.

- -
✅ 1. Read source 6. How surprised are you by this source?

2. Israel had to withdraw from land they had conquered. Does this mean they gained little from the Suez-Sinai War?
- -

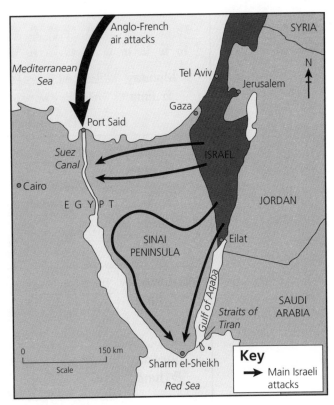

▲ Fig. 11.1 The Suez–Sinai War, 1956.

The Six-Day War, 1967	
Events leading to war	After Suez, Israel continued to modernise its army aided by the USA, Britain, France and West Germany. The Arabs continued to receive military support from the USSR.
	Border skirmishes continued between the Israelis and Palestinian guerrilla groups such as Fatah. This was a constant problem for those living in border settlements.
	At the 1964 Cairo Conference, the Palestine Liberation Organisation (PLO) was created.
	Following the overthrow of its government, Syria became more violently anti-Israeli and border raids continued. On 11 May 1967, Israel's Prime Minister warned that it would strike back against Syria if the attacks continued.
	The following day an untrue story began to spread throughout the Arab countries. According to the information passed by the USSR to Syria and Egypt, Israel was massing its armed forces on the Syrian border ready to attack. Was the Russian government misinformed or lying?
	Nasser put 100,000 troops on alert and on 16 May increased tension by ordering the UN force that had been patrolling the Israeli–Egyptian border since 1956 to leave Egyptian territory.
	On 23 May, Nasser closed the Gulf of Aqaba to Israeli ships. Israel regarded this as an act of aggression.
	By 28 May Egypt, Jordan, Syria, Iraq and Lebanon were among the eight Arab states ready to attack.
	On 5 June the Israeli air force took off. It was war again!

Events of the war		
Monday 5 June	Israeli air force bombed and destroyed almost all Egyptian planes while they were still on the ground.	
	Both the Jordanian and Syrian air forces were virtually crippled.	
Tuesday 6 June	Israeli troops entered Sinai and the West Bank.	
	In a race to the Suez Canal, the Israelis decimated the Egyptian military capability.	
	There was heavy fighting between Israelis and Jordanians for control of the West Bank of the River Jordan and Jerusalem.	
Wednesday 7 June	The Israelis won control of Sinai and Jerusalem.	
	A UN demand for a ceasefire with Egypt was accepted by Israel. Jordan accepted the proposed ceasefire.	
Thursday 8 June	Israel won control of the West Bank.	
	Egypt accepted the UN demand of a ceasefire after suffering a heavy defeat in Sinai.	
Friday 9 June	Israel attacked Syria, taking the Golan Heights.	
Saturday 10 June	Syria accepted the UN proposal of a ceasefire.	

Results of the war	
	The Israelis were fighting for their nation's survival and achieved a brilliant victory against Arabs armed with modern Soviet weaponry. The speed of attack and the pre-emptive air strike planned by Moshe Dayan had been crucial.
	The speed of dealing with Egyptian and Jordanian forces brought an early ceasefire. This allowed Israel to divert all its attention to Syria and the Golan Heights.
	In six days, Israel had managed to triple its size and increase its security.
	The Arabs were more hostile than ever, still refusing to recognise Israel.
	The eastern part of Jerusalem was captured. The holy city was now under Israeli control for the first time in nearly 2,000 years.
	The conflict created the issue of the plight of over one million Palestinian Arabs living in Gaza, the West Bank, East Jerusalem and the Golan Heights. The UN started to explore ways to achieve a lasting peace.

▲ Table 11.4 The Six-Day War

Source 7

| The existence of Israel is an error which we must put right. This is our opportunity to wipe out the disgrace which is Israel which has been with us since 1948. Our goal is clear – to wipe Israel off the map. |

▲ The President of Iraq speaking on the radio before the start of the Six-Day War.

✔ Read source 7. How far does it suggest war in the Middle East was inevitable?

The Yom Kippur War, 1973	
Events leading to war	The Arabs had been humiliated in the Six-Day War and wanted to regain their pride. Nasser died in 1970 to be replaced by Anwar Sadat.
	In order to regain Sinai, Sadat was willing to recognise the state of Israel. The Israelis had no wish to open discussions. Sadat had hoped the US would use its influence but this did not happen.
	Support for Sadat came from Saudi Arabia and Syria for a further war, especially as the Israelis were increasing their control over Sinai and the Golan Heights.
	The final straw for Sadat was the building of new Jewish settlements in the occupied territories.
Events of the war	On 6 October 1973, Egyptian and Syrian forces launched an attack. It was the Jewish holiday of Yom Kippur. Large numbers of Israeli forces were on holiday and the Israelis were caught by surprise.
	Part of Sinai was taken back, Israeli forces were defeated on the Golan Heights and Soviet-supplied surface-to-air missiles were effective against the Israeli air force.
	It took the Israelis three days to mobilise fully. Once mobilised (9 October) the Israelis: • recaptured the Golan heights within two days • pushed the Egyptians back across the Suez Canal, cutting off their Third Army • were aided by US President Nixon who refused to broker a ceasefire until Israel regained all its lost territory.
	Oil was a factor in this war as well. • Arab oil-producing states decided to reduce oil production until Israel withdrew from lands they had occupied since 1967. • Saudi Arabia banned oil exports to the US. Supplies to Europe were reduced significantly.
	A joint US–Soviet initiative through the UN brought fighting to an end on 24 October.
Results of the war	The war showed again the military superiority of the Israelis and their ability to inflict huge casualties on their opponents despite the vulnerabilities highlighted by the surprise attack.
	The oil embargo was a powerful economic weapon resulting in rising prices in the west and damage to economies of a number of nations. There was a view that a solution to the problems in the Middle East should be solved.
	Egypt and the USA developed closer relations. This was a change in US policy.
	Israel realised that lasting security could only be achieved by diplomacy.

▲ Table 11.5 The Yom Kippur War, 1973

How significant was superpower involvement in Arab–Israeli conflicts?

The involvement of the USA	• Support to Israel started with its creation.
	• In its early days, Israel relied more on France for economic and military support. Indeed, the USA tried to limit arms sales to Israel and its Arab neighbours.
	• Under Eisenhower, US policy moved towards finding a lasting peace.
	• The Israel invasion of Egypt in 1956 shocked and concerned the USA who insisted Israel withdraw from its position in the Sinai desert.
	• In 1957, US support for non-communist regimes in the Middle East gave more positive support to Israel's security.
	• Driven by the fear of communist expansion in the region, military loans had reached record levels by the end of the 1960s.
	• President Johnson adopted a strongly pro-Israel policy, with major arms deals and the protection of Israel's gains following the 1967 war.
	• The most significant military contribution was in the Yom Kippur War, where the USA responded quickly to replace large numbers of tanks destroyed in the surprise attack.
	• The USA played a key role in the ending of the war of 1973 driven by the oil issue and a need to maintain good relations with the USSR. President Nixon and his National Security Adviser Henry Kissinger organised settlements between Egypt and Israel, and Syria and Israel in the early months of 1974.
The involvement of the Soviet Union	• During the early years of Israel's existence, Stalin saw the possibility of an ally in the Middle East. Also he was keen to reduce British influence in the region.
	• By 1955, within the context of the Cold War, America's refusal to supply arms to Egypt opened the way for Czechoslovakia, a Soviet ally.
	• Links with Nasser and Egypt were strengthened with financial aid given for the Aswan Dam project and diplomatic support during the Suez Crisis of 1956. They exploited this to the full, deflecting attention away from the invasion of Hungary.
	• In 1967, the USSR passed on intelligence to Egypt about the build-up of Israeli forces on the Syrian border. This information proved to be false. Did the USSR intend to provoke a war in the Middle East at a time when the USA was distracted by Vietnam?
	• The Soviet Union supported Egypt before the Yom Kippur War, providing surface-to-air missiles and anti-tank weapons. This enabled the Egyptians to prevent Israel using its air superiority to the full.
	• The USSR was involved in brokering a ceasefire after which relations between the two countries deteriorated.

▲ Table 11.6 Involvement of the USA and to Soviet Union in Arab-Israeli conflicts

Source 8

"Double, Double . . ."

▲ A cartoon published in Britain in November 1967. It is commenting on the involvement of America and Russia in the Arab–Israeli conflict.

✔ Look at source 8. What is the cartoonist's message?

How important was oil in changing the nature of the Arab–Israeli conflict?

Increasingly since 1953, the USA had become reliant on the Middle East for oil. The economic stability of the US and her European allies largely depended on events in the Middle East. The Six-Day War of 1967 illustrated the vulnerability of the USA when Libya increased the price of its oil.

In 1973 President Nixon stated that, "Oil without a market does not do a country much good". The Arab states defied this view. Saudi Arabia at first increased oil prices by 70% as well as reducing supplies to any country supporting Israel during the war. When the USA doubled their support for Israel, the members of OPEC (Organisation of Petroleum-Exporting Countries) led by the Saudis implemented a complete embargo of oil supplies.

Over 12 months prices of oil in the US increased 387%, triggering a rise in unemployment and an economic crisis. The embargo was removed in March 1974.

The embargo illustrated the vulnerability of the west to changes in cost and supply, resulting in America starting a programme to become self-sufficient in oil by 1980. New energy sources in other regions in the 1980s, coupled with falling consumption of oil, resulted in a buyers' market as opposed to the OPEC members being able to hold the world to ransom.

Resolving its oil problems did not change America's desire to see peace in the region. Indeed US policy was more concerned with the fear of increasing Soviet influence in the Middle East.

By the 1990s, how far had problems which existed between Israel and her neighbours been resolved?

Israeli–Palestinian attempts at peacemaking in the 1970s

After the Yom Kippur War of 1973 Egypt was the first of the Arab states to appear willing to recognise the state of Israel. Similarly, Yasser Arafat and some PLO leaders were less determined to remove the state of Israel. In 1974 Arafat was invited to speak at the United Nations. There were many who showed sympathy but also many Israelis who were furious at the United Nations. The main issues still remained.

In 1977, Sadat surprised the world by going to Israel to discuss peace. The following month, Begin went to Egypt and peace talks were started.

In September 1978, following a slowdown in the talks, Sadat and Begin went to Camp David, the retreat of the US President, to meet President Carter. A framework for peace was drawn up. The main points were:

- Israeli forces to be withdrawn from Sinai
- Egypt to regain all of Sinai within three years
- Israeli shipping to have free passage through the Suez Canal and the Straits of Tiran.

In March 1979, a peace treaty was signed confirming the points agreed at Camp David. Both sides recognised the other's right to have secure, recognised boundaries.

Despite this breakthrough, the Palestinian problem still remained as the interests of other Arab states had been ignored. Egypt was suspended from the Arab League and Sadat assassinated.

Source 9

> The difference between a revolutionary and the terrorist lies in the reason for which each fights. Whoever stands by a just cause and fights for liberation from invaders and colonialists cannot be called a terrorist. Those who wage war to occupy, colonise and oppress other people are the terrorists. The Palestinian people had to resort to armed struggle when they lost faith in the international community, which ignored their rights, when it became clear not one inch of Palestine could be regained through exclusively political means.
>
> The PLO dreams and hopes for one democratic state where Christian, Jew and Muslim live in justice and equality. I appeal to the General Assembly to accompany the Palestinian people in the struggle to attain the right of self-determination. I have come bearing an olive branch and a freedom fighter's gun. Do not let the olive branch fall from my hand.

▲ An extract from Arafat's speech to the UN, November 1974.

> ✔ Look at source 9. How useful is this source to an historian studying the Arab-Israeli conflict? Discuss your ideas.

Israeli–Palestinian attempts at peacemaking in the 1990s

By the end of 1991 the prospect of peace for the region still seemed far off. The resistance group Hezbollah inflicted heavy casualties on the Israelis.

In 1991, the PLO broke away from the rest of the Arab world to support Iraqi dictator Saddam Hussein against a US-led coalition.

In October 1991, Israel met with delegations from Arab countries to renew the peace process. Secret talks in Oslo, away from the glare of the media, were started.

From these talks "The Declaration of Principles" was signed. It included:

- Israel recognising the PLO as the "representative of the Palestinian people"
- a phased withdrawal of Israeli troops from Gaza and the West Bank
- elections to be held for the new Palestinian Authority.

In May 1994, the new Authority was given control of Gaza and Jericho, and later the Palestinian area of the West Bank. This was perceived in Israel as a triumph in diplomacy for Shimon Peres as he gave up less than was demanded.

Also in 1994, Jordan signed a peace treaty with Israel, settling disputes over their borders.

Israel's relations with Syria remained bitter. Opposition continued to be shown through violence on both sides. Despite this the Middle East Peace Accord was signed which stated:

- Israel would withdraw from many West Bank towns
- talks on the status of Jerusalem, West Bank and Gaza would start the following year
- Israel would maintain control of its civilian settlements
- the status of Hebron would be decided at a later date.

Fundamental differences still remained, including the status of Jerusalem.

Lebanon

In 1949 Lebanon had to find room for 100,000 Palestinian refugees fleeing from Egypt.

From 1968 the PLO based themselves in Lebanon, launching daily cross-border attacks on Israel. The Israelis carried out reprisal raids, the most spectacular in 1968 when Israeli troops landed at Beirut airport in helicopters, blowing up 13 Lebanese aircraft.

The attacks, and reprisals, continued. After the Munich Olympics, Israel killed 118 suspected PLO guerrillas in a raid.

In 1978, 26,000 Israeli troops invaded with the aim of taking control of southern Lebanon. This was in response to the PLO killing Israeli civilians in a bus hijack. In an attempt to restore peace, the United Nations sent a peacekeeping force.

Following continued attacks the UN organised a ceasefire in July 1981.

In June 1982 a large Israeli military force carried out a full-scale invasion with the aim of removing the PLO. Civilian casualties were high. The invasion saw the dispersal of the PLO.

Public opinion condemned Israel for a massacre within the refugee camps. By 1985, the last of the Israeli forces had left Lebanon.

Exam-style questions

1. Describe events in 1956 which contributed to the Suez Crisis.
2. What were the results of the Yom Kippur War of 1973?
3. Why did the Six-Day War of 1967 take place?
4. How far, by the 1990s, had problems which existed between Israel and her neighbours been resolved?
5. How important was oil in changing the nature of the Arab-Israeli conflict?
6. How significant was the role of the USA compared to that of the Soviet Union in Arab-Israeli conflicts?

11.3 What was the impact of the Palestinian refugee issue?

Why were there so many Palestinian refugees?

The events of 1947 and 1948 created a huge refugee crisis. Around 700,000 Arabs left their homes, going mostly to the West Bank, Gaza Strip, Jordan, Syria or Lebanon. Most refugees were forced to live in camps under atrocious conditions.

Some argued that the Israelis carried out a deliberate policy of expulsion in order to occupy as much of Palestine as possible. Others put a case for Arab leaders encouraging a mass exodus in order to gain public support for their cause. The Arabs had also rejected the Partition Plan.

The refugee crisis worsened as a result of the 1967 war, as refugees fled from Sinai, Gaza and the West Bank. Jewish settlers moved in so the refugees could not return.

Out of the bitterness and frustration arose the PLO.

How effective was the PLO in promoting the Palestinian cause?

From its beginnings until 1976

In 1959, Al-Fatah was formed, launching guerrilla raids into Israel.

In 1964, Fatah and other resistance groups combined to form the Palestinian Liberation Organisation (PLO). The PLO was dedicated to using force to gain the return of the Palestinian homeland.

After the defeat of the Arab states in the 1967 war, the PLO increasingly deployed terrorist methods against Israel and western companies.

At the same time Egypt and Syria were more concerned about lands they had lost and less concerned about the Palestinian refugees. This convinced many Palestinians that they were on their own in fighting for their homeland.

Following the war most refugees went to Jordan. Fatah began to recruit volunteers from the refugee camps. Raids into Israel increased followed by full-scale Israeli reprisal attacks. At this stage thousands were joining the resistance fighters.

In 1968, Yasser Arafat became leader of the PLO. He wanted to limit raids
to Israeli territory, although they achieved very little. Extremist Palestinians
were unhappy with this and carried out attacks on other parts of the world.

	Attacks carried out by the PLO and their results	
	Palestinian terrorism	**Outcome**
December 1968	An Israeli passenger plane attacked at Athens airport. One person was killed.	The Israelis attacked and destroyed 13 aircraft at Beirut airport.
September 1970	Four planes hijacked by Palestinian extremists. Three were flown to Dawson Field, Jordan. While passengers were set free, the planes were blown up.	Jordan feared international intervention. King Hussein decided to rid Jordan of the PLO. During Palestinian resistance 10,000 of them were killed. The PLO moved to Syria and Lebanon.
November 1971		In revenge for their expulsion, the Jordanian Prime Minister was murdered by Black September terrorists.
September 1972	Black September kidnapped 11 Israeli athletes taking part in the Olympic Games. All the athletes were killed.	The Palestinians got massive publicity for their cause. They failed to gain the release of 200 of their comrades who were in prison in Israel. The Israelis gained their revenge by carrying out reprisal raids, killing 200 refugees. The PLO became terrorists in the eyes of the western press.
October 1972	Black September hijacked a Lufthansa plane, demanding the release of those jailed for their part in the Munich Olympics attack.	
1974		The Arab League declared the PLO to be the "sole legitimate representative of the Palestine people". Arafat was invited to speak at the United Nations.
July 1976	An Air France Flight was hijacked by PFLP terrorists and flown to Entebbe, Uganda. The 104 Jewish passengers were threatened with death unless Palestinian prisoners around the world were released. An Israeli special-forces unit killed the hijackers and rescued all but three of the hostages.	Again much publicity was gained but not the release of prisoners. People in Europe began to ask if the guerrillas were in fact terrorists or freedom fighters.

▲ Table 11.7 Attacks carried out by the PLO and their results

Source 10

▲ A photograph showing planes being blown up at Dawson's Field, Jordan in September 1970.

Source 11

Tuesday September 5 1972

MURDER AT THE OLYMPICS

Arab terrorists gun down Israelis in Munich village — hold 13 as hostages

▲ Headlines from a British newspaper published in 1972.

> ✅ Look at sources 10 and 11. Which source is more useful as evidence of the activities of the PLO guerrilla groups?

In the 1980s

Following their expulsion from Jordan in 1970, most of the PLO forces moved to Lebanon and from here continued to launch attacks on Israel.

In March 1978, following a PLO attack on a bus carrying Israelis which killed 34, Israel invaded south Lebanon. In June 1982, Israel again invaded Lebanon with the goal of destroying the PLO. By August the PLO had moved to Tunisia.

Although the PLO had been accepted as the voice of the Palestinians, the use of force against the Israelis had brought little success. Arafat turned to diplomacy, attempting to build better relations with the US and Jordan. Negotiations for a homeland came to nothing.

In late 1987, young Palestinians started an uprising against the Israelis. This was known as the "Intifada". The Israeli forces faced demonstrations and stone throwing which provoked a violent backlash from Israel. The Palestinian Intifada lasted until 1990, signalling there would be no peace in the region without a solution to the Palestinian problem. Israel responded with an "iron fist" policy. Over 500 Palestinians were killed and well-documented stories of Israeli brutality appeared in the national press. Foreign governments and the UN were publicly critical.

Israel and Arafat

After leaving Lebanon, Arafat was forced to rethink his methods. He wanted a compromise with Israel but had to avoid appearing to be a traitor to the cause.

In December 1988, Arafat publicly accepted the existence of Israel and rejected the use of terrorism. The Americans, welcoming this change, invited the PLO for talks.

Some Israelis, including many in the Labor Party, welcomed the PLO change of policy. Others, including the Likud Party, were distrustful, claiming it was a trick and that the PLO had not really changed. They still feared the destruction of Israel.

Why did Arab states not always support the Palestinian cause?

Jordan expelled the PLO in 1970. At the time the PLO were carrying out terrorist violence and King Hussein feared Israeli reprisals. He also thought the PLO was acting as though it ruled most of Jordan.

When in Lebanon, the PLO continued to attack Israel. For every attack came an Israeli response. The Maronites of the government condemned them, refusing to accept the power of the PLO. The Muslims in the government gave their support to the PLO. This division led to a full-scale civil war in which 40,000 people were killed and large areas of Beirut destroyed. The war came to an end when the Syrians invaded to defeat and expel the PLO.

Egypt abandoned the PLO completely after making peace with Israel in 1979.

There were financial costs involved in funding the PLO. An annual figure of $250 million was agreed in 1978 but only Saudi Arabia paid its share.

Other reasons for this reluctance to support the PLO included the following.

- Some Arab states saw the Middle East crisis as an opportunity to gain ascendancy over their Arab neighbours. The PLO became a tool for individual states.

- The PLO caused problems for the governments of Arab states including Jordan and Lebanon.

- Arafat's change of strategy towards a diplomatic route cost him the support of Syria.

- Arafat's decision to support Saddam Hussein in Kuwait was disastrous as it placed the PLO in opposition to a coalition of the USA and Arab states.

- The rise of extremists after 1991 led to several Arab states negotiating individually with Israel.

How did international perceptions of the Palestinian cause change over time?

United Nations' view	The United Nations responded quickly to the initial problem, providing basic amenities. The policies of Israel and the conflicting demands of the Arab states made the work almost impossible. By the middle of the 1950s the operation effectively ceased as an acceptable solution could not be found.
USA's view	By the end of the 1980s it was clear to the US administration that there could be no lasting peace in the Middle East without a resolution to the Palestinian issue. In 1993 negotiations started in Oslo between Palestinian and Israeli representatives.
Perceptions of the PLO	The upsurge of violence by the PLO led to widespread condemnation. Arafat was criticised for allowing the attacks. Fortunes improved when the PLO was recognised by the Arab League in 1974 and Arafat was allowed to address the UN. Backing from African and Asian states at the UN strengthened their position. The following years saw the PLO return to international isolationism as support from Arab states was lost.

▲ Table 11.8 Changing views of the Palestinian cause

Exam-style questions

1. Describe what happened at the Olympic Games of 1972.
2. Why were towns on the West Bank a source of tension between Israeli and Palestinians?
3. Why was the PLO formed?
4. How effective has the PLO been in promoting the Palestinian cause?
5. How important has the lack of support for the PLO from Arab states been in the preservation of the state of Israel?

11.4 Why has it proved impossible to resolve the Arab–Israeli issue?

Why has the United Nations been unable to secure a lasting peace?

The United Nations has made many attempts to resolve the situation.

- The UN tried to redraw the original partition plan, but again this was not accepted. A UN mediator was assassinated following this rejection.
- In 1949 the UN was involved in supervising the fragile peace following the fighting. The UN failed to achieve its goal of lasting peace because neither side wanted it.
- Between 1956 (the Suez War) and 1982 (the Israeli invasion of Lebanon) the UN acted as peacemaker, for example, ordering the British and French forces to leave Suez. More often it was ineffective as America held the position of power in the region. Its vulnerability was highlighted when prior to the Six-Day War they allowed Nasser to dictate that they withdraw from Egypt.
- After the Six-Day War the UN introduced Resolution 242. Unfortunately the issue of Israel's newly captured territories remained a stumbling block to negotiation. This resolution remains the basis of all attempts at peace.
- In 1973 the UN went to Egypt in a peacekeeping capacity.
- In 1978 the UN oversaw the withdrawal of Israel from Lebanon. This happened again in 1982 when protection and humanitarian aid was offered to the civilian population. However, the intervention of the USA gradually reduced the UN's role.
- The different focus of the UN General Assembly and the UN Security Council has undermined attempts to achieve peace.
- The UN has been accused of having an anti-Israeli bias. This can be exemplified by Yasser Arafat's address in 1974 and a UN Resolution, passed in 1975, which equated Zionism with racism. (This was revoked in 1991.)
- Since the end of the Cold War the UN had failed to make a significant contribution to peace in the region. One reason for this is the increasing American intervention in peacekeeping and the decline in Soviet influence.
- In addition, the nature of the conflict has changed from a conflict between nations to one between ethnic groups such as Fatah and Hamas. The second change has come with radicalisation of the conflict, with extremists on both sides showing a willingness to use violence.

How far have international diplomatic negotiations improved Israel's relations with Arab states and the Palestinians?

In 1978 at Camp David, a framework for peace was agreed. Six months later Egyptian and Israeli leaders signed a peace treaty recognising the right of each other to live in peace within recognised, secure boundaries. The Accords were bitterly opposed by some Arab countries including Libya and Syria. While this represented a great breakthrough, the Palestinian issue still remained.

At the Madrid Conference of 1991, the USA persuaded the Israelis and Palestinians to hold face-to-face talks. Progress was limited and disrupted by extremist violence.

The Oslo Peace Agreement of 1993 paved the way for self-government for the Palestinians. The Agreement was intended to build trust and confidence between Palestinians and the Israelis. The main issues to be resolved over the next five years were:

- o the future of Jerusalem, as both wanted it as their capital
- o what would happen to the Jewish settlements in the occupied territories?
- o would Palestinian refugees have a right to return to their homes from Lebanon, Jordan, Syria and other Arab countries?
- o an independent Palestinian state – not only was the idea of "independence" a big issue but what area would it cover? Was it to be all, or part, of Palestine? All of Palestine would mean the end of Israel.

In 2000 President Clinton tried to revive the peace process but the talks ended with no significant progress over the issues outstanding from 1998.

In April 2004 President George W. Bush presented his "road map" for peace. This depended on an end to violence but the Palestinian bombings and Israel assassinations continued.

How have divisions within Israel affected the peace process?

Political obstacles

During the period 1948–67, the Labor Party dominated Israeli politics. The focus at that time was ensuring survival and building a democratic state.

- The election of the Likud government in 1977 gave greater prominence to religion.
- Both parties have maintained the hard-line stance in relation to denying the right of Palestinians to self-determination and the rejection of the notion of an independent Palestinian state.
- For much of the period neither party would negotiate directly with the PLO. This only changed in 1994.
- The aims of the two parties differ. Likud has consistently pursued a goal of creating a "Greater Israel" thus denying any claims over the West Bank, while the Labor party believes Israel's security would be best served by achieving a peaceful resolution. This hard-line stance of Likud was highlighted by Menachem Begin during the Camp David agreement discussions, while Yitzhak Rabin's Labor party brought a different approach to the discussion following the election of 1992.
- In 1996, the newly elected government opposed any further negotiations with Arafat and the Palestinian Authority.

Other obstacles to peace

- Ethnic groups came from Arab countries and Europe, many not speaking Hebrew, and found it difficult to find work or to achieve more senior positions. This discrimination was resented and they turned against Labor and towards Likud.
- There is a difference between religious and non-religious Jews and the link to the Orthodox Jews' belief in relation to the establishment of Israel being part of God's plans.

- In November 1995, following an Israeli peace rally in Tel Aviv, Prime Minister Rabin was shot dead. The assassin was a member of an Israeli group opposed to any peace with Palestinians. After a series of suicide bombings on crowded buses the hardliners gained more support.

- A second Intifada started in September 2000. The underlying cause was the frustration and anger of Palestinians in the occupied territories of the West Bank and Gaza. Limited progress had been made towards peace, and violence in the form of Israeli reprisals to Palestinian suicide bombing continued.

- In March 2002, Ariel Sharon launched "Operation Defensive Shield" in response to Hamas killing 29 Israelis in a suicide bombing. Raids were carried out inside Palestinian towns and refugee camps on the West Bank and Gaza. Targeted assassinations were introduced.

✔ In a small group produce a mind map to illustrate the difficulties faced in reaching a solution to the Arab–Israeli issue. Select one aspect of your map and prepare a presentation.

How have rivalries among Palestinians affected progress towards a settlement?

The PLO was created in 1964. Its dominant group was Fatah. The aim of the organisation was to achieve a homeland for Palestinian people. Following early use of violence, Arafat turned to a more peaceful approach after leaving Lebanon.

As a result of its expansion from Lebanon in 1982, its dominance has been challenged. Hamas (Islamic Resistance Movement) was formed in 1987, emerging as the most prominent rival to the PLO, pledging violence to achieve its declared aim – the destruction of Israel. Following the murder of 29 Palestinians in a mosque in Hebron, Hamas launched a campaign of violence against Israel. They used mainly suicide bombers. They carried out bus bombings in early 1996, killing nearly 60 Israelis. Arafat was blamed for not controlling the militants, with Israel moving troops back into Gaza and the West Bank. Curfews were imposed and border crossings closed between Israel and the occupied territories. This was to prevent suicide bombers but it prevented many Palestinians going to work.

Hezbollah ("the Party of God") was formed in 1982. One of its aims was to turn Lebanon into an Islamic state.

Abbas replaced Arafat, who died in 2004, and in February 2005 he persuaded Palestinian militants to call a halt to their bombings. Israeli and Palestinian leaders met in Egypt and called a halt to violence. In the summer, Jewish settlers and troops withdrew from Gaza. The Jewish settlements on the West Bank still remained as a barrier to peace.

In the Palestinian elections of 2006, Hamas won a majority of seats but refused to recognise the state of Israel. As a result Israel and the USA, together with many European governments, refused to have any dealing with Hamas.

In July 2006 Lebanese Hezbollah militants crossed into Israel and captured two Israeli soldiers. They demanded the release of hundreds of freedom fighters and Palestinians held in Israeli jails, but were refused. Israeli air attacks followed with the militants hitting back by launching missiles. Almost one thousand Lebanese civilians were killed. In August the UN arranged a ceasefire and deployed a peacekeeping border force.

Prospects for peace

The main issue, the Palestinian problem, still remains at the centre of the conflict.

Peace will be difficult unless leaders of both sides control their extremists who are opposed to compromise. The Israeli extremists believe they must retain the West Bank while extremist Palestinians believe that all of Palestine should be returned, even if this means the destruction of Israel.

Unlike Egypt and Jordan, Syria has never made a peace treaty with Israel. The Golan Heights, captured in 1967, remain in Israeli hands.

Full US support would be required to reach a resolution. America is the one country that is able to exert enough pressure and, as a giver of aid to Israel, would have a huge influence.

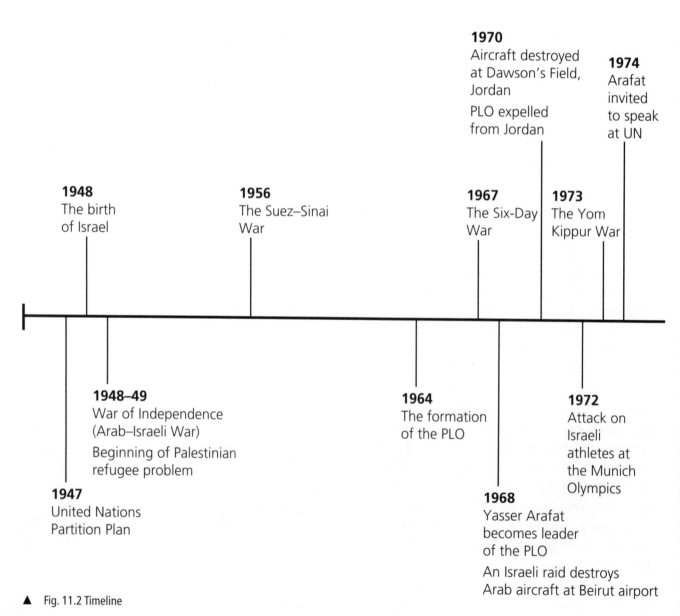

▲ Fig. 11.2 Timeline

Exam-style questions

1. Describe the role of the United Nations in attempting to secure a lasting peace.
2. What political divisions within Israel have affected the peace process?
3. Why were discussions at Camp David in 1978 important?
4. How far have divisions within Israel affected attempts to bring peace to the Middle East?
5. How important has the role of America been in the Middle East since 1956?

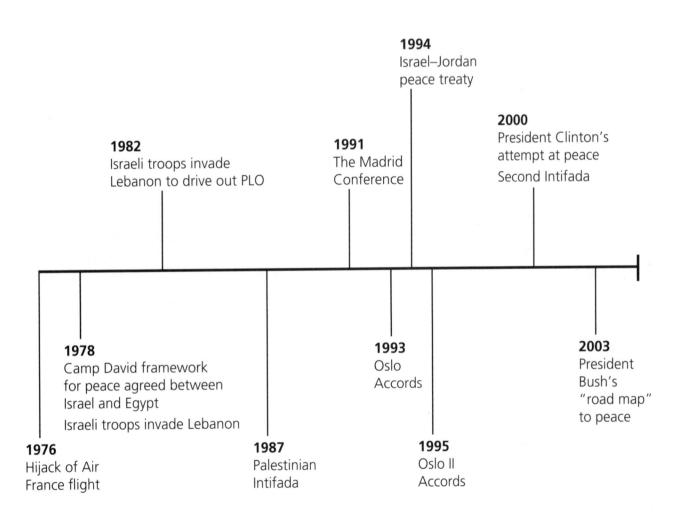

1982
Israeli troops invade Lebanon to drive out PLO

1991
The Madrid Conference

1994
Israel–Jordan peace treaty

2000
President Clinton's attempt at peace
Second Intifada

1976
Hijack of Air France flight

1978
Camp David framework for peace agreed between Israel and Egypt
Israeli troops invade Lebanon

1987
Palestinian Intifada

1993
Oslo Accords

1995
Oslo II Accords

2003
President Bush's "road map" to peace

Index

Page numbers in *italics* refer to question sections.

A

Abyssinia 21–3
Afghanistan 85
Agent Orange 69
Anschluss 3, 7
  Anschluss with Austria, 1938 31–2
appeasement 24, 26
  arguments against appeasement 34
  arguments for appeasement 33
Arabs 165
  Arab rejection of UN plans to partition
    Palestine 167–8
  causes of conflict between Jews and Arabs in
    Palestine 165–6
  international diplomatic negotiations 185–6
  why did Arab states not always support the
    Palestinian cause? 183–4
Arafat, Yasser 178, 181, 183, 184, 185, 186, 187
Armenia 8
Attlee, Clement 42
Austria 100
  Anschluss with Germany, 1938 31–2
  Treaty of St Germain 7
Austro-Hungarian Empire 1, 7

B

Battle of Jutland, May–June 1916 112–113
Battle of the Marne 102
Battle of the Somme, July 1916–November 1916
  106–9
  General Haig 108
  significance 107
Battle of Verdun 105
Battle of Ypres 103
Bay of Pigs invasion 57
Belgium 100, 101, 103
Ben-Gurion, David 169
Berlin Blockade 46
  airlift 48
  causes of the blockade 47
  consequences of the blockade 49
  options available to the western Allies 48
  Stalin's motive 48
Berlin Wall 80–1, 85
Bolsheviks 1, 2, 5, 28, 40
Brezhnev, Leonid 78, 82
Britain 1, 2, 5, 8, 100
  British Expeditionary Force (BEF) 101–3
  declaration of war on Germany in September
    1939 38–9
  First Gulf War 95
  Israeli-Palestinian conflict 165–7
  Suez Crisis, 1956 171–3
Bulgaria 1, 17
  Treaty of Neuilly 8
Bush, George W. 186

C

capitalism 40, 48–9
Carter, Jimmy 178
Castro, Fidel 57, 64
Chamberlain, Neville 35
chemical weapons 69
Chernobyl disaster 86
China 20, 51–5
Churchill, Winston 41, 42–3
Clemenceau, Georges 1, 2, 4
Clinton, Bill 186
Cold War 40, *50*, 86
  Berlin Blockade 46–9
  Berlin Wall 80–1
  breakdown of the USA–USSR alliance 40–3
  history of hostility 40–1
  removal of common enemy 40
  USA reaction to Soviet expansion 45–6
  USSR control of eastern Europe 43–44
  who was to blame? 49–50
collective security 18
COMECON 49
COMINFORM 43, 45, 49
communism 28, 40, 48–9, 51
  America and events in Cuba, 1959–62 57–64
  America and events in Korea, 1950–53 51–6
  American involvement in Vietnam 65–72
  Germany, 1918–45 125, 129, 132, 134, 135
conscription 3
Cuban missile crisis 57, *64*
  aftermath of the crisis 64
  thirteen days of crisis 60–1
  USA reaction to Cuban revolution 57–8
  what options did Kennedy have? 59
  who won? 63
  why did Kennedy react as he did? 61–2
  why did Kruschev put nuclear missiles into
    Cuba? 58
  why did tensions develop between Cuba and
    America? 57
Czechoslovakia 7, 17, 79
  opposition to Soviet control 76–8, 79
  Sudetenland invasion 35–6

D
demilitarised zones 3
Depression 19, 132, 152, 156
disarmament 3, 17, 26
Dubcek, Alexander 76–7

E
Ebert, Friedrich 124
economic sanctions 16
Eisenhower, Dwight 65, 74, 176

F
financial sanctions 16
First Gulf War 96–9
    consequences of the war 98–9
    course of the war 97–8
    reasons for invasion of Kuwait 96
    wider-world reaction to invasion of Kuwait 97
First World War 1–11, 100, *103, 111, 119, 123*
    aircraft 110
    armistice 123, 124
    artillery 110
    attempts at breakthrough, 1915 105
    Battle of Jutland, May–June 1916 112–113
    Battle of the Marne 102
    Battle of the Somme, July 1916–November
        1916 106–9
    Battle of Verdun 105
    conditions in Germany towards the end of the
        war 122–3
    deadlock 103
    first Battle of Ypres 103
    Gallipoli campaign, 1915 115–17
    gas 109
    how successful was the British Expeditionary
        Force (BEF)? 102
    impact of United States entering the war 120
    machine guns 109
    offensives of 1917 110–11
    race to the sea 102–3
    Schlieffen Plan 101
    stalemate on the Western Front 103–4, 111
    submarine warfare 114
    tanks 109
    technological developments 109–10
    who won the war at sea? 112
    why did Russia leave the war in 1917? 117–19
    why did the Schlieffen Plan fail? 101–2
    why did the United States enter the war? 120
    why was the German offensive of 1918
        unsuccessful? 121–2

France 1, 2, 4, 8, 17, 100
    declaration of war on Germany in September
        1939 38–9
    First Gulf War 95
    occupation of the Ruhr 5, 126–7
    Suez Crisis, 1956 171–3
Franco, Francisco 30

G
Gallipoli campaign, 1915 115–16
    results of the campaign 116–17
Germany 1, 2, 17, 100, 124
    Berlin Blockade 46–9
    Berlin Wall 80–1, 85
    Britain and France declare war on Germany
        38–9
    First Gulf War 95
    Freikorps 5, 125, 126
    Germany in 1948 47
    impact of the Treaty of Versailles on Germany
        up to 1923 5–6
    Kapp Putsch 5, 125, 126
    key terms of the Treaty of Versailles 3, 126
    lebensraum 24, 28
    Nazi regime 137–43
    Schlieffen Plan 101–2
    "stab in the back" myth 24
    Weimar Republic 5, 124–9
    why did revolution break out in October 1918?
        122–3
    why was Hitler able to dominate Germany by
        1934? 130–6
    why was the German offensive of 1918
        unsuccessful? 121–2
Gorbachev, Mikhail 83–5
Greece 8, 17
guerilla warfare 68
Gulf Wars 87, *99*
    First Gulf War 96–9
    Iran–Iraq War, 1980–88 92–6
    Iranian revolution 91–2
    rise of Saddam Hussein 88–9
    Saddam Hussein's rule in Iraq 89–91

H
Haig, Douglas 108, 110
Hitler, Adolf 20, 22, 124, 130–1, *136*
    foreign policy actions from 1933 to 1936 29
    foreign policy actions from 1936 to 1939 30

foreign policy objectives 27–8
how did Hitler become Chancellor in January 1933? 134
how did Hitler consolidate his power in 1933–34? 134–5
importance of Poland 38
Mein Kampf 27, 131
Night of the Long Knives, June 1934 136
what happened in the elections of 1932? 133
why was Hitler able to become Chancellor by 1933? 132–3
Ho Chi Minh 65, 68, 72
Hoare-Laval Pact 22
Hoover, Herbert 154, 155, 156
humanitarian issues 17
Hungary 7, 79
actions planned by Nagy's government 74
reasons for opposition to Soviet control 74
USSR reaction to opposition 75–6
why did the Hungarians think they would be successful? 74–5

I
ideological differences 40
communism and capitalism 48–9
Iran 91
dissatisfaction with the Shah's modernisation programme 91–2
opposition to foreign influence 91
resentment at autocratic and repressive government 92
Iran–Iraq War, 1980–88 92
Ayatollah Khomeini's opposition to Saddam Hussein 94
consequences of the war 94–5
course of the war 94
domination of the Gulf 93
Islamic Revolution 93
Saddam's view 95–6
territorial disputes 93
Western involvement in the war 94–5
Iraq 8, 17
Iran–Iraq War, 1980–88 92–6
Iraq and its neighbouring countries 87
Saddam Hussein's rule in Iraq 89–91
Islamic Revolution 93, 94, 95
Israeli-Palestinian conflict 165, *170*, 171, *180*, *184*, *189*
Arab rejection of UN plans to partition Palestine 167–8

attempts at peacemaking in the 1970s 178
attempts at peacemaking in the 1990s 179
causes of conflict between Jews and Arabs in Palestine 165–6
civil war in Palestine 168–9
divisions within Israel 186–7
end of the Second World War 166–7
how significant was superpower involvement in Arab–Israeli conflicts? 176–7
impact of the Palestinian refugee issue 180–4
importance of oil 177–8
international diplomatic negotiations 185–6
Israeli success in 1948–49 war 169
Lebanon 179
Palestine handed over to the United Nations 167
prospects for peace 188–9
rivalries among Palestinians 187–8
significance of the 1948–49 war 170
Six-Day War, 1967 173–5
Suez Crisis 171–3
war of independence 169
why has the United Nations been unable to secure a lasting peace? 185
Yom Kippur War, 1975 175
Italy 7, 8, 13, 26
invasion of Abyssinia 21–3

J
Japan 26
invasion of Manchuria 20–1
Jaruzelski, Wojciech 82
Jews 165
establishment of Jewish state of Israel 165–70
Jews in Nazi Germany 130, 131, 132, 133, 135, 137, 141
Final Solution 138, 143
Kristallnacht 139
Johnson, Lyndon B. 67, 71, 175

K
Kellogg-Briand Pact 17
Kemal, Mustapha 8
Kennedy, John Fitzgerald 57–64, 66, 67
Khomeini, Ayatollah Khomeini 92
Iran–Iraq War, 1980–88 92–6
Kim Il-Sung 52
Korean War 51–2, *56*
attitude of the USA to the invasion of South Korea 53–4

consequences for the United Nations 55–6
course of the war 55
how did the United Nations become involved? 53
results for USA 56
why did North Korea invade South Korea? 52–3
Kruschev, Nikita 57–64, 73, 74, 75
Kurds 89–90, 93, 94
Kuwait 94, 96–9

L
League of Nations 3, 13, *23*
aims of the League 13–14
collective security 18
consequences of failures in the 1930s 26
failures in the 1930s 20–3
membership 18
organisation and structure of the League 15–16
powers of the League 16
successes and failures in the 1920s 16–17, 19
unanimous decisions 18
World Depression 19
Lebanon 179
Lithuania 13
Lloyd George, David 1, 2, 4, 5
Locarno Treaties 17, 128

M
MacArthur, Douglas 53, 54, 55, 56
Manchuria 20–1
mandates 3
Mao Zedong 52, 55
Marshall Aid 45–6
military sanctions 16
moral condemnation 16
Munich Conference, 29 September 1938 35–6
Mussolini, Benito 17, 20, 21–2
My Lai 67, 71

N
Nagy, Imre 74, 75
napalm 69
Nasser, Gamal 171, 172, 173, 175, 176, 185
Nazis 24, 129, *136*
did most people in Germany benefit from Nazi rule? 142
Final Solution 143
Hitler as Chancellor 134–6
how did the coming of war change life in Nazi Germany? 143
how effectively did the Nazis deal with their opponents? 137–8
how much opposition was there to the Nazi regime? 137
key points from Nazi Party objectives published in 1920 130
Munich Putsch, 1923 130–1
Nazi-Soviet pact 37–8
Reichstag Fire 134
status of the Nazi Party by the end of the 1920s 131
Storm Troopers (SA) 130, 131, 132, 135, 136
use of culture and mass media 138–9
was Nazi Germany a totalitarian state? 140
what happened in the elections of 1932? 133
why did the Nazis benefit from the Depression? 132
why did the Nazis persecute many groups in German society? 139–40
why did the Nazis succeed in elections? 132–3
women and the family in Nazi Germany 142
young people in Nazi Germany 137, 140–2
New Deal 158, *164*
banks 158
changes after 1933 160
farmers 159
industry 159
opposition 160–2
poor relief 159
successes and failures 162–4
Tennessee Valley Authority (TVA) 159
unemployed 158, 162–3
Nixon, Richard 67, 71–2, 175, 177

O
OPEC (Organisation of Petroleum-Exporting Countries) 177
outbreak of Second World War 24, *39*
appeasement 33–4
Britain and France declare war on Germany 38–9
failure of League of Nations 26
Hitler's foreign policy 27–32
long-term consequences of 1991–23 peace treaties 25
main causes 25
Munich Conference, 29 September 1938 35–6
Nazi-Soviet pact 37–8
Sudetenland 35

P

Palestine 8, 165–70
  civil war in Palestine 168–9
  international diplomatic negotiations 185–6
  rivalries among Palestinians 187–8
Palestinian refugees 179, 180
peace treaties 1–11
  long-term consequences 25
plebiscites 3
PLO (Palestine Liberation Organization) 178, 179
  attacks carried out by the PLO and their results 181–3
  how effective was the PLO in promoting the Palestinian cause? 180–1
  international perceptions of the Palestinian cause 184
  Israel and Arafat 183
  why did Arab states not always support the Palestinian cause? 183–4
Poland 7, 17
  Catholic Church 82
  how important was Solidarity? 82–3
  Polish Corridor 38
  Solidarity 81
  why did the communist government agree to meet the demands of Solidarity? 81
  why was action taken against Solidarity? 82
Potsdam Conference, July-August 1945 42–3
Prohibition 149–50

R

Reagan, Ronald 86
reparations 3
Rhineland 3
"Roaring Twenties" 147
Romania 7, 8
Roosevelt, Franklin Delano 41, 42, 150
  New Deal 158–64
  why did Roosevelt win the election of 1932? 155
Russia 1, 2, 100
  impact of participation in the First World War 118
  impact of participation in the First World War on civilian populations 119
  why did Russia leave the war in 1917? 117–18

S

Sadat, Anwar 175, 178
Saddam Hussein 87, 179, 184
  building up a power base 87
  Iran–Iraq War, 1980–88 92–6
  military expansion 90–1
  personality cult 90
  purges and terror 89
  road to presidency 87–8
  totalitarianism 91
  waging war on his own people 89–90
sanctions 16, 20
sappers 103, 104
Schlieffen Plan 101–2
search and destroy raids 69, 70
Shah of Iran 91–2
Shiite Moslems 89–90, 94
Six-Day War, 1967 173–5
snipers 102
Solidarity 81–3
South America Peru Columbia Bolivia Paraguay 17
Soviet Russia 1
Soviet Union see USSR
Spanish Civil War 30
Stalin, Joseph 37, 40–1, 42, 43, 52, 73, 74, 83, 175
  Berlin Blockade 46–8, 49
Storm Troopers (SA) 130, 131, 132, 135
  Night of the Long Knives 136
strategic bombing 69
Stresemann, Gustav 127–8, 132
Suez Crisis, 1956 171–3
Sunni Moslems 89–90, 94

T

Tet Offensive 67, 71
Treaty of Brest-Litovsk 2, 6, 123
Treaty of Lausannes 8
Treaty of Neuilly 8
Treaty of Sèvres 8
Treaty of St Germain 7
Treaty of Trianon 7
Treaty of Versailles 1, 28, 124, 125, 128
  Anschluss 3
  disarmament 3, 126
  reparations 3, 126–7
  territorial decisions 3
  War Guilt (article 231) 3, 126
  Rhineland 3
trench warfare 103
  dangers 104
Truman Doctrine 45

Truman, Harry S. 42, 53, 54, 55, 166, 167, 168
Turkey 1, 17
    Treaty of Lausannes 8
    Treaty of Sèvres 8

U
unanimous decisions 18
United Nations 53, 55–6, 97
    Israeli-Palestinian conflict 167–8
    unable to secure a lasting peace in the Israeli-Palestinian conflict 185
USA 1, 2, 4, 144, *146*, *151*
    agriculture in the 1920s 145–6
    America and events in Korea, 1950–53 51–6
    breakdown of alliance with USSR 40–3
    causes and consequences of the Wall Street Crash 152–7
    did all Americans benefit from the boom in the 1920s? 146
    economic boom in the 1920s 144–5
    end of the arms race 86
    entertainment opportunities in the 1920s 147
    First Gulf War 95
    how far did the roles of women change during the 1920s? 150–1
    how significant was superpower involvement in Arab–Israeli conflicts? 176–7
    how successful was the New Deal? 158–64
    how widespread was intolerance in the 1920s? 148
    impact of entering the First World War 120
    industrial performance in the 1920s 145
    loans to Germany 128, 129, 132
    Prohibition 149–50
    role in starting the Cold War 50
    USA reaction to Soviet expansion in eastern Europe 45–6
USSR 40, 52
    Berlin Wall 80–1
    breakdown of alliance with USA 40–3
    Brezhnev Doctrine 78
    collapse of Soviet control over eastern Europe 83–5
    Cuban Missile Crisis 57–64
    end of the arms race 86
    how significant was superpower involvement in Arab–Israeli conflicts? 176–7
    Korean War 51–3, 55
    opposition to Soviet control in Czechoslovakia 76–8, 79
    opposition to Soviet control in Hungary 74–6, 79
    opposition to Soviet control in Poland 81–3
    role in starting the Cold War 49–50
    Six-Day War, 1967 173–5
    Soviet expansion in eastern Europe 43–4, 73
    USA reaction to Soviet expansion in eastern Europe 45–6
    USSR in world affairs 41
    war in Afghanistan 85

V
Versailles Settlement 1, *12*
    background to the Versailles Settlement 1–2
    could the treaties be justified at the time? 8–11
    how were Germany's allies affected by peace treaties? 7–8
    impact of the Treaty of Versailles on Germany up to 1923 5–6
    main terms of the Treaty of Versailles 3
    motives and aims of the "Big Three" 2
    why did the victors not get everything they wanted? 4–5
Vietnam War 65, *72*
    American military tactics 69–70
    end of war 71–2
    human and economic cost 71
    main events of the Vietnam War 67
    Operation Rolling Thunder 67, 69
    press and media 71
    problems faced by America 70
    protests against the war 71
    results of war 72
    strategic villages 69
    Vietcong military tactics 68
    Vietnamisation 67
    why did America become involved in Vietnam? 65–6
    why did American involvement increase? 65–6
    why did the USA withdraw? 71

W
Walesa, Lech 81–2
Wall Street Crash 129, 132, *157*
    how far was speculation responsible for the Wall Street Crash? 152–3
    impact on the economy 153–4
    social consequences 154–5
    what did Hoover do to combat the Great

Depression? 156
why did Roosevelt win the election of 1932?
155
War Guilt (article 231) 3, 5
Warsaw Pact 74, 75, 76, 77, 78, 79, 84
weapons of mass destruction (WMD) 98
Weimar Republic 5, 124, *129*
achievements of the Weimar period 128–9
challenges faced by the new government
125–6
constitutional organisation 125–6
crisis in the Ruhr 126–7
how did Germany emerge from defeat at the
end of the First World War? 124
impact of the Treaty of Versailles 126
political instability 129
recovery after 1923 under Stresemann 128
renewed economic crisis 129
Western Front 103–4
Wilson, Woodrow 1, 2, 4, 13, 18, 120

Y
Yalta Conference, February 1945 41
Yom Kippur War, 1973 175
Yugoslavia 7, 8, 43, 44

Z
Zionism 165, 166, 167, 170, 185